First World War
and Army of Occupation
War Diary
France, Belgium and Germany

17 DIVISION
52 Infantry Brigade
Northumberland Fusiliers
9th Battalion
6 July 1915 - 31 July 1917

WO95/2013/1

The Naval & Military Press Ltd
www.nmarchive.com
Published in association with The National Archives

Published by

The Naval & Military Press Ltd

Unit 10 Ridgewood Industrial Park,

Uckfield, East Sussex,

TN22 5QE England

Tel: +44 (0) 1825 749494

www.naval-military-press.com

www.nmarchive.com

This diary has been reprinted in facsimile from the original. Any imperfections are inevitably reproduced and the quality may fall short of modern type and cartographic standards.

© Crown Copyright
Images reproduced by permission of The National Archives, London, England, 2015.

Contents

Document type	Place/Title	Date From	Date To
Heading	WO95/2013/1		
Heading	17th Division 52nd Infy Bde 9th Bn North'd Fus. Jly 1915-Jly 1917.		
Heading	52nd Inf. Bde. 17th Div. Battn. disembarked Boulogne from England 15.7.15. 9th Battn. The Northumberland Fusiliers. July (6/31.7.15) 1915 Attached: Appendix "A".		
War Diary	Hursley Park	06/07/1915	15/07/1915
War Diary	Boulogne France	16/07/1915	17/07/1915
War Diary	Arques	17/07/1915	18/07/1915
War Diary	Hazebrouck	19/07/1915	19/07/1915
War Diary	Godewaersvelde	20/07/1915	21/07/1915
War Diary	near Ouderdom	22/07/1915	22/07/1915
War Diary	near Ouderdom	23/07/1915	23/07/1915
War Diary	Ouderdom	24/07/1915	30/07/1915
War Diary	Chateau 1 1/2m. n.e. of Dickebusch	31/07/1915	31/07/1915
Miscellaneous	Appendix: A	26/07/1915	26/07/1915
Heading	52nd Inf. Bde. 17th Div. 9th Battn. The Northumberland Fusiliers. August 1915 Attached: Appendix "B".		
War Diary	Chateau 1 1/2 m. N.E. of Dickebusch	01/08/1915	01/08/1915
War Diary	Trenches 'P' Sector South of Sr. EL01	02/08/1915	13/08/1915
War Diary	Ridge Wood	14/08/1915	20/08/1915
War Diary	Vierstraat	21/08/1915	31/08/1915
Miscellaneous	Appendix "B".		
Heading	52nd Inf. Bde. 17th Div. 9th Battn. The Northumberland Fusiliers. September 1915		
War Diary	La Clytte	01/09/1915	05/09/1915
War Diary	Ridgewood	06/09/1915	10/09/1915
War Diary	Vierstraat	11/09/1915	17/09/1915
War Diary	Vierstraat (Fine Trenches)	17/09/1915	21/09/1915
War Diary	La Clytte	22/09/1915	28/09/1915
War Diary	Ridgewood	29/09/1915	01/10/1915
Miscellaneous	Appendix. C.		
Miscellaneous	Appendix D 5th Corps. Summary of Information.-No 143. 26/9/15.	27/09/1915	27/09/1915
Heading	52nd Inf. Bde. 17th Div. 9th Battn. The Northumberland Fusiliers. October 1915 Attached: List of Casualties.		
War Diary	Ridgewood	01/10/1915	01/10/1915
War Diary	Hill 60	02/10/1915	04/10/1915
War Diary	Dickebusch	05/10/1915	05/10/1915
War Diary	Godwaersvelde	06/10/1915	22/10/1915
War Diary	1 1/2 Miles S.W. of Vlamertinghe G.18a.4.5.	23/10/1915	30/10/1915
War Diary	Trenches Sanctuary Wood	30/10/1915	31/10/1915
Miscellaneous	Casualties During October 1915.		
Heading	52nd Inf. Bde. 17th Div. 9th Battn. The Northumberland Fusiliers. November 1915		
War Diary	Sanctuary Wood	01/11/1915	09/11/1915
War Diary	2000 Yards S.W. of Vlamertinghe.	10/11/1915	15/11/1915

War Diary	2000 yds S.W. of Vlamertinghe to Hooge	16/11/1915	16/11/1915
War Diary	Hooge	17/11/1915	23/11/1915
War Diary	Camp 2000 Yards S.W. of Vlamertinghe.	24/11/1915	30/11/1915
Miscellaneous	Appendix E	01/12/1915	01/12/1915
Heading	52nd Inf. Bde. 17th Div. 9th Battn. The Northumberland Fusiliers. December 1915		
Heading	War Diary of 9th (S) Bn. North'd Fusiliers From 1 Dec. To 31 Dec 1915 Volume 1.		
War Diary	Camp 1000 Yds. S.W. Of Vlamertinghe.	01/12/1915	01/12/1915
War Diary	Hooge	02/12/1915	06/12/1915
War Diary	Ouderdom And Kruistraat	07/12/1915	09/12/1915
War Diary	Camp 1000 Yds S.W. Of Vlamertinghe	10/12/1915	17/12/1915
War Diary	Hooge	18/12/1915	23/12/1915
War Diary	Belgian Chateau. Krvistraat.	24/12/1915	25/12/1915
War Diary	Ypres.	26/12/1915	31/12/1915
Miscellaneous	Appendices "F" "G" "H" "I" "J"		
Miscellaneous	Appendix F O.C. 9th Northumberland Fusiliers 10th Lancashire Fusiliers	22/12/1915	22/12/1915
Miscellaneous	Appendix: G. Christmas Messages from His Majesty The King.		
Miscellaneous	Appendix H. To all Concerned.	20/12/1915	20/12/1915
Miscellaneous	Appendix I G.O.C. 5th Corps.	21/12/1915	21/12/1915
Miscellaneous	Appendix J. Casualties 9th Northd Fus.		
Heading	9th Northumb: Fus: January 1916 Vol 7		
War Diary	Ypres	01/01/1916	02/01/1916
War Diary	Hooge	03/01/1916	07/01/1916
War Diary	On March	08/01/1916	08/01/1916
War Diary	La Panne	09/01/1916	31/01/1916
Miscellaneous	Appendix K Summary of Casualties, January. 1916		
War Diary	La Panne	01/02/1916	05/02/1916
War Diary	Reninghelst	06/02/1916	06/02/1916
War Diary	Trenches "P" Sector S. of St Eloi	07/02/1916	16/02/1916
War Diary	Dickebusch	17/02/1916	21/02/1916
War Diary	Reninghelst	22/02/1916	23/02/1916
War Diary	Trenches Right Sub. Section.	24/02/1916	26/02/1916
War Diary	Trenches Right-sub-section, left. Sector N. of Ypres Commines Canal	27/02/1916	29/02/1916
Miscellaneous	Appendix L		
Heading	9th Northumb Vol 7		
War Diary	Trenches n of Ypres Commines Canal	01/03/1916	01/03/1916
War Diary	Reninghelst	02/03/1916	03/03/1916
War Diary	Dickebusch	04/03/1916	06/03/1916
War Diary	St. Eloi (Trenches)	07/03/1916	09/03/1916
War Diary	Reninghelst	10/03/1916	11/03/1916
War Diary	Near Meteren	12/03/1916	19/03/1916
War Diary	La Creche area	20/03/1916	20/03/1916
War Diary	Armentieres	21/03/1916	21/03/1916
War Diary	Trenches Right Centre Sector	22/03/1916	30/03/1916
War Diary	Armentieres	31/03/1916	31/03/1916
Miscellaneous	Appendix M. Casualties:- 9th Bn. Northd Fusiliers		
War Diary	Armentieres	01/04/1916	07/04/1916
War Diary	Trenches	08/04/1916	15/04/1916
War Diary	Armentieres	16/04/1916	23/04/1916
War Diary	Trenches	23/04/1916	30/04/1916
Miscellaneous	Appendix N. Casualties 9th Northumberland Fus.		
Heading	9th Northumberland. Fus: Vol: 6		

War Diary	Trenches Before Armentieres.	01/05/1916	01/05/1916
War Diary	Armentieres	02/05/1916	09/05/1916
War Diary	Trenches	10/05/1916	15/05/1916
War Diary	Armentieres	16/05/1916	16/05/1916
War Diary	Estaires	17/05/1916	17/05/1916
War Diary	Morbecques	18/05/1916	18/05/1916
War Diary	Racquinghem	19/05/1916	19/05/1916
War Diary	St Martin au Laert	20/05/1916	31/05/1916
War Diary	St Martin au Laert.	01/06/1916	11/06/1916
War Diary	Coisy	12/06/1916	26/06/1916
War Diary	Coisy Heilly	27/06/1916	27/06/1916
War Diary	Heilly	28/06/1916	30/06/1916
Heading	52nd Inf. Bde. 17th Div. 9th Battn. The Northumberland Fusiliers. July 1916		
Heading	War Diary of 9th Service Bn. Northumberland Fusiliers From 1st July 1916 to 31st July 1916.		
War Diary	In Bivouac Bois Des Tailles	01/07/1916	01/07/1916
War Diary	Morlancourt	02/07/1916	03/07/1916
War Diary	In Trenches E. of Becourt Chateau	04/07/1916	04/07/1916
War Diary	In Trenches	05/07/1916	05/07/1916
War Diary	Quadrangle & Hedge Line Trenches	06/07/1916	07/07/1916
War Diary	Meaulte	08/07/1916	08/07/1916
War Diary	Ville-Sous-Corbie	09/07/1916	10/07/1916
War Diary	Riencourt	11/07/1916	15/07/1916
War Diary	Vauchelles	16/07/1916	16/07/1916
War Diary	Les-Domarts	17/07/1916	17/07/1916
War Diary	Vauchelles	18/07/1916	23/07/1916
War Diary	In Bivouac Near Dernancourt	24/07/1916	31/07/1916
Miscellaneous	Appendices.		
Miscellaneous	A Form. Messages And Signals.		
Miscellaneous	Fourth Army. Special Order Of The Day.	12/07/1916	12/07/1916
Miscellaneous	Special Order Of The Day by General Sir Douglas Haig, G.C.B., K.C.I.E., K.C.V.O., A.D.C. Commander-in-Chief, British Armies in France.	17/07/1916	17/07/1916
Miscellaneous	Special Order Of The Day by General Sir Douglas Haig, G.C.B., K.C.I.E., K.C.V.O., A.D.C. Commander-in-Chief, British Armies in France.	27/07/1916	27/07/1916
Miscellaneous	17th Division. Special Order.	13/07/1916	13/07/1916
Miscellaneous	Address by Major General P.R. Robertson, C.M.G. to the 17th. Division on the occasion of presentation of Military Medals, 27th. July 1916.	27/07/1916	27/07/1916
Miscellaneous	Special Order Of The Day by General Sir Douglas Haig, G.C.B., K.C.I.E., K.C.V.O., A.D.C. Commander-in-Chief, British Armies in France.	18/07/1916	18/07/1916
Miscellaneous	Special Order Of The Day by General Sir Douglas Haig, G.C.B., K.C.I.E., K.C.V.O., A.D.C. Commander-in-Chief, British Armies in France.	07/07/1916	07/07/1916
Miscellaneous	Order of the Day by Lieut. Col H. Bryan C.M.G. Coming 9th North'd Fusiliers 26.7.16	26/07/1916	26/07/1916
Miscellaneous	Casualty Returns.		
Miscellaneous	Remained at Duty		
Miscellaneous	Herewith Casualty Return		
Heading	52nd Brigade. 17th Division. 1/9th Battalion Northumberland Fusiliers August 1916		
Heading	War Diary 9th Northumberland Fusiliers August 1916. Vol 12		

War Diary	In Bivouac near Dernancourt	01/08/1916	01/08/1916
War Diary	In Trenches	02/08/1916	06/08/1916
War Diary	Pommier Trench	07/08/1916	08/08/1916
War Diary	In Bivouac near Fricourt	09/08/1916	10/08/1916
War Diary	Trenches	11/08/1916	12/08/1916
War Diary	Pommiers Redoubt.	13/08/1916	13/08/1916
War Diary	Camp Deoncourt	14/08/1916	14/08/1916
War Diary	Dernancourt I Fienvilles	15/08/1916	15/08/1916
War Diary	Fienvillers Barly	16/08/1916	16/08/1916
War Diary	Barly Grouche Luchuel	17/08/1916	17/08/1916
War Diary	Grouche. Luchuel	18/08/1916	19/08/1916
War Diary	Souastre & St Amand	20/08/1916	20/08/1916
War Diary	Souastre	21/08/1916	21/08/1916
War Diary	Souastre	22/08/1916	27/08/1916
War Diary	Trenches	28/08/1916	31/08/1916
Miscellaneous	To O i/c N.A.I.S. 2	03/08/1916	03/08/1916
Miscellaneous	To Officer i/c N.A.I.S. 2.		
Miscellaneous	To Officer i/c N.A.I.S. 2.	05/08/1916	05/08/1916
Miscellaneous	To Officer i/c N.A.I.S. 2.	08/08/1916	08/08/1916
Miscellaneous	To Officer i/c N.A.I.S. 2.	09/08/1916	09/08/1916
Miscellaneous	To Officer i/c N.A.I.S. No 2.	09/08/1916	09/08/1916
Miscellaneous	To Officer i/c N.A.I.S. No 2.	12/08/1916	12/08/1916
Miscellaneous	To Officer i/c N.A.I.S. 2.	17/08/1916	17/08/1916
Miscellaneous	To Officer i/c N.A.I.S. No 2.	17/08/1916	17/08/1916
Miscellaneous	To Officer i/c N.A.I.S. 119.	17/08/1916	17/08/1916
Miscellaneous	To Officer i/c N.A.I.S. 2.	19/08/1916	19/08/1916
Miscellaneous	To N.A.I.S. no 2	21/08/1916	21/08/1916
Miscellaneous	Officer i/c New Army Inf Base 2. Base Herewith Casualty Report.	31/08/1916	31/08/1916
Miscellaneous	Officer i/c New army Intersection No 2 Herewith Casualty Report	25/08/1916	25/08/1916
Miscellaneous	Officer i/c New Army Inf Section 2 Base Herewith Casualty Report	26/08/1916	26/08/1916
Miscellaneous	Officer i/c New Army Inf Sect 2. Base Herewith Casualty Report	31/08/1916	31/08/1916
Miscellaneous	Special Order of the Day by General Sir Douglas Haig, G.C.B., K.C.I.E., K.C.V.O., A.D.C. Commander-in-Chief, British Armies in France.	04/08/1916	04/08/1916
Miscellaneous	Special Order Of The Day by General Sir Douglas Haig, G.C.B., K.C.I.E., K.C.V.O., A.D.C. Commander-in-Chief, British Armies in France.	05/08/1916	05/08/1916
Miscellaneous	Special Order.	05/08/1916	05/08/1916
Miscellaneous	Special Order. Award Of Military Medal.	26/07/1916	26/07/1916
Heading	War Diary Of 9th (S) Bn Northumberland Fusiliers From 1st September 1916 to 30th September 1916 Vol 13		
War Diary	Trenches	01/09/1916	04/09/1916
War Diary	Trenches Souastre	05/09/1916	05/09/1916
War Diary	Souastre	06/09/1916	09/09/1916
War Diary	Souastre Souastre Camp	10/09/1916	10/09/1916
War Diary	Souastre Camp	11/09/1916	21/09/1916
War Diary	Souastre Camp Mondicourt	21/09/1916	21/09/1916
War Diary	Souastre Camp Mondicourt Barly	22/09/1916	22/09/1916
War Diary	Barly Heirmont	23/09/1916	23/09/1916
War Diary	Hiermont Millancourt	24/09/1916	24/09/1916
War Diary	Millancourt	25/09/1916	30/09/1916

Miscellaneous	Special Order of the Day by General Sir Douglas Haig, G.C.B., G.C.V.O., K.C.I.E., A.D.C. Commander-in-Chief, British Armies in France.	22/09/1916	22/09/1916
Heading	War Diary From 1st to 31st October 9th (S) Bn Northumberland Fusiliers Volume I.		
War Diary	Millencourt	01/10/1916	08/10/1916
War Diary	Millancourt Conteville	09/10/1916	09/10/1916
War Diary	Conteville Barly	10/10/1916	10/10/1916
War Diary	Barly Mondicourt	11/10/1916	11/10/1916
War Diary	Mondicourt	12/10/1916	18/10/1916
War Diary	Mondicourt Le Souich	19/10/1916	19/10/1916
War Diary	Le Souich	20/10/1916	21/10/1916
War Diary	Le Souich Coisy	22/10/1916	22/10/1916
War Diary	Coisy Daours	23/10/1916	23/10/1916
War Diary	Daours	24/10/1916	26/10/1916
War Diary	Daours Sand Pits Camp	27/10/1916	27/10/1916
War Diary	Sano Pits Camp	28/10/1916	30/10/1916
War Diary	Camp S.23 B.22.	31/10/1916	31/10/1916
Heading	War Diary Of 9th (S) Bn. Northumberland Fusiliers From 1st November 1916. To 30th November 1916.		
War Diary	Trenches	01/11/1916	03/11/1916
War Diary	H Camp Carnoy	04/11/1916	04/11/1916
War Diary	H Camp	05/11/1916	06/11/1916
War Diary	Trenches	07/11/1916	10/11/1916
War Diary	Trenches "W" Camp	10/11/1916	10/11/1916
War Diary	W Camp "H" Camp	11/11/1916	11/11/1916
War Diary	W Camp "H" Camp Citadel	12/11/1916	12/11/1916
War Diary	Citadel	13/11/1916	13/11/1916
War Diary	Citadel Hangest	14/11/1916	14/11/1916
War Diary	Hangest Breilly	15/11/1916	15/11/1916
War Diary	Breilly	16/11/1916	30/11/1916
Miscellaneous	Special Order Of The Day By General Sir Douglas Haig, G.C.B., G.C.V.O., K.C.I.E., A.D.C. Commander-in-Chief, British Armies In France.	22/11/1916	22/11/1916
Miscellaneous	War Diary. November. 9th Battn. The Northd Fus: Casualties November. Appendix 6		
Miscellaneous	Officer i/c Regular Inf Sec 3 Base 131 Herewith Casualty Report please		
Miscellaneous	Officer i/c Regular Inf Sec. 3 Base Herewith Casualty Report		
Miscellaneous	Officer i/c Regular Inf Sect 3 Base Herewith Casualty Report	23/11/1916	23/11/1916
Miscellaneous	Officer i/c Reg Infantry Sec 3 Base Herewith Casualty Report please	21/11/1916	21/11/1916
Miscellaneous	Casualty Report Continued No. 131.		
Heading	War Diary Of The 9th (S) Bn. Northumberland Fusiliers. From 1st December 1916 to 31st December 1916 Volume XVIII		
War Diary	Breilly	01/12/1916	12/12/1916
War Diary	On the Move	13/12/1916	13/12/1916
War Diary	Meaulte	14/12/1916	22/12/1916
War Diary	Camp	23/12/1916	24/12/1916
War Diary	Trenches	25/12/1916	26/12/1916
War Diary	Camp	27/12/1916	30/12/1916
War Diary	Trenches	31/12/1916	31/12/1916

Miscellaneous	Appendix T War Diary Officer i/c Regular Infantry Section Base Herewith Casualty Report please	28/12/1916	28/12/1916
Miscellaneous	Special Order of the Day by General Sir Douglas Haig, G.C.B., G.C.V.O., K.C.I.E., A.D.C. Commander-in-Chief, British Armies in France.	24/12/1916	24/12/1916
Miscellaneous	A Form. Messages And Signals.	16/12/1916	16/12/1916
Miscellaneous	Special Order Of The Day by General Sir Douglas Haig, G.C.B., G.C.V.O., K.C.I.E., A.D.C. Commander-in-Chief, British Armies in France.	25/12/1916	25/12/1916
Miscellaneous			
Heading	War Diary of 9th (S) Battn the Northumberland Fus. From Jany 1st: 1917 to Jany 31st 1917. (Volume)		
War Diary	Trenches	01/01/1917	01/01/1917
War Diary	Camp	02/01/1917	05/01/1917
War Diary	Trenches	06/01/1917	08/01/1917
War Diary	Camp	09/01/1917	13/01/1917
War Diary	Trenches	14/01/1917	15/01/1917
War Diary	Camp	16/01/1917	16/01/1917
War Diary	Billets	17/01/1917	28/01/1917
War Diary	Camp	29/01/1917	31/01/1917
Miscellaneous	Appendix U		
Miscellaneous	To Officer i/c Regular Infantry Section 35 Base	10/01/1917	10/01/1917
Miscellaneous	To Officer i/c Regular Infantry Section Base.	17/01/1917	17/01/1917
Miscellaneous	To O i/c Regular Infantry Section 3	23/01/1917	23/01/1917
Heading	War Diary The 9th (S) Battn of the North Fusiliers for the month of February 1917. Volume XX From 1-2-17 to 28-2-17		
War Diary	Trenches	01/02/1917	02/02/1917
War Diary	Camp	03/02/1917	06/02/1917
War Diary	Trenches	07/02/1917	08/02/1917
War Diary	Dugouts (Combles)	09/02/1917	09/02/1917
War Diary	Camp	10/02/1917	12/02/1917
War Diary	Trenches	13/02/1917	14/02/1917
War Diary	Camp	15/02/1917	18/02/1917
War Diary	Trenches	19/02/1917	20/02/1917
War Diary	Camp	20/02/1917	20/02/1917
War Diary	Billets	21/02/1917	28/02/1917
Miscellaneous	Appendix V. Casualties incurred during February.		
Miscellaneous	To O i/c Regular Infantry Section	03/02/1917	03/02/1917
Miscellaneous	To O i/c Regular Infantry Section 3.	10/02/1917	10/02/1917
Miscellaneous	Officer i/c Regular Infantry Section 3 Base	15/02/1917	15/02/1917
Miscellaneous	To O i/c Regular Infantry Section 141.	16/02/1917	16/02/1917
Miscellaneous	To Officer i/c Regular Infantry Section No 3	26/02/1917	26/02/1917
Heading	War Diary of the 9th (S) Bn. Northumberland Fusiliers From 1st March 1917. to 31st March 1917. Volume XXI.		
Miscellaneous	To 52nd Bde:	01/04/1917	01/04/1917
War Diary	Billets	01/03/1917	31/03/1917
Heading	War Diary of the 9th (S) Battn. The Northd Fusiliers From April 1st 1917 To April 30th 1917 Volume XXII		
Miscellaneous	To 52nd Bde:	30/04/1917	30/04/1917
War Diary	Billets	01/04/1917	09/04/1917
War Diary	Bivouac	10/04/1917	10/04/1917
War Diary	Billets	11/04/1917	11/04/1917
War Diary	Trenches	12/04/1917	18/04/1917
War Diary	Billets	19/04/1917	20/04/1917

War Diary	Trenches	21/04/1917	25/04/1917
War Diary	Billets	26/04/1917	30/04/1917
War Diary	Billets	01/04/1917	09/04/1917
War Diary	Bivouac	10/04/1917	10/04/1917
War Diary	Billets	11/04/1917	11/04/1917
War Diary	Trenches	12/04/1917	18/04/1917
War Diary	Billets	19/04/1917	20/04/1917
War Diary	Trenches	21/04/1917	25/04/1917
War Diary	Billets	26/04/1917	30/04/1917
Miscellaneous	Casualties incurred by the 9th (S) Bn. the Northd Fus: during the month of April 1917. Appendix X		
Miscellaneous	Casualty Report No 145		
Miscellaneous	To Officer i/c Regular Infantry Section No 3.	27/04/1917	27/04/1917
Miscellaneous	Special Order of the Day by Major General P.R. Robertson, C.E., C.M.G., Commanding 17th Division. 27th April, 1917.	27/04/1917	27/04/1917
Miscellaneous	Special Order Of The Day By Field-Marshal Sir Douglas Haig, G.C.B., G.C.V.O., K.C.I.E., Commander-in-Chief. British Armies in France.	24/04/1917	24/04/1917
Miscellaneous	Special Order Of The Day By Field-Marshal Sir Douglas Haig. G.C.B., G.C.V.O., K.C.I.E., Commander-in-Chief. British Armies in France.	20/04/1917	20/04/1917
Miscellaneous	Special Order Of The Day By Field-Marshal Sir Douglas Haig. G.C.B., G.C.V.O., K.C.I.E., Commander-in-Chief. British Armies in France.	12/04/1917	12/04/1917
Miscellaneous	To Officer i/c Regular Infantry Section No 3	02/04/1917	02/04/1917
Miscellaneous	To Officer i/c Regular Infantry Section 3	20/04/1917	20/04/1917
Miscellaneous	To Officer i/c Regular Infantry Section No 3	30/04/1917	30/04/1917
Miscellaneous	Special Order Of The Day By Field-Marshal Sir Douglas Haig. G.C.B., G.C.V.O., K.C.I.E., Commander-in-Chief. British Armies in France.	12/04/1917	12/04/1917
Heading	War Diary Of The 9th (S) Bn. Northumberland Fusiliers. From 1st May 1917. To 31st May 1917.		
Heading	To 52nd Infy Bde Hewitt War Diary For May 1917.	02/06/1917	02/06/1917
War Diary	Billets	01/05/1917	01/05/1917
War Diary	Camp	02/05/1917	03/05/1917
War Diary	Reserve Trenches	04/05/1917	06/05/1917
War Diary	Reserve Line	07/05/1917	09/05/1917
War Diary	Support Trenches	10/05/1917	11/05/1917
War Diary	Front Line	12/05/1917	14/05/1917
War Diary	Reserve	15/05/1917	16/05/1917
War Diary	Support Trenches	17/05/1917	19/05/1917
War Diary	Front Line	20/05/1917	23/05/1917
War Diary	Support	24/05/1917	24/05/1917
War Diary	Camp	25/05/1917	27/05/1917
War Diary	Reserve Line	28/05/1917	28/05/1917
War Diary	Reserve	29/05/1917	29/05/1917
War Diary	Camp	30/05/1917	30/05/1917
War Diary	Billets	31/05/1917	31/05/1917
Miscellaneous	To O i/c R.I.S. 3 Appendix Y 147.	12/05/1917	12/05/1917
Miscellaneous	To Officer i/c Regular Infantry Section No 3.	26/05/1917	26/05/1917
Miscellaneous	Special Order of the Day by General Sir Edmund Allenby, K.C.B., Commanding Third Army.	25/04/1917	25/04/1917
Miscellaneous	Special Order Of The Day By Field-Marshal Sir Douglas Haig. G.C.B., G.C.V.O., K.C.I.E., Commander-in-Chief. British Armies in France.	28/05/1917	28/05/1917

Heading	9th (S) Bn North'd Fus War Diary From 1st June 1917 To 30th June 1917 Vol 22		
Miscellaneous	To 52nd Infy Bde. Herewith War Diary for the month of June 1917		
War Diary	In Billets	01/06/1917	01/06/1917
War Diary	Billets	02/06/1917	20/06/1917
War Diary	Camp	21/06/1917	21/06/1917
War Diary	Trenches	22/06/1917	26/06/1917
War Diary	In Reserve line	27/06/1917	30/06/1917
Miscellaneous	To Officer i/c Regular Infantry Section 149.	24/06/1917	24/06/1917
Miscellaneous	To Officer i/c Regular Infantry Section 150.	25/06/1917	25/06/1917
Miscellaneous	To Officer i/c Regular Infantry Section 151.	28/06/1917	28/06/1917
Miscellaneous	Special Order Of The Day By Field-Marshal Sir Douglas Haig. G.C.B., G.C.V.O., K.C.I.E., Commander-in-Chief. British Armies in France.	05/06/1917	05/06/1917
Miscellaneous	Special Order Of The Day By Field-Marshal Sir Douglas Haig. G.C.B., G.C.V.O., K.C.I.E., Commander-in-Chief. British Armies in France.	08/06/1917	08/06/1917
Miscellaneous	Special Order Of The Day By Field-Marshal Sir Douglas Haig. G.C.B., G.C.V.O., K.C.I.E., Commander-in-Chief, British Armies in France.	11/06/1917	11/06/1917
Miscellaneous	Special Order Of The Day By Field-Marshal Sir Douglas Haig. G.C.B., G.C.V.O., K.C.I.E., Commander-in-Chief, British Armies in France.	12/06/1917	12/06/1917
Heading	War Diary of 9th (S) Bn The Northumberland Fusiliers 1st July 1917 to 31st July 1917		
Miscellaneous	To 52nd Infy Bde.	11/08/1917	11/08/1917
War Diary	Trenches	01/07/1917	03/07/1917
War Diary	Support Trenches	04/07/1917	07/07/1917
War Diary	Reserve Camp	08/07/1917	15/07/1917
War Diary	Trenches	16/07/1917	20/07/1917
War Diary	Support Trenches	21/07/1917	24/07/1917
War Diary	Trenches	25/07/1917	27/07/1917
War Diary	Support Trenches	28/07/1917	31/07/1917
Miscellaneous	To O i/c R.I.S. 3. 153	09/07/1917	09/07/1917
Miscellaneous	To O i/c R.I.S. 3. Base G. 154	22/07/1917	22/07/1917
Miscellaneous	To O i/c R.I.S. 3. 155	23/07/1917	23/07/1917
Miscellaneous	To O i/c R.I.S. 3 Base 156	26/07/1917	26/07/1917
Miscellaneous	To O i/c R.I.S. 3 Base 157	27/07/1917	27/07/1917
Miscellaneous	O i/c R.I.S. 3 157	31/07/1917	31/07/1917
Miscellaneous	Special Order Of The Day By Field-Marshall Sir Douglas Haig, K.T., G.C.B., G.C.V.O., K.C.I.E., Commander-in-Chief, British Armies in France.	25/07/1917	25/07/1917
Miscellaneous	Special Order Of The Day By His Majesty The King.	14/07/1917	14/07/1917
Miscellaneous	Operation Order 9th Northumberland Fusiliers	18/07/1917	18/07/1917

WO 2013/1

17TH DIVISION
52ND INFY BDE

9TH BN NORTH'D FUS.
JLY 1915-JLY 1917.

To 34 Div 103 Bde

52nd Inf.Bde.
17th Div.

Battn. disembarked
Boulogne from
England 15.7.15.

9th BATTN. THE NORTHUMBERLAND FUSILIERS.

J U L Y

(6/31.7.15)

1 9 1 5

Attached:

Appendix "A".

Army Form C. 2118

WAR DIARY
or
INTELLIGENCE SUMMARY
(Erase heading not required.)

9th Northumberland Fusiliers

Instructions regarding War Diaries and Intelligence Summaries are contained in F.S. Regs., Part II. and the Staff Manual respectively. Title Pages will be prepared in manuscript.

Place	Date	Hour	Summary of Events and Information	Remarks and references to Appendices
HURSLEY PARK	6.7.15	11.30 a.m.	Orders received from Headquarters, 52nd Inf. Bde. that the 17th Division was to be held in readiness to proceed on Active Service. 2nd Lieut. M.G. PATTEN embarked at SOUTHAMPTON for HAVRE.	
do.	6.7.15	7.15.	The Battalion halted at HURSLEY PARK, WINCHESTER.	
do.	14.7.15	4 a.m.	Major G.P. WESTMACOTT, 2 officers and 108 rank & file; including the Machine Gun Section and Transport, with 66 horses, left HURSLEY PARK at 4 a.m. for SOUTHAMPTON. The party embarked at 9 p.m. for HAVRE.	
do.	15.7.15	3.15. p.m.	The Battalion marched from HURSLEY PARK to WINCHESTER and entrained for FOLKESTONE by half battalion. The first train leaving at 3.15.p.m. The second at 4.10.p.m. Strength 25 Officers and 2 attached (Medical Officer and Chaplain) 880 rank and file. The battalion embarked on the "INVICTA" left FOLKESTONE at 9.10.a.m. and landed at BOULOGNE at 11 p.m.	
BOULOGNE FRANCE	16.7.15	1.a.m.	Arrived in Camp at BOULOGNE and halted for the day.	
do.	17.7.15	1.30 a.m.	Marched from Camp at BOULOGNE at 1.30.A.M. to PONT DE BRIQUES and entrained at 3.15.a.m. joining up with HAVRE party under Major WESTMACOTT. Arrived at ARQUES at 6.20.a.m. the battalion going into billets.	
ARQUES	17.7.15		Halted in billets at ARQUES.	

Army Form C. 2118

2

9th Northumberland Fusiliers

WAR DIARY, or INTELLIGENCE SUMMARY

(Erase heading not required.)

Place	Date	Hour	Summary of Events and Information	Remarks and references to Appendices
ARQUES	18.7.15	9 a.m.	Paraded at 9.a.m. and marched, leading 52nd Inf. Bde., to HAZEBROUCK arriving at 1.P.M. and went into billets in the Hospital Nouvelle.	
HAZEBROUCK	19.7.15	9.30 a.m.	Left HAZEBROUCK at 9.30.a.m. and marched via CAESTRE to GODEWAERSVELDE arriving at 1.15. p.m. Went into close billets. Battalion headquarters in bivouac.	
GODEWAERSVELDE	20.7.15	—	In close billets. At 2 P.M. the 52nd Inf. Bde. was inspected by LIEUT. GENERAL Sir HERBERT PLUMER, K.C.B. Commanding the 2nd Army, British Exp. Force.	
do.	21.7.15	—	In close billets. Left GODEWAERSVELDE at 8.15.p.m. and marched by a circuitous route, about 16 miles, to temporary huts in camp 2 miles N.E. of OUDERDOM on OUDERDOM — VLAMERINGHE road. Arrived in camp at 3.A.M. A tiring march for men and horses through hilly country in difficult rout' roads. Lt. Col. H. St.G. THOMAS highly commanded the excellent march discipline maintained en route.	
Near OUDERDOM near OUDERDOM	22.7.15	—	Halted in temporary huts.	
	23.7.15	—	Halted in temporary huts. The C.O. 2nd in Command and Adjutant visited Battalion 1/2 Can. of 1st half Battn. trenches holding a section of front line trenches south of St. ELOI. Four platoons were in the trenches for 24 hours under instruction.	
do.	24.7.15	—	Halted as on previous day. Four platoons were in the trenches occupied by the	

Army Form C. 2118

WAR DIARY
or
INTELLIGENCE SUMMARY
(Erase heading not required.)

9th Northumberland Fusiliers (3)

Place	Date	Hour	Summary of Events and Information	Remarks and references to Appendices
OUDERDOM	24.7.15	—	1st Battn. Northd. Fusiliers for 24 hours. Orders were received from 151st Brigade to form a "Minor Salient" of 1 Officer: 3 N.C.Os and 20 men. Great activity observed from 5 – 7 p.m. on part of allied and enemy air craft between YPRES and Sc. ELOI.	
do.	25.7.15	—	Shelled in temporary trenches. Four platoons were under instruction in the trenches as on two previous occasions for 24 hours. Orders received to form a grenadier party of 4 Officers: 4 N.C.Os and 80 men. Allies and enemy air craft active between 5 and 7 p.m. One hostile aeroplane was shelled and brought down in lines occupied by IV Army Corps.	
do.	26.7.15	—	Shelled as before. Four platoons were under instruction as on previous days for 24 hours. The trenches they occupied in conjunction with 1st Batt. North. Fusiliers was heavily bombarded by H.E. shell between 5.30 – 7 p.m. The battalion sustained the first casualties this day as follows: 5 killed; 19 wounded; 1 died of wounds	See appendix "A"
do.	27.7.15	—	Shelled as before. Four platoons were under instruction in 151st fire and support trenches as on previous days for 24 hours.	
do.	28.7.15	—	Shelled at OUDERDOM. "B" Company went into 151st trenches occupied by 1st Batth. North. Fus. line for period of 48 hours. (instructional)	
do.	29.7.15	—	At OUDERDOM. "B" Company in firs trenches.	

Army Form C. 2118

(4)

WAR DIARY
or
INTELLIGENCE SUMMARY
(Erase heading not required.)

Instructions regarding War Diaries and Intelligence Summaries are contained in F.S. Regs., Part II. and the Staff Manual respectively. Title Pages will be prepared in manuscript.

Place	Date	Hour	Summary of Events and Information	Remarks and references to Appendices
OUDERDOM	30.7.15	2.20 P.M.	The 52nd Inf. Bde. were ordered to go into billets at Chateau N.E. of DICKEBUSCH to form a reserve to 14th Division which was hard pressed at ZOUAVE Wood near HOOGE. The Battn. moved at 3 P.M. and bivouacked in field. Battalion in rear of Battles in YPRES sector was heavily shelled and vigorously replied during the night 30 - 31st	
CHATEAU 12m. N.E. of DICKEBUSCH	31.7.15		in bivouac near Chateau. Three S.A.A. wagons handed over to Brigade Reserve. Four Officers sent to reconnoitre approaches from YPRES and ZILLEBEKE to ZOUAVE Wood. Again heavy artillery duel by night. The 6th Bn of Cameron since landing on 16th July, are — 5 killed; 1 died of wounds, 9 wounded	see Appendix

Appendix. A

WAR DIARY
or
INTELLIGENCE SUMMARY
(Erase heading not required.)

Army Form C. 2118

Place	Date	Hour	Summary of Events and Information	Remarks and references to Appendices
			Casualties during month of July. 1915.	

Killed

10222 C.Q.M.S. H.L. Jackson C coy. 26/7/15
13337 Cpl J.R. Bawn C coy. 26/7/15
9/7611 Cpl N. Young C coy 26/7/15
10479 L/Cpl R.S. Wilson C coy. 26/7/15
18275 Pte T. Thompson C coy. 26/7/15

Died of Wounds

14785 Pte E. Shane C coy. 26/7/15

Wounded

15913 Pte A. Curry C coy.
11436 Pte T. Dial C coy.
14791 Pte J. Garbutt C coy.   } 26/7/15
13083 Pte J. Watson C coy.
16008 Pte W. Jarvis C coy.

15912 Pte J. Hood
14556 Pte H. Ford
13245 Pte J.W. Kemp   } 26/7/15
10365 L/C R. Bronley

Total Killed 5
D. of W. 1
Wounded 9

52nd Inf. Bde.
17th Div.

9th BATTN. THE NORTHUMBERLAND FUSILIERS.

A U G U S T

1 9 1 5

Attached:

Appendix "B".

Army Form C. 2118.

WAR DIARY
or
INTELLIGENCE SUMMARY.
(Erase heading not required.)

9/Northumberland Fusiliers.

Instructions regarding War Diaries and Intelligence Summaries are contained in F.S. Regs., Part II. and the Staff Manual respectively. Title pages will be prepared in manuscript.

August 1915

Place	Date	Hour	Summary of Events and Information	Remarks and references to Appendices
CHATEAU 1½ m. N.E. of DICKEBUSCH	1.8.15		The 52nd Inf. Bde. this night took over area 7. 9th Inf. Bde. The 9th Northd. Fus. took over the sector occupied by 1st Northd. Fus between 9 P.M. and 1 A.M. "B" Coy. was detached to form part of a composite reserve battalion. The front held by the Battn. extends from the VIERSTRAAT - POPERINGHE road to a point 250x S.W. of St. ELOI.	9 Brigade
Trenches "P"Sector South of St. ELOI	2nd & 6th August		The battalion was in the front trenches during this period with one company "B" with the composite reserve in RIDGE WOOD. Headquarters of the Battn. were at WILTSHIRE Farm. On 6th August a draft of 1 Sergt, 1 Corpl. & 28 men joined from 15 (Service) Battalion.	
do.	7/8 August	9 P.M. to 3 A.M.	"Dummy" starting parallels and "assembly posts" were dug in "P" sector with a view to lead the enemy to draw troops from HOOGE to resist an assault. The work was done in front of the wire entanglements without sustaining a casualty.	

1875 Wt. W593/826 1,000,000 4/15 J.B.C. & A. A.D.S.S./Forms/C. 2118.

T2134. Wt. W708-776. 500000. 4/15. Sir J. C. & S.

WAR DIARY
or
INTELLIGENCE SUMMARY

(Erase heading not required.)

Army Form (5)

9' Northumberland Fusiliers

Instructions regarding War Diaries and Intelligence Summaries are contained in F.S. Regs, Part II. and the Staff Manual respectively. Title Pages will be prepared in manuscript.

Place	Date	Hour	Summary of Events and Information	Remarks and references to Appendices
Trenches "P" Sector South of St. ELOI	8/9 August	2.30 & 3.15 a.m.	The battalion stood to arms during the heavy artillery bombardment which preceded the successful assault at HOOGE.	
do.	10/13 August	-	No special incident occurred during this period. The battalion continued to hold "P" Sector.	
RIDGE WOOD	14/20 August	-	On 14 August the Battalion came into Reserve at RIDGEWOOD. One company ("B") rejoined on disbandment of composite battalion. The Brigadier Commdg S.20 Inf. Bde. inspected the Battalion on 18" & intimated that the G.O.C. 17 Div. had expressed himself as completely satisfied with the manner in which the first tour of duty in the trenches had been performed. The Brigadier was pleased to commend the general "turn-out" of the men after their arduous work in the firing line.	
VIERSTRAAT	21" August	10.P.M.	The Battalion was relieved at RIDGEWOOD by 12" Battn. Manch. Regt. The reliefs being completed by 10 P.M. The trenches M1, M2, M3, M1.G, M2.A, M4, M5, N1, N2, N2A and N7 were taken over by A, B & C Coys. The VIERSTRAAT defences were taken over by D. Coy; with Battn. Hd. Qrs at a farm 800 yds. N.W. of VIERSTRAAT. The pri trenches and VIERSTRAAT defences were taken over from 10" Lancashire Fusiliers, the reliefs being completed by 12. midnight on 21st –	

WAR DIARY
or
INTELLIGENCE SUMMARY

(Erase heading not required.)

9th Northumberland Fusiliers (6)

Place	Date	Hour	Summary of Events and Information	Remarks and references to Appendices
VIERSTRAAT	22nd August	—	Battn. Engaged in reconstruction and improvement of trenches and building dug-outs to provide accommodation for Head Quarters. G.O.C. 17th Division visited and inspected VIERSTRAAT defences. 2nd in Command and Adjt. visited fire trenches.	
do.	23rd August	—	This day a draft from 15th Battn. joined at VIERSTRAAT. Strength 1 Sergt. 1 Corpl. 38 men. Work on fire trenches and dug-outs continued.	
do.	24th August	—	C.O. & 2nd in Command visited fire trenches. Work as on previous day.	
do.	25th August	.	Large scheme carried in VIERSTRAAT main salient. VIERSTRAAT lines of trenches visited and inspected by G.O.C. 17th Division. "D" Coy. was this night relieved in the VIERSTRAAT posts by a Coy. 10th Lan. Fus. 16 pounds amm. firing into hostile reserves for rifle block of 16 front held by 50th Inf. Bde.	
do.	26th August	.	G.O.C. 17th Division and Brigadier 52nd Inf. Bde. met at Battln. Head quarters and compared notes. O.C. 9th North. Fusiliers. This night the 93rd Field Coy. R.E. commenced wire of ditch proposed to be constructed in front of fire trenches.	
do.	27th August		The O.C. & 2nd in command inspected VIERSTRAAT defensive posts. Work of wiring ditch continued this night by R.E. officers.	

Army Form C. 2118

(7).

9th Northumberland Fusiliers

WAR DIARY
or
INTELLIGENCE SUMMARY
(Erase heading not required.)

Instructions regarding War Diaries and Intelligence Summaries are contained in F.S. Regs, Part II. and the Staff Manual respectively. Title Pages will be prepared in manuscript.

Place	Date	Hour	Summary of Events and Information	Remarks and references to Appendices
VIERSTRAAT	28th August	—	The O.C. and 2/C in Command visited and inspected the fire trenches. G.O.C. visited Battn. H.Q. 17th Divn. On at 3.15 P.M. & proceeded to inspect VIERSTRAAT subsidiary line on the night 28/29 Lieut. BLIGH, R.E. was killed in front of R. trenches while laying out line of ditch to be constructed in front of fire trenches. Screen erected on VIERSTRAAT – WYTSCHAETE road about 300° S.E. of VIERSTRAAT.	
do.	29th August	—	O.C. inspected screen erected on night of 28/29. Heavy rain P.M. Work on trenches and dugouts continued.	
do.	30th August	—	No incidents. Work on trenches and dugouts continued as on previous days.	
do.	31st	—	At about 6.0 P.M. "C" Coy sustained casualties in trench N7. 3 killed. 3 wounded by rifle grenade landing in harness. This night the Battln. was relieved in the trenches and at VIERSTRAAT by 10th Lan. Fusiliers. Relief completed by 12 midnight. The W.D. casualties from 1st to 31st August were – killed 6 wounded-following- killed 3 wounded 22	Total 31 see appendix B

APPENDIX "B".

RANK	REG NO.	NAME	CASUALTY	DATE	REMARKS
L.Cpl.	5299	Leake C	Killed	1·8·15	
"	12886	Sweeney. P	Wounded	1·8·15	
Pte	13265	Trewick. J.E	Wounded	1·8·15	
"	13145	Cuthbert. R.	Died of Wounds	2·8·15	Wounded 1·8·15
"	13141	Anderson R.B	Killed	9·8·15	
"	4120	Taylor. J.T.	Wounded	8·8·15	Rejoined
"	15316	Archer. A.H	Wounded.	9·8·15	
"	5220	Leslie G.K.	Wounded.	10·8·15	Rejoined
Cpl.	13178	Jerram. T.	Died of Wounds	14·8·15	
Pte	12880	Forster. J.W	Died of Wounds	14·8·15	
"	5205	Jones. W.	Wounded.	14·8·15	
"	12232	Travers. J.R	Wounded	20·8·15	Rejoined.
"	12255	Wilson. G.	Wounded	20·8·15	Rejoined
"	11375	Robinson. G	Killed	23·8·15	
"	12994	Allen. P.	Wounded.	22·8·15	
"	12983	Main. A	Wounded	22·8·15	
"	12165	Hamilton. S.B	Wounded	23·8·15	Rejoined
"	5220	Leslie G.K.	Wounded	23·8·15	
C.S.M.	9605	Smith. J.W	Wounded	26·8·15	
Pte	12214	Bolam. W	Wounded	26·8·15	
"	12131	Norris. R.H	Wounded	26·8·15	
L.Cpl	14800	Tickner. S.	Wounded	26·8·15	Rejoined
Pte	12156	Tinn. H.	Wounded	26·8·15	Rejoined
"	13326	O'Dowd. J.	Wounded.	31·8·15	
"	16355	Sandy	Wounded	31·8·15	
"	15906	Whittaker. J.	Killed	31·8·15	
"	10668	Elston. D.	Killed	31·8·15	
"	12263	Harrison A	Killed	31·8·15	
"	13166	Dick. J.	Wounded	31·8·15	
"	13267	Nelson. J	Wounded	31·8·15	
"	10675	Smith. R.	Wounded	31·8·15	

2. NETT. RETURN OF WASTAGE.

Officers 1. Capt H.W.R. Haselhurst.
Other Ranks 48.

3. RETURN OF DRAFTS RECEIVED DURING MONTH OF AUGUST
30. N.C.O's & men Taken on Strength.   6.8.15.
40 N.C.O's & men Taken on Strength   23.8.15.

70 TOTAL NUMBER OF REINFORCEMENTS.

4. TOTAL STRENGTH OF BATTALION ON AUGUST 31ST 1915.

Officers 29   Other Ranks 996
         Grand Total.   1025.

52nd Inf.Bde.
17th Div.

9th BATTN. THE NORTHUMBERLAND FUSILIERS.

S E P T E M B E R

1 9 1 5

Attached:

Appendices "C" & "D".

Army Form C. 2118.

WAR DIARY
or
INTELLIGENCE SUMMARY.   9/Northumberland Fusiliers.

(Erase heading not required.)

September 1915

Place	Date	Hour	Summary of Events and Information	Remarks and references to Appendices
LA CLYTTE	1st Sept		In reserve at LA CLYTTE. Battn. marched in relays to RENINGHELST for hot bath and change of underclothing. Heavy rain.	
do	2d Sept		Heavy rain. Battn. mostly engaged on fatigues.	
do	3d/4th Sept		In reserve. Heavy rain. Battn. on fatigues.	

Army Form C. 2118
(8)

WAR DIARY or INTELLIGENCE SUMMARY

(Erase heading not required.)

9th Northumberland Fusiliers

Place	Date	Hour	Summary of Events and Information	Remarks and references to Appendices
LA CLYTTE	5th Sept	-	At 10 P.M. the Battalion relieved 9th West Riding at RIDGEWOOD and BOIS CARRE, LA BRASSERIE, defence posts. 'A' Coy. + 3 Platoons 'B' Coy. in RIDGEWOOD. one Platoon 'B' Coy. at LA BRASSERIE; 'C' Coy. in VIERSTRAAT defence posts; 'D' Coy. at BOIS CARRE. Headquarters at RIDGEWOOD.	See Appendix C
RIDGEWOOD	6th Sept	-	Two casualties (wounded) in 'C' Coy. at VIERSTRAAT. Two casualties in Kemport convoy proceeding YPRES. Three killed, seven wounded in transport convoy proceeding YPRES - DICKEBUSCH - YPRES. 2 heavy draught horses killed and wagons destroyed by shell-fire. This day about 6.45 p.m. Captain H.B. Knott was fatally wounded in Western Redoubt, BOIS CARRE and fell in ambulance to POPERINGHE where he arrived at 10 P.M.	
do.	7th Sept	-	Captain H.B. Knott died of wounds at 1.40 a.m. This loss was very sincerely and deeply mourned by all ranks. Two men of 'C' Company killed by shrapnel at VIERSTRAAT.	
do.	8th Sept	-	BOIS CARRE defences. Western, Eastern and Southern Redoubt visited by 2nd in Command + Adjt.	
do.	9th "	-	In Brigade Reserve at RIDGEWOOD.	
do.	10th "	-	The Battalion this day took over the position as on 21st August from 10th Lan. Fus. One Company "A" being into mobile reserve at the Batt. Headquarters 800 yds. N.W. of VIERSTRAAT. The reliefs were completed without incident by 10 P.M.	

Army Form C. 2118

(9)

WAR DIARY or INTELLIGENCE SUMMARY

9th Northumberland Fusiliers

(Erase heading not required.)

Instructions regarding War Diaries and Intelligence Summaries are contained in F.S. Regs., Part II. and the Staff Manual respectively. Title Pages will be prepared in manuscript.

Place	Date	Hour	Summary of Events and Information	Remarks and references to Appendices
VIERSTRAAT	11.9.15	-	The C.O. and 2nd in Command visited the fire trenches 10.A.M. to 3.30 P.M.	
do.	12.9.15	-	The Brigadier and C.O. visited the fire trenches 9.30. to 1 P.M. The G.O.C. 17" Div. inspected VIERSTRAAT defended localities, and afterwards (5.45.P.M) conferred with C.O.	
do.	13.9.15	-	Trenches visited by 2nd in Command 9.45.a.m. to 1.30.P.M. From 3.P.M. to 24.10.P.M. "B" Battery, 120th N.W. of VIERSTRAAT was heavily shelled. No casualties occurred. No. of projectiles (8.5) was 36: shells used armour piercing.	
do.	14.9.15	-	The C.O. + Adjt. visited fire trenches 10.a.m to 2.15 p.m.	
do.	15.9.15	-	The C.O. + 2nd in Command visited fire trenches 9.30.a.m to 1.30.P.M.	
do.	16.9.15	-	The C.O. + Adjt. with O.C. 93rd Field Coy. R.E. visited the trenches 9.45 a.m to 2 P.M. The German artillery on the ___ and from previous days shelled our above an hour (namely beginning at noon) the dummy screens in position at four points near POPPY LANE. The expenditure of ammunition was considerable + the damage done to screens in clay was repaired by working parties by night. No casualties occurred.	
do.	17.9.15	-	Trenches visited by 2nd in Command 9.30.a.m. to 2.P.M. The support trench No.8. + reinforcing fire trenches were shelled by a new form of H.E. shrapnel fired from mortar. Positions	

WAR DIARY or INTELLIGENCE SUMMARY

9" Northumberland Fusiliers

Army Form C. 2118

Place	Date	Hour	Summary of Events and Information	Remarks and references to Appendices
VIERSTRAAT (this includes)	17.9.15 (continued from page 9)	—	9 the hostile w/E pieces of fire were collected by O.C. "C" Company & sent to 52nd Inf. Bde. for investigation.	
do.	18.9.15	—	The C.O. & Capt. visited the fire trenches 10 a.m. to 2 P.M.	
do.	19.9.15	—	At about 9 A.M. the Enemy put 6 heavy shell (probably 8.9 in.) in vicinity of Bn. Headquarters VIERSTRAAT. No damage, no casualties.	
do.	20.9.15	—	On night of 20/21, a patrol of "B" Coy got up to Enemy's wire opposite M3 trench. The entanglements reported very strong. Knife-rests but deep & not - fastened together. The wire was found to be three ply & impervious to ordinary wire cutters. Bank about 1½ m. long.	
do.	21.9.15	—	The Battalion was relieved in the fire trenches by 10 "Lan. Fus. The relief being completed without incident by 7.25 P.M. Headquarters arrived at LACLYTTE at 10 P.M. for four days rest. The C.O. & 2 i/c Command visited the fire trenches 9.45. am to 1.30. P.M. A Coy of 22nd Canadian Regt. was found to be under instruction in L. trenches in right of our line.	
LA CLYTTE	22.9.15	—	Battalion at rest LA CLYTTE. The Enemy positions were bombarded in front of 17 Division especially BOIS QUARANTE; PICADILLY FARM, & HOLLANDSCHESCHUUR FARM. Enemy wire reported to be severely damaged.	
do.	23.9.15	—	At LA CLYTTE at 4 P.M. Enemy position again heavily bombarded as on previous day. At midnight 23/24 the Battalion went into 50" Inf. Bde. and was 5" Corps Reserve with	

WAR DIARY or INTELLIGENCE SUMMARY

9th Northumberland Fusiliers

Army Form C. 2118

Place	Date	Hour	Summary of Events and Information	Remarks and references to Appendices
LA CLYTTE	23.9.15 (continued from page 10)		in readiness to move at an hour's notice. The enemy front opposite 19th Division was again heavily bombarded 4 P.M. to 4.45 P.M.	
do.	24.9.15	—	Battalion confined to Camp in readiness to move as 5th Corps reserve with 50th Inf. Bde.	
do.	25.9.15	—	(Requisite transport inspected at LA CLYTTE at 2 P.M.) At 11.6 a.m. 7.M. Commander in Chief telegraphed "The C in C makes known to be informed that he feels confident that they will realize how much depends on their success in the forthcoming operations depends upon the individual efforts of each Officer, N.C.O. & man. He wishes them to be conveyed verbally by all Company Commanders." Ends. A telegram received at 10.40 a.m. begins "Gas and Smoke opened in front of first and Indian Corps. 5th Brigade found German trenches in front of GIVENCHY. MEERUT division captured German front line and reports 100 enemy parties surrendering. 8th Division captured German second line trench.	
do.	26.9.15	—	Sunrise service 9.30 a.m. after parade the C.O. read further telegrams received reporting success of British and French attack near LA BASSEE and in CHAMPAGNE respectively. The attack on 5th Corps front near HOOGE was at first successful but it was not found possible to retain possession of captured trenches. Two Officers and 167 German prisoners were captured in this attack. Particulars are given in the attached summary marked "Appendix D"	Appendix D.

1875 Wt. W593/826 1,000,000 4/15 J.B.C. & A. A.D.S.S./Forms/C. 2118.

Army Form C. 2118

(12)

WAR DIARY
or
INTELLIGENCE SUMMARY 9th Northumberland Fusiliers

(Erase heading not required.)

Place	Date	Hour	Summary of Events and Information	Remarks and references to Appendices
LA CLYTTE	27.9.15	—	Battalion still in 5th Corps Reserve. Received orders from 52nd Inf. Bde. at 9.22 AM "Following Ulpain (Brigadier General BENYON). Following Ulpain captured whole of 1st & 2nd line trenches along a front of 21 kilometres. They have captured also in "CHAMPAGNE" in same date 18,000 prisoners & 31 guns. British forces withstood enemy counter attack about and including LOOS. By 11am drawing upon in enemy reserve we have greatly aided 115 French. We captured on 25" and 26", 2,600 prisoners; 9 guns, and many machine guns. Our aeroplanes bombed and derailed train E. of DOUAI and another laden with troops at ROSULT. Also burnt station at VALENCIENNES. Ends.	48 ests.
LA CLYTTE	28.9.15	—	Battalion still in 5th Corps Reserve. Battalion Drill in morning. Proceeded to Ridgewood in afternoon to be in 52nd Bde Reserve taking over from 9th Duke of Wellingtons Regt. B coy proceeded to take over O5, P5 and S8 being attached to 51st Bde. Reliefs completed without incident.	
Ridgewood	29.9.15		At RIDGEWOOD reserve to the 52nd Inf. Bde. (see appendix)	
RIDGEWOOD	30.9.15		At RIDGEWOOD in BRIGADE RESERVE. Received orders at 11.5am that the Brigade	
RIDGEWOOD	1.10.15		Received orders that battalion was to take over trenches 37 to 40 inclusive and including Support and Reserve trenches and R7 and R8, (see appendix). opposite HILL 60.	

J.V. Bryan
Major
Comdt 9th N.F. Bn.

APPENDIX. C.

Reg'tl Number	Rank	Name	Casualty	Date	Remarks
	Capt	Knott H.B.	Died of wounds	7-9-15	Wounded 6-9-15
13102	Pte	McKinney J.	Killed	6-9-15	
13120	"	Cottiss W.J.	Killed	6-9-15	
13130	"	Barron B.	Killed	6-9-15	
10433	"	Adams J.	Killed	6-9-15	
6904	"	Shiel J.J.	Killed	6-9-15	
4779	"	Miller W.J.	Died of wounds	6-9-15	Wounded 6-9-15
1469	"	Hornsby G.	Wounded	6-9-15	
10634	"	Moffatt A.	Wounded	6-9-15	
13016	"	Gibbons G.	Wounded	6-9-15	
13888	L/Cpl	Scott W.P.	Wounded	6-9-15	
13125	Pte	Donaghey T.	Wounded	6-9-15	Rejoined.
13106	Pte	Thompson J.	Wounded	6-9-15	Rejoined.
13142	L/Cpl	Oakley J.	Wounded	7-9-15	
13155	"	Eales R.	Wounded	8-9-15	
9124	Sgt	Evans J.	Wounded	1-9-15	
15389	Pte	Needham A.	Wounded	10-9-15	
12302	Pte	Kilnshurst A.P.	Wounded	16-9-15	
13194	"	Henderson W.	Killed	18-9-15	
13140	Cpl	Whent A.	Wounded	24-9-15	
14989	Pte	Hawkridge J.	Wounded	25-9-15	
12982	"	Usher C.E.	Killed	28-9-15	Accidentally
11345	"	Slater J.W.	Wounded	29-9-15	

(2) Nett Return of Wastage.

Officers 1. Capt. H.B. Knott.
Other Ranks. 29.

(3) Return of Drafts received during September.
30 N.C.O's & men taken on Strength 27-9-15

(4) Total Strength of Battalion on September 30th
Officers.   24.
Other Ranks   990
                1014.

APPENDIX D

5th Corps.

SUMMARY OF INFORMATION. - No 143.

26/9/15.

ALLIED FRONT.

British. Yesterday morning an attack was carried out by our 1st Army. East of GIVENCHY the German first line trenches appear to have been captured without much difficulty. But in this section our Troops were bombed out of them later in the day. South of the LA BASSEE Canal, however, considerable progress was made although a heavy counter attack about midnight drove us back a short distance N.W. of HULLUCH. This morning our line ran through FOSSE No 8 (South of AUCHY-LA-BASSEE) cross roads just west of HULLUCH, down LENS main road as far as Hill 70 where Germans still hold redoubt on crest of the hill, and thence south of LOOS to our original line at FOSSE No 5. This represents an advance of 2000 - 3000 yards on a front of about 6000 yards. We captured 8 German field guns and took 2200 prisoners. The advance is being resumed today.

5th Corps Front. Yesterday morning we attacked the enemy in the vicinity of HOOGE and BELLEWARDE FARM. A considerable number of German trenches were captured but it was not found possible to hold them. 167 German prisoners, including 2 officers, were taken.

French. After a bombardment lasting several days the French assumed the offensive yesterday morning in CHAMPAGNE, and captured the whole first line of German trenches on a front of 25 to 30 kilometres. The attack was made from the line North of ST HILAIRE LE GRAND - SOUAIN - PERTHES-LES-HURLUS and VIRGINY. By evening the French had reached the line AUBERIVE - NAVARIN FARM - MAISON DE CHAMPAGNE FARM - HILL 190, an advance in some places of three to four kilometres. During the day between 7,000 and 8,000 prisoners were taken.

RUSSIA.

Following the recapture of LUTZK, where 4,000 prisoners were taken, the Russians have gained two more important successes. East of VILNA the enemy were driven from the town of VILEIKA, and are reported to have lost several thousand prisoners, fifteen field guns, and over twenty machine guns. On the OGINSKI Canal and the JASIOLDA, North of the PRIPET marshes, where Von MACKENSEN on his own admission has been compelled to withdraw on account of a Russian encircling movement, the Russians have driven the Germans in retreat and have occupied LOGICHIN, 15 miles North of PINSK.

BALKANS.

Martial Law is to be proclaimed in Greece. Mobilization is proceeding and the military measures now enforced are greeted with enthusiasm. In Bulgaria on the other hand the mobilization is characterized by an absence of fervour.

GERMANY.

The Allies' recent raid on STUTTGART is exciting general protest throughout Germany. The Duke of WURTEMBURG has expressed intense indignation in a telegram which he has sent to the Burgomaster. Nothing has been disclosed as to the results of the raid but there is ground for believing that the number killed and wounded is greater than in the KARLSRUHE raid. The German press calls for an immediate raid of a deadly character on PARIS by way of retaliation.

27/9/15. SUN rises 5.43 a.m. Sets 5.37 p.m.
         MOON "   6.36 p.m. " 10.38 a.m.

52nd Inf.Bde.
17th Div.

9th BATTN. THE NORTHUMBERLAND FUSILIERS.

O C T O B E R

1 9 1 5

Attached:

List of Casualties.

WAR DIARY
or
INTELLIGENCE SUMMARY
(Erase heading not required.)

Army Form C. 2118

9th Wilts Fusiliers 13

Place	Date	Hour	Summary of Events and Information	Remarks and references to Appendices
	1915		Received orders that battalion was to take over trenches 37 to 40 inclusive	
RIDGEWOOD	1 Oct	—	as 17th Division was relieved to take over part of line held by 46th Division. Battalion left RIDGEWOOD at 5.15 p.m. and relieved 5th North Staffords in these trenches. The relief was completed by 12.15 p.m. One casualty in C coy whilst altering the trenches on railway cutting. Previously the same afternoon Germans had blown up a mine in Trench 40, killing 2 officers and one man of Royal Engineers. These trenches were S.W. of HILL 60 about 2000 yards from HOOGE salient. They were very good trenches- in the greater portion of the line only 80 yards from GERMAN trenches.	
HILL 60	2 Oct		B coy started working to occupy crater made by mine explosion in trench 40. Whilst working in this crater incurred 3 casualties, 2nd Lt L.R. Burrows and Pte Ord being killed and 4/c Taylor wounded. 2 Lt Burrows was fatally shot whilst going to the assistance of Pte Ord. The loss of such an excellent and promising officer was deeply felt by all ranks. Two other men were also killed this day, one in trench 40 and one in own trench. Owing to the proximity of the enemy lines many rifle grenades and bombs were exchanged, but not much shelling took place with the exception of 7.7. The enemy opposite this line of trenches appeared to be very good troops with good morale and were very active snipers.	

WAR DIARY
or
INTELLIGENCE SUMMARY
(Erase heading not required.)

Army Form C. 2118

9th North'n Fus

14

Place	Date	Hour	Summary of Events and Information	Remarks and references to Appendices
HILL 60	3 Oct.		Still in same trenches. Work was continued uninterrupted on craters. Many rifle grenades were thrown during day into enemy trenches. One casualty in D coy whilst using West's Spring Bomb throwers.	
HILL 60	4 Oct.		No noteworthy incident occurred during day. The battalion was relieved by 8 Gordon Highrs and 7th Seaforth Highrs & 26th Infy Bde, two very weak battalions. Relief was carried out by 11.45 pm without incident. The battalion marched to Brigade Transport Depot DICKEBUSCH arriving there about 2 pm, bivouacing in the field for the night.	
DICKEBUSCH	5 Oct.		The battalion was refitted and clothed during the morning as far as stores would permit. Brigade marched at 7.30 pm in brigade route to GODWAERSVELDE via RHENINGHELST, WESTOUTRE and BOESCHEPE. The battalion was allotted billets in GODWAERSVELDE and neighbouring farms, the whole division being "in rest".	
GODWAERSVELDE	6 Oct.		Battalion in rest billets. Interior economy was carried out all day. The rest after 3 months with B.E.F. was much appreciated by all ranks.	

Army Form C. 2118

WAR DIARY
or
INTELLIGENCE SUMMARY

(Erase heading not required.)

9th Notts Fus.

Instructions regarding War Diaries and Intelligence Summaries are contained in F. S. Regs., Part II. and the Staff Manual respectively. Title Pages will be prepared in manuscript.

Place	Date	Hour	Summary of Events and Information	Remarks and references to Appendices
GODWAERSVELDE	7 Oct.		Battalion in rest. Bombing Practice, Route march by Companies and Physical drill carried out	
GODWAERSVELDE	8 Oct.		Battalion in rest. Bombers increased in numbers, 1 N.C.O and 7 men per Platoon.	
GODWAERSVELDE	9 Oct.		At Rest.	
GODWAERSVELDE	10 Oct.		At Rest.	
GODWAERSVELDE	11 Oct.		At Rest.	
GODWAERSVELDE	12 Oct.		At Rest.	
GODWAERSVELDE	13 Oct.		At Rest.	
GODWAERSVELDE	14 Oct.		At Rest.	

WAR DIARY
or
INTELLIGENCE SUMMARY
(Erase heading not required.)

Army Form C. 2118

9th N. Lakd Fus 16

Place	Date	Hour	Summary of Events and Information	Remarks and references to Appendices
GODESWAERVELDE.	1915			
	15 Oct.		at Rest.	
	16 Oct.		at Rest.	
	17 Oct.		at Rest.	
	18 Oct.		at Rest.	
	19 Oct.		at Rest.	
	20 Oct.		at Rest.	
	21 Oct.		at Rest. During all this period at rest, the battalion was in Army Reserve. Opportunity was taken to give great attention to practicing the attack, also bomb-throwing was extensively practised. Major Viscount Howick assumed command of the battalion in the absence on the sick list of Lt.-Col. H. St. G. Thomas	
GODESWAERVELDE	22 Oct.		The battalion left GODESWAERVELDE Good at 9.30 p.m. and marched in Brigade to G.18.a.4.5. (Sheet 28) to remain in DIVISIONAL RESERVE there. The battalion marched via BOESCHEPE and N.W. of RHENINGHELST, on to the POPERINGHE–VLAMERTINGHE road.	

Army Form C. 2118

9th Notts & Derby

17

WAR DIARY
or
INTELLIGENCE SUMMARY
(Erase heading not required.)

Place	Date	Hour	Summary of Events and Information	Remarks and references to Appendices
1/2 Miles S.W. VLAMERTINGHE G.16.a.4.5.	23 Oct.		In Reserve.	
	24 Oct.		In Reserve.	
	25 Oct.		In Reserve.	
	26 Oct.		In Reserve.	
	27 Oct.		His Majesty the King inspected portions of 2nd Army at RHENINGHELST, each battalion of 52nd Bde sent 2 N.C.O.s and 18 men, this battalion being also represented by Capt. & Adjt. J.P. Chenevix Trench. The battalion still remained in reserve.	
	28 Oct.		In Reserve. Officers proceeded to Salient S. of HOOGE to go round trenches B1, B2 and A12, also redoubts R4, R5 in SANCTUARY WOOD preparatory to battalion taking over this portion of the line. Major H. Bryan C.M.G. assumed command of the battalion.	
	29 Oct.		In Reserve	
	30 Oct.		Battalion proceeded to take over trenches A12, B1, B2 and redoubts R4, R5 in SANCTUARY WOOD in SALIENT S. of HOOGE. These trenches were taken over by 10 p.m. and relief completed without incident	

Army Form C. 2118

9th Notts & Derbys 18

WAR DIARY
or
INTELLIGENCE SUMMARY
(Erase heading not required.)

Place	Date	Hour	Summary of Events and Information	Remarks and references to Appendices
TRENCHES SANCTUARY WOOD	1915 30 Oct.		The disposition of the battalion was as follows:- A coy in A1, 2 and B1, ½ platoons of B coy in B2, remainder of coy in SANCTUARY WOOD, D coy in Redoubts R4 and R5, C coy in reserve in SANCTUARY WOOD. Battalion Headquarters being in MAPLE COPSE. These trenches were taken over from 16th Bn. Sherwood FORESTERS. The unit on our right being 12th MANCHESTER REGT. and on our left 10th LANCASHIRE FUSILIERS.	
	31 Oct.		Quiet day. Scarcely any shelling. No casualties. Enemy working party was located on which artillery opened fire	

H Munro Stuart
Captain Adjt
9th N&D'shire

31/11/15

Casualties during October 1915.

Regt. Number	Rank	Name	Date	Casualty	Remarks
6707	2/Lt	Burrows E.L.	2.10.15	Killed	
5722	Pte	Guilford J.	1.10.15	Died of Wounds	
12198	"	Kenrod J.	1.10.15	Killed	
12206	"	Kay R.M.	2.10.15	Killed	
11316	"	Ord B.P.D.	2.10.15	Killed	
2235	L/Cpl	Wrightson S.B.	2.10.15	Wounded	
12198	Pte	Smith E.	2.10.15	Wounded	
12328	"	Swith E.J.	2.10.15	Killed	
5570	L/Sgt	Pigeon P.J.	4.10.15	Wounded	
14628	Pte	Easton G.	8.10.15	Wounded	
15614	"	Veal H.R.	2.10.15	Wounded	
2330	"	Atkinson N.	1.10.15	Wounded	
18702	"	Nicholson J.	29.10.15	Wounded	While attached to Bde. to date given in report.

Bug J.

Killed Statement: 8
Wounded: 6
Total: 14

52nd Inf.Bde.
17th Div.

9th BATTN. THE NORTHUMBERLAND FUSILIERS.

N O V E M B E R

1 9 1 5

Attached:

Appendix "E".

WAR DIARY
INTELLIGENCE SUMMARY

Army Form C. 2118
Page 18.

Place	Date	Hour	Summary of Events and Information	Remarks and references to Appendices
SANCTUARY WOOD	1 Nov	—	Battalion still in occupation of trenches on salient S. of HOOGE. Enemy somewhat more active and we had 2 casualties (vide appendix E)	
	2 Nov.	—	Heavy rains all day and much damage done to trenches which were flooded to a considerable depth. Commanding officer visited Bde HdQrs and urged the need of close co-operation between infantry and field and howitzer batteries whenever suitable targets were reported from observation post.	
	3 Nov	—	C coy relieved this day by A coy in A.12 trench. One casualty (vide appendix E) Good progress made in letting off flood water. Heavy rain again fell.	
	4 Nov	—	Another wet day. One man and subsidiary communication trenches fell in in many places. 3 casualties (vide appendix E)	
	5 Nov	—	Continuation of heavy rains. After consultation with C.O.s of Field and Howitzer batteries, it was arranged to co-operate in shelling enemy positions at STIRLING CASTLE where large working parties had been seen from our observation post.	

WAR DIARY or INTELLIGENCE SUMMARY

(Erase heading not required.)

Army Form C. 2118

Page 19

Place	Date 1915	Hour	Summary of Events and Information	Remarks and references to Appendices
SANCTUARY WOOD	6 Nov.		Weather improved. Artillery bombardment mainly on enemy's second line from 6 a.m. to 6.45 a.m. Heavy mist unfortunately prevented accurate observation but many heavy shell fell in and about STIRLING CASTLE. The orders for the relief of the battalion on the 7th were this day cancelled.	
	7 Nov.		Enemy this day retaliated heavily especially on B2 trench, only one casualty (see Appendix E). Bombardment continued intermittently from 2.30 pm till 4pm.	
	8 Nov.		Our guns initiated bombardment at 10 a.m. to which enemy promptly replied with guns and trench mortars. Special attention being given to trench B2 and GORDALLS (C.T.) Casualties 5 all B coy (vide appendix E)	
	9 Nov.		On night 9/10 Nov. battalion was relieved as follows — Trench A12 7th ROYAL SCOTS FUSILIERS, Trenches B1 and B2 by 11th ROYAL SCOTS. MACHINE guns by 10th ARGYLL and SUTHERLAND HIGHRS Relief completed at 11.35 pm during very heavy rain. Headquarters left MAPLE COPSE at 1 a.m. on 10th and arrived in camp at OUDERDOM (censored) at 5 a.m.	

Army Form C. 2118

Page 20

WAR DIARY
or
INTELLIGENCE SUMMARY
(Erase heading not required.)

Place	Date 1915	Hour	Summary of Events and Information	Remarks and references to Appendices
	9 Nov.		The last company arriving in camp at 6.30 a.m.	
2000 yards S.W. of VLAMERTINGHE	10 Nov		At 2.30 p.m. battalion moved camp to G.18.a.4.5. and went into Divisional reserve. Lt-Col Thomas this day resumed command of the battalion on return from leave of absence vice Major H. Bryan C.M.G.	
—do—	11 Nov		In DIVISIONAL RESERVE; this day battalion had use of baths at POPERINGHE.	
—do—	12 Nov.		In DIVISIONAL RESERVE.	
—do—	13 Nov		In DIVISIONAL RESERVE.	
—do—	14 Nov		In DIVISIONAL RESERVE. 2nd in command and 4 company officers visited the trenches at HOOGE preparatory to taking over from 6th DORSET REGT.	
—do—	15 Nov		In DIVISIONAL RESERVE. Advance parties were sent to HOOGE trenches	

WAR DIARY or INTELLIGENCE SUMMARY

Army Form C. 2118
Page 21

Place	Date 1915	Hour	Summary of Events and Information	Remarks and references to Appendices
2000yds S.W. of VLAMERTINGHE	16 Nov		On night 16/17 Nov. battalion relieved 6 Dorset Regt. in the left centre sector of HOOGE defences. Relief complete by 9.11 p.m. Dispositions as follows. Trenches C4 and C5 held by C company, C6 and C7 by D coy, trench C7S by 2 platoons A coy. At battalion	
HOOGE.			headquarters (HALF-WAY HOUSE) 2 platoons of A coy in reserve. at KRUISTRAAT B company J. Trenches on our immediate right were occupied by 12th MANCHESTER REGT. 52 INF BDE and those on our left by 7 LINCOLN REGT. 51 INF BDE. During the relief march through the town heavily shelled when the battalion marched through the town but we were fortunate to escape with no casualties	
HOOGE	17 Nov		Owing to recent heavy rains the trenches taken over were in a deplorable condition, average depth of mud and water being about 2 feet. Throughout the day rain, hail and sleet fell continuously. Communication by day (except by telephone) between	

WAR DIARY or INTELLIGENCE SUMMARY

Page 22

Place	Date 1915	Hour	Summary of Events and Information	Remarks and references to Appendices
HOOGE	17 Nov	—	Battalion headquarters and the firing line was entirely cut off, all communication trenches having fallen in. One Casualty (vide appendix E)	
HOOGE	18 Nov	—	Enemy aeroplanes were very active about 8.30 a.m. when 4 bombs were dropped behind trench C7, no damage was done. It was brought to notice of brigade that the ground in the vicinity of HOOGE village and W. of that point along YPRES-MENIN road remains an uncleared battlefield affording scope for the activities of the Salvage Corps. Three Casualties (vide appendix E)	
HOOGE	19 Nov	—	A profusion of signallers, bombers and machine gun section of 9th WEST RIDING REGT came to the trenches preparatory to relief. The severe weather during the past 2 days resulted in several cases of trench feet. An observation post was established in the Gable.	
HOOGE	20 Nov	—	Number of trench feet reported to-day was again excessive, bringing the total number from night 16/17th up to 40. A dug-out at Battalion Headquarters received a direct hit from 5.9 Howitzer shell resulting casualties being 5 killed, 1 died of wounds and 5 wounded (vide appendix E)	

WAR DIARY
or
INTELLIGENCE SUMMARY
(Erase heading not required.)

Army Form C. 2118

Page 23

Place	Date 1915	Hour	Summary of Events and Information	Remarks and references to Appendices
HOOGE	20 Nov	—	The battalion was relieved on night 20/21st Nov by 9th Battalion WEST RIDING regiment, relief was completed by 9.15 p.m without incident. The battalion went into BRIGADE reserve in the RAMPARTS LILLE GATE YPRES.	
HOOGE.	21 Nov	—	BRIGADE reserve at YPRES. The battalion was distributed as follows — Battalion Hdqrs and C coy in the ramparts. A coy in the cellars beneath the GENERAL POST OFFICE. B coy in cellars of convent adjoining RUE RICHES-CLAIRE, D coy in cellars in the RUE DE LILLE	
HOOGE	22 Nov		BRIGADE reserve. 2 casualties (vide appendix E) were sustained by night working parties.	
HOOGE	23 Nov		BRIGADE reserve. Battalion was relieved on night 23/24th Nov by 7th YORKSHIRE regt 51st BDE, relief being completed without incident by 7p.m. Battalion then going into DIVISIONAL reserve	

INTELLIGENCE SUMMARY

Page 24

Place	Date	Hour	Summary of Events and Information	Remarks and references to Appendices
Camp 2000 yards S.W. of VLAMERTINGHE	1915 24 Nov		DIVISIONAL RESERVE at camp G.18 a 4.5. 2000 yards S.W. of VLAMERTINGHE. Battalion had use of DIVISIONAL baths throughout the day.	
	25 Nov		In DIVISIONAL RESERVE.	
	26 Nov		In DIVISIONAL RESERVE. LT. COL H. St. G. THOMAS assumed temporary command of 52nd Inf. Bde vice BRIG-GEN. H.C. SURTEES CB MVO DSO on leave of absence. Major H BRYAN CMG assumed command of the battalion	
	27 Nov		In DIVISIONAL RESERVE.	
	28 Nov		In DIVISIONAL RESERVE	
	29 Nov		In DIVISIONAL RESERVE	
	30 Nov		In DIVISIONAL RESERVE	

J. Chevenix-Trench
Capt & Adjt
9 N. Fus.

1/12/15

Appendix E

Regtl Number	Rank & Name	Date of Attack	Casualty	Remarks
9720	Pte McGill	1-11-15	Wounded	
12299	L/Cpl Viner T.H.	1-11-15	do	
12155	" Muse J.	3-11-15	Killed	
12189	Pte Stevenson R.	4-11-15	Wounded	
14863	" Boyd K.P.	4-11-15	do	
13105	" Thompson G.	4-11-15	do	
10588	" Palmer J.	7-11-15	do	
12104	" Sewer S.	8-11-15	Killed	
12356	L/Cpl Milne C.D.	8-11-15	Wounded	
12205	Pte Charlton C.S.	8-11-15	do	
12529	" Dunn R.O.	8-11-15	do	
12187	" Mitchell J.	8-11-15	do	
10436	" Riley J.	8-11-15	do	accidentally
10746	" Boardman E.	18-11-15	Killed	
13026	" Lawrence J.	17-11-15	Wounded	
13208	" Nichol J.S.	18-11-15	Killed	
10417	" McGuigan S.	18-11-15	Wounded	
15138	L/Cpl Mills J.	20-11-15	Killed	
13029	" Waters J.A.	20-11-15	do	
12377	" Smith F.	20-11-15	do	
12947	Pte Daglish R.	20-11-15	do	
14526	" Reynolds J.	20-11-15	do	
10486	" Balmer J.	20-11-15	Died of wounds	Wounded 20/11/15
13357	Cpl Hornby J.	20-11-15	Wounded	
13073	L/Cpl Peach E.	20-11-15	do	
7045	Pte Meadows J.	20-11-15	do	
15031	" Mottershaw A.	20-11-15	do	
5196	" Otway C.H.	20-11-15	do	
13175	" Bartlett J.	29-11-15	do	
10474	" Hayes J.	29-11-15	do	
16279	" Bell W.	6-11-15	do	
12283	Sgt Logie G.M.L.	5-11-15	do	
	2/Lt Patten M.E.	5-11-15	do	Whilst at Bombing School Terdeghen Accidental.

Statement

Killed	10
Wounded	23
Total Casualties	33 x Includes 1 Officer

H. Cheney Thrush
Capt & Adjt
9th Yorkshires

1/12/15

52nd Inf.Bde.
17th Div.

9th BATTN. THE NORTHUMBERLAND FUSILIERS.

D E C E M B E R

1 9 1 5

Attached:

Appendices "F", "G", "H", "I" & "J".

Confidential

A.G 3rd Ech: Base.

I herewith enclose War Diary of 9th Northumberland Fusiliers for the period 1st to 31st December 1915.

J H Bryan
Lieut-Colonel
Cmdg 9th North'd Fusiliers.

January 12th 16.

Confidential
War Diary
of
9th (S) Bn: North'd Fusiliers
from 1 Dec. to 31 Dec 1915
Volume 1.

Army Form C. 2118

WAR DIARY
or
INTELLIGENCE SUMMARY
(Erase heading not required.)

9 Northumberland Fusiliers

page 25

Place	Date	Hour	Summary of Events and Information	Remarks and references to Appendixes
CAMP 1000 yds. S.W. of VLAMERTINGHE	1 Dec.	—	In Divisional Reserve. Advance Party (Machine Gun section, Bombers and Signallers) proceeded to the trenches occupied previously on 16th November.	
HOOGE	2 Dec.	—	The battalion relieved 6th DORSET REGT in the left half of the right sector of HOOGE defences. The dispositions being as on 16th November. The relief was completed by 8.50 p.m. without incident or casualties.	
HOOGE	3 Dec.	—	In the firing line. A scheme for the defence of the half sector held by the battalion was prepared for approval by O.O.C. 17th Division. Weather very wet but mild.	
HOOGE	4 Dec.	—	In firing line. A working party on enemy support trench opposite C4 was effectively shelled by trench howitzer. The enemy showed no enterprise.	
HOOGE	5 Dec.	—	In firing line. Weather still very wet. Great difficulty in keeping water down in trenches. Battalion Headquarters was heavily shelled (5.9 H.E.) from 2 p.m. till 2.20 p.m. No casualties.	

WAR DIARY 9th North Fusiliers
INTELLIGENCE SUMMARY
Page 26

Army Form C. 2118

Place	Date	Hour	Summary of Events and Information	Remarks and references to Appendices
HOOGE	6 Dec	—	The battalion was relieved in the trenches by 9th WEST RIDING REGT. The relief was completed without incident by 9.30 p.m. The battalion proceeded to KRUISTRAAT and huts at OUDERDOM being disposed as follows. Headquarters and 1½ coys at OUDERDOM and 2½ companies at KRUISTRAAT. This day Lieut-Colonel H. St. G. THOMAS left the battalion on promotion and appointment as A.A and Q.M.G. CALAIS	
OUDERDOM and KRUISTRAAT	7 Dec		In BRIGADE reserve. Nightly fatigue parties on HOOGE sector. Very wet weather.	
OUDERDOM and KRUISTRAAT	8 Dec		In BRIGADE reserve. Major BRYAN accompanied by a Staff Officer 17th DIV. visited the FRENCH army of the NORTH in the vicinity of ELVERDINGHE and BOESINGHE with a view to studying the methods adopted by the FRENCH for prevention of "chilled feet".	

WAR DIARY
or
INTELLIGENCE SUMMARY

Army Form C. 2118

9th NORTHUMBERLAND FUSILIERS   page 27.

Place	Date	Hour	Summary of Events and Information	Remarks and references to Appendices
OUDERDOM and KRUISTRAAT	9 Dec.		In BRIGADE reserve	
CAMP 1000 yds S.W. of VLAMERTINGHE	10 Dec.		In DIVISIONAL reserve. The battalion this day moved from OUDERDOM and KRUISTRAAT to the depot.	
CAMP 1000 yds S.W. of	11 Dec.			
	12 Dec.			
	13 Dec.		In DIVISIONAL reserve	
VLAMER-TINGHE	14 Dec.			
	15 Dec.			
Camp 1000 yds S.W. of VLAMERTINGHE	16 Dec.		In DIVISIONAL reserve. The battalion found a working party of 500 men and constructed during the night 16/17 Dec. a sand-bag breastwork forming a communication trench W. of HOOG E.	

WAR DIARY or INTELLIGENCE SUMMARY

9th Northumberland Fusiliers page 28

Army Form C. 2118

Place	Date	Hour	Summary of Events and Information	Remarks and references to Appendices
CAMP 1000 yds S.W. of VLAMERTINGHE	17 Dec		In DIVISIONAL reserve. The usual advance party of Machine gun section, Battalion Runners, and Signallers left for the trenches occupied by the battalion in the front line of the HOOGE sector.	
CAMP HOOGE	18 Dec		This day the battalion relieved 6th DORSET regiment in the firing line taking up the same front as on 2nd December. The relief was completed without incident by 8 p.m.	
HOOGE	5:30am 19 Dec		The enemy began a violent artillery bombardment of YPRES, VLAMERTINGHE and the whole area held by 17th Division. The bombardment was accompanied by a gas attack from the North and a hail of gas and lachrymatory shells from North from Fort and from HILL 60. The bombardment continued incessantly during the whole of the 19th and 20th. No enemy infantry attack was launched on sector held by the battalion. Gas helmets were at once put on by all ranks - no casualties from gas poisoning resulted. In the HOOGE sector the attack was confined to reserve	

WAR DIARY of 9 Northumberland Fusiliers

INTELLIGENCE SUMMARY

page 29.

Place	Date	Hour	Summary of Events and Information	Remarks and references to Appendices
			and support areas, special attention being devoted to the exits from YPRES and the communication trenches leading to the HOOGE sector, with the result that the casualties sustained by troops coming up in support were far greater than those of the troops in the firing line. The Signalling Sergeant, Sergt FULLER and the battalion signallers went out from battalion headquarters and succeeded under heavy shell fire in bringing in 3 wounded men of the 9th WEST RIDING regiment.	
HOOGE.	20 Dec		The artillery bombardment, though rather less intense, continued from midnight 19th till midnight 20th. The enemy shortened his range and covered the area between the exits from YPRES and the CULVERT, MENIN ROAD with a storm of shells which were mainly ineffective as the troops in support were in the trenches assigned to them. As on the previous day the casualties in the firing line were comparatively trifling. This day Pte HEDLEY. T of A coy performed a gallant act in bringing to safety a man of the 18th LANCASHIRE FUSILIERS who was shot in the back by a bullet at a point about 200 yards E. of the CULVERT on the MENIN ROAD, though in full	

WAR DIARY
or
INTELLIGENCE SUMMARY

9th Northumberland Fusiliers page 30

Place	Date	Hour	Summary of Events and Information	Remarks and references to Appendices
(continued)	20 Dec		views of the enemy and under heavy fire, Pte HEDLEY went unaided to the man's assistance, and brought him in and administered first aid.	
HOOGE	21 Dec		The enemy bombardment continued from midnight 20th and ceased abruptly at 7.15 a.m. on the 21st. The total casualties sustained by the battalion up to midnight on the 20th were only 11 and up to the end of the bombardment 13 viz killed 2 O.R. Died of Wounds 1 O.R. Wounded 10 O.R. In rendering a report to the Brigadier 52nd Infy Bde on the operations, the O.C. Battalion concluded as follows "All ranks behaved extremely well under trying conditions and the general feeling was one of regret that no opportunity was given to repel an enemy infantry attack."	
HOOGE	22 Dec		A comparatively quiet day. Beyond some artillery activity on both sides the day was uneventful.	
HOOGE	23 Dec		The battalion was relieved by the 9th Duke of Wellingtons Regt, the relief was completed at 1.35 a.m. on 24th without incident. At 4 a.m. on	

WAR DIARY
or
INTELLIGENCE SUMMARY
(Erase heading not required.)

Army Form C. 2118

page 31

Place	Date	Hour	Summary of Events and Information	Remarks and references to Appendices
	23 Dec.		The morning of the 23rd a bomb attack was successfully carried out in conjunction with 10th LANCASHIRE FUSILIERS on the enemy trenches opposite C3 and C4. 70 bombs were thrown into the enemy trenches by our squads which returned without casualties. The names of LIEUT. H.D. HASLAM who led the main attack and Sergt. MCCONNELL who led the support were brought to the notice of the G.O.C. 17th Division (vide appendix F)	
BELGIAN CHATEAU. KRUISTRAAT.	24 Dec.		On relief from the trenches the battalion was disposed as follows:— KRUISTRAAT. Battalion Hdqrs and 2½ companies. OUDERDOM huts. 1 company Strong points T.H. and I.K. 2 platoons. On Christmas Eve the battalion found working parties as usual.	
BELGIAN CHATEAU KRUISTRAAT.	25 Dec.		A message of Christmas greeting from HIS MAJESTY the KING was received and promulgated (copy attached). Christmas messages were also received from G.O.C. 17th Division and Brigadier 52nd Infy Bde.. The Chaplain (Rev. Norman WRIGHT) conducted Divine service at 2.30 pm.	

WAR DIARY or INTELLIGENCE SUMMARY

Army Form C. 2118

9th North Shropshire
page 32.

Place	Date 1915	Hour	Summary of Events and Information	Remarks and references to Appendices
YPRES.	26 Dec.		This day the battalion relieved 6th DORSET regiment in the RAMPARTS, MENIN GATE YPRES, being attached as reserve to the 57 & 2nd Bde under Brigadier-Genl R.B. FELL. Relief was completed by 6.30 pm without incident. The dispositions being as follows. In the RAMPARTS - Battalion Hdqrs, A and D Companies; in the CONVENT D company; at the ÉCOLE B company.	
YPRES	27 Dec		In the RAMPARTS. The battalion found working parties from 5.30 pm till midnight.	
YPRES	28 Dec.		Enemy artillery shelled YPRES intermittently all day. Working parties at night.	
YPRES	29 Dec.		Heavy enemy bombardment began at 12.25 pm and continued till 4.30 pm. A large number of lachrymatory shells fell near the RAMPARTS and the effect of the gas was severely felt.	
YPRES	30 Dec.		Enemy again shelled YPRES from 10.40 am till noon. The demolition of the [?] afterwards hastened by some shells of 42 centimetre	

WAR DIARY or **INTELLIGENCE SUMMARY**

9 North'd. Page 33

Place	Date	Hour	Summary of Events and Information	Remarks
YPRES	1915 31 Dec.		In RAMPARTS, YPRES – an uneventful day.	
			Appendices	
			F. re Bombing Enterprise	
			G. Christmas message from HIS MAJESTY	
			H. Message from G.O.C. 17th Div. referring to operations 19 Dec.	
			I. Message from G.O.C. 2nd Army referring to operations of 19 Dec.	
			J. Casualties	

J A Bryan
Lieut Col.
Comdg
9 North'd Fusiliers

APPENDICES

"F"
"G"
"H"
"I"
"J"

Appendix F.

Copy

52nd Inf. Bde.
52.G.
480.

O.C. 9th Northumberland Fusiliers
10th Lancashire Fusiliers

The Brigadier wishes all concerned to be informed of his appreciation of the manner in which the Bombing Expedition was carried out this morning.

He congratulates the 9th North^d Fus. and 10th Lancs. Fus. on the careful planning of the enterprise, and the initiative shown by the junior officers and their men in its execution.

He will be pleased to bring the names of the leaders to the notice of the Divisional General.

(sgd) S.R. Shirley, Captain.
Brigade Major.
52nd Infantry Brigade.

22.12.15.

Appendix G.   JHB 20.12.15.

Christmas Message from His Majesty The King.

The following message has been received:—

"Another Christmas finds all the resources of the Empire still engaged in War, and I desire to convey on my own behalf, and on behalf of the Queen, a heartfelt Christmas greeting and our good wishes for the New Year to all who, on Sea and Land, are upholding the honour of the British name. In the officers and men of my Navy, on whom the security of the Empire depends, I repose, in common with all my subjects, a trust that is absolute. On the officers and men of my Armies, whether now in France, in the East, or in other fields, I rely with an equal faith, confident that their devotion, their valour and their self-sacrifice will, under God's guidance, lead to Victory and an honourable Peace. There are many of their comrades now, alas, in hospital and to these brave fellows, also, I desire, with the Queen, to express our deep gratitude and our earnest prayers for their recovery.

Officers and men of the Navy and Army, another year is drawing to a close, as it began, in toil, bloodshed and suffering; but, I rejoice to know that the goal to which you are striving draws nearer into sight.

MAY GOD BLESS YOU AND ALL YOUR UNDERTAKINGS."

GEORGE, R.I.

The following reply has been despatched:—

To:—HIS MAJESTY THE KING,
   Buckingham Palace,
      London.

The Army in France under my Command desires to be allowed to express its warmest thanks to Your Majesty and to Her Majesty the Queen for the gracious message received. On behalf of the troops I respectfully beg Your Majesties to accept the most heartfelt good wishes of all ranks for Xmas and the New Year and an expression of their firm and lasting determination to prove themselves worthy of the great trust which Your Majesty reposes in us.

From:—SIR DOUGLAS HAIG.

Christmas Day, 1915.

1st Printing Co., R.E. G.H.Q. 2000

Appendix H.

Copy.

To all Concerned.

The Major General Commanding 17th Division wishes to express his appreciation of the manner in which all ranks and all units have fulfilled their various duties during yesterday's gas attack.

Not only is credit due to batteries and battalions in the front trenches but also to the battalions who came up from the rear and made their way through heavy shelling to the support trenches, to Engineers and signallers who worked hard throughout the day to keep communications intact, to ambulance and medical personnel who worked hard throughout to collect the wounded, to transport, ammunition, and ration parties who carried out their arduous duties in spite of all risks and to all others who assisted in their various ways in the operations.

He feels sure the Division will do equally well should the enemy make any further attacks.

(Sgd) A.H. Marindin.
Lieut. Col.
G.S. 17th Division.

20.12.15.

Appendix 1

Copy

2nd Army
G.939.

G.O.C. 5th Corps.

I should be glad if you will express to the troops of the 5th Corps my appreciation of their steadiness under the very difficult and trying circumstances which attended the "gas attack" and heavy shelling by the Germans on the 19th inst.

It was owing to the steadiness of the troops that the attack failed completely.

(Sgd) Herbert Plumer
General
Commanding 2nd Army.

21.12.15.

Appendix J.
Casualties 9th North'd Fus.

Regt. No.	Rank	Name	Date of Casualty	Casualty	Remarks
96	Sgt.	Marshall. W.	4/12/15	Wounded	Accidentally
871	Pte.	Ogle. J.W.	7.12.15	Wounded	
886	"	Maxwell. R.	14.12.15	Wounded	
128	"	Pryde. J.	18.12.15	Killed	
879	"	Parkinson G.	19.12.15	Wounded	
273	"	Lowcock. R.B.	20.12.15	Killed	
191	Sgt.	Medlin. A.F.	20.12.15	Died of Wounds	Wounded 20.12.15
179	Sgt.	Graham. W.J.	20.12.15	Wounded	
14	Pte.	Whamer. J.	20.12.15	Wounded	
545	"	Thorpe. F.	20.12.15	Wounded	Accidentally
040	Cpl.	Cafferty. W.	21.12.15	Wounded	
993	Pte.	Anderson A.	21.12.15	Wounded	
039	"	Watson. W.	21.12.15	Wounded	
260	"	Nuitt J.H.	21.12.15	Wounded	
254	"	Fairlam. J.T.	21.12.15	Wounded	
899	"	Stobart. W.	21.12.15	Wounded	
812	"	Sweddle. W.	21.12.15	Died of wounds	Wounded 20.12.15
475	Sgt.	McKeag. R.	19.12.15	Died	Died in hospital. Nephritis
222	Pte.	Lowes R.	23.12.15	Wounded	
280	"	Taylor. F.	23.12.15	Died of wounds	Wounded 23.12.15
177	"	Towns W.	23.12.15	Wounded	
065	"	Ahlstead. G.	23.12.15	Wounded	
54	"	Lutin. D.	23.12.15	Wounded	
320	"	Bonner. C.	23.12.15	Wounded	
301	"	Vincent. J.	23.12.15	Wounded	
336	"	Crooks. W.	19.12.15	Wounded	
120	"	Taylor. J.	20.12.15	Shell shock	
034	"	Oscroft. B.	20.12.15	Shell shock	

Statement
- Killed — 2
- Died of Wounds — 3
- Died — 1
- Wounded — 22
- Total = 28

Strength of Bn. on 31.12.15.
- Officers — 28
- O.R. — 822
- Total = 850

9th Hothmuh: Two:
Vol 2?
Jany 1916

17th
52 Ryle

Army Form C. 2118

Page 33

WAR DIARY
or
INTELLIGENCE SUMMARY
(Erase heading not required.)

9th Northumberland Fusiliers

Place	Date	Hour	Summary of Events and Information	Remarks and references to Appendices
YPRES	1916 1st Jany.		In Ramparts (MENIN GATE) attached to 51st Inf. Bde. Intermittent enemy activity during day & retaliation.	
do.	2nd Jany.		In Ramparts. Orders received to relieve 6th Dorsets (50th Bde) on night of 3/4th. Intermittent Artillery actions. Letter received from Brig. General FELL Comdg. 51st Bde. expressing appreciation of work done during the period 15th Dec–1st Jany. Fusiliers had been attached to his Brigade.	
HOOGE	3rd Jany.		The Battalion relieved the 6th Dorset Regt. in trenches C4, C5, C6, C7 & 1st support and reserve trenches. Trenches IH + IK was also occupied. Relief completed without incident by 8.55 p.m. 2nd March. Regt. on left 10th Sherwood Foresters. The Batt. is attached to 50th Inf. Bde. Brigadier General BANON.	
do.	4th Jany.		Brigadier 50th Inf. Bde. visited Batt. H.Q. and trenches. Working parties out repairing wire found to be much damaged by enemy artillery. One casualty (wounded) ✗	✗ See Appendix K
do.	5th Jany.		Trenches visited by Brigadier and G.S.O.1 of V Corps. Batt. H.Q. heavily shelled between 12.30 and 2.30 p.m. out of 60 shells about 50 were blind. Casualties three wounded	

WAR DIARY
or
INTELLIGENCE SUMMARY 9th Northumberland Fusiliers

Page 34

Army Form C. 2118

Place	Date	Hour	Summary of Events and Information	Remarks and references to Appendices
HOOGE	1916 6' Jan		In trenches, a comparatively quiet day. Nothing of special interest. At 10th Regt., 1st 9th E. Surrey Regt. relieved 9th 24th Division arrived and took over 1st Camp. (Lt. Col. de la Fontaine Commanding) Casualty, one wounded.	
do.	7 Jan.		At 10 Dept., 1st 9th R. Sussex Regt. arrived and took over Camp from 9th E. Surrey Regt. The Battn. was relieved in 10 trenches by 1st 9th E. Surrey Regt. and marched to POPERINGHE to entrain for AUDRICQ (France) 10/17 Division being into rest. The Regtl. Transport marched via Camp 15 GODEWAERSVELDE and there entrained. The Batn. left billets arrived at POPERINGHE at intervals between 12 midnight and 3 a.m. Casualties, two wounded.	
on march	8 Jan.		The Batt. entrained at POPERINGHE at 9.45 A.M. proceeded up with Transport train at GODEWAERSVELDE, arriving at AUDRICQ at 1.15 P.M. After detraining, 1st Batt. marched to LA PANNE, arriving at 4.15 P.M., and went into open billets at LA PANNE; LE COMMUNE and LA COMMUNE.	
LA PANNE	9 Jan.		In rest. Divine service parade at 11. a.m.	

Army Form C. 2118

WAR DIARY
or
INTELLIGENCE SUMMARY
9th Northumberland Fusiliers

Page 35

(Erase heading not required.)

Place	Date	Hour	Summary of Events and Information	Remarks and references to Appendices
LA PANNE	13th Jan 1916		in rest. The Battalion was engaged in reorganizing; interior economy; physical training; route marches; elementary musketry; rifting.	
do.	14th Jan.		transport.	
do.	15th Jan.		Model trenches at TILQUES visited by Officers. Lecture on work elsewhere at TILQUES divisional school.	
do.	16th Jan.		Divine Service. Infantry Commanding Officers of 17th Division visited II Army transport at HAZEBROUCK.	
do.	17th Jan.		Continuation of work programme. LEWIS 'A' Coy. proceeded on detachment to OSTOVE to work on railway sidings.	
do.	18th Jan.		The 50th, 51st & 52nd Inf. Bdes. were inspected during a route march by the II Army Commander, General H. Plumer.	
do.	19th Jan		The Battalion carried out the programme of work laid down on the lines of the proposed between 10th and 14th January.	
	20th Jan.			

Army Form C. 2118

WAR DIARY
or
INTELLIGENCE SUMMARY 9th Northumberland Fusiliers
(Erase heading not required.)

Page 36

Instructions regarding War Diaries and Intelligence Summaries are contained in F.S. Regs., Part II. and the Staff Manual respectively. Title Pages will be prepared in manuscript.

Place	Date	Hour	Summary of Events and Information	Remarks and references to Appendices
LA PANNE	1916 27' Jan'.		The Battalion hdQR. part in a Brigade Tactical Exercise. "A" Coy. returned from detachment.	
do.	28' Jan'.		Continuation of programme of work. (vide anti)	
do.	29' Jan'.		Demonstration of "Gas" attack under 17th Divisional arrangements. Its effects apparent. Lecture by G.S.O. 9' Division on 15 enemy of LOOS.	
do.	30' & 31st Jan'.		The battalion engaged on programme of work as on 28th.	

J.F. Bryan
Lieut. Col.
Comdg.
9th Northd. Fusiliers

1875 Wt. W593/826 1,000,000 4/15 J.B.C. & A. A.D.S.S./Forms/C. 2118.

Appendix K

Summary of Casualties. January 1916

Regt. No	Rank & Name	Coy.	Date	Casualty
13251	Pte. Lemon. J.	C	4.1.16	Wounded
8704	Cpl. Symington. J.	D	5.1.16	- do -
6902	Pte. Scofield. R.	D	5.1.16	- do -
16300	" Clarkson. W.S	D	5.1.16	- do -
12355	" Wilson. A.	B	6.1.16	- do -
10611	L/c. Frazer. W.	C	7.1.16	- do -
13025	Pte. Stoker. E.	A	7.1.16	- do -
13065	" Ahlstedt. G.	D	18.1.16	Died of wounds
12196	" Hardy. C.E	B	27.1.16	Accidentally wounded
13179	Sgt. Graham. W.J.	A	30.1.16	Died of wounds

Statement

Died of wounds   2.
Wounded   8.
Total Casualties. 10.

Reinforcements

Officers.   2   28.1.16.
Other ranks.   47   29.1.16.

Strength of Battalion on 31.1.16.

Officers   28.
Other ranks.   884.

WAR DIARY or INTELLIGENCE SUMMARY

Army Form C. 2118

9th Northamptonshire

Page 37

Place	Date 1916	Hour	Summary of Events and Information	Remarks and references to Appendices
LA PANNE	1st Feb		The 73rd Brigade demonstrated an attack on enemy trenches, at 11 a.m. During the afternoon B. & C. Coys practised the attack over the same ground.	
do	2nd Feb.		The Batt. was engaged in carrying out programme of work laid down for rest period.	
do	3rd Feb		Continuation of programme of work. Orders received that the Batt. is to be held in readiness for instant move.	
do	4th Feb.		Orders received to entrain at AUDRUICQ on the morning of the 5th. The transport left LA PANNE at 10.30 p.m.	
do	5th Feb	12.30 a.m.	The Batt. paraded at 12.30 a.m. arrived at AUDRUICQ at 2.10 a.m. and were entrained by 2.55 a.m. The Batt. and transport arrived at POPERINGHE at 6.30 a.m. where a halt of 4 hours was made for rest and a meal. The Batt. and transport arrived at RENINGHELST at 12.10 p.m. and took over camp "D" from 7th Batt. Shropshire L.I. Infantry.	
RENINGHELST	6th Feb.		The Batt. paraded at 3.15 p.m. and marched via La CLYTTE and DICKEBUSCH to "P" trenches south of ST ELOI. The trenches between ones from 12th Batt. West Yorkshire Reg. (Lt Col CAMPBELL) were P, P2, P3, P2a, P.H, P4a, P4b, 05 and strong point S.8. The relief	

WAR DIARY or INTELLIGENCE SUMMARY

Army Form C. 2118

9th Northumberland Fusiliers

Page 38

Place	Date	Hour	Summary of Events and Information	Remarks and references to Appendices
Trenches P. Such S. of ST ELOI.	7th Feb.		was completed by 8.40 pm without incident. Batt on our right is the 21st Canadian Regiment, 4th Brigade, 2nd Canadian Division; on our left is the 9th Batt West Riding Reg. 52nd Infantry Brigade, 17th Division. The enemy - probably Saxons - show little activity.	
do.	8th Feb.		A quiet day in the trenches. The day passed without incident. The trenches were inspected by Brig. Gen. H.C. Surtees commanding 52nd Inf Bde. and Col. Carpenter C.R.E. 17th Division.	
do.	9th Feb.		This day the 20th Canadian Reg. relieved the 21st Canadian Reg on our right. A quiet day, two casualties.	see appendix L
do.	10th Feb.		This day the trenches were visited by the G.O.C. 17th Division. 14 N.C.Os and men, having been granted commissions as 2nd Lieuts proceeded on leave.	
do.	11th Feb		A quiet day. A patrol under Lieut. P. Robinson did good work.	
do.	12th Feb.		The C.O. and officers 10th West York Reg. visited the trenches prior to our relief on the night of the 14/15th	

WAR DIARY or INTELLIGENCE SUMMARY

Army Form C. 2118

9th Northumberland Fusiliers

Page 29

Place	Date	Hour	Summary of Events and Information	Remarks and references to Appendices
Trenches "P" Sector S. of ST ELOI	13th Feb		The trenches from section and the Batt Grenadiers were relieved by the 10th West Yorkshire Reg. A German officer and two men were shot by our snipers. The 30 OR 16 ORs and from Coy. took over the MG emplacements in P.2.a. and S.8.	
do.	14th Feb		The officers dug-out in S8 was hit direct by a 7.7 HE. The dug-out was partially wrecked, and an officer (Lieut R.Vt. DALLAS) slightly wounded. Orders counter-manding relief, then in progress, received at 6.55 p.m. The 10th West Yorkshire Reg. withdrew and took up the position in G.H.Q.2nd line trenches in outpost. The enemy about 6 p.m. having explored some of the trenches held by the 51st Brigade on our left, north of the YPRES-COMINES Canal, from which two counter attacks failed to dislodge them, the situation in the "P" Sector remained Quiet, except that S.8 was heavily shelled between 6 and 6.30 p.m.	
do.	15th Feb		Situation in "P" Sector remains unchanged. 10th Batt West Yorkshire Reg. being in support in SCOTTISH WOOD, a counter attack by 6th Batt Dorset Reg. on lost trenches failed. Heavy rain fell all night, and arms between the hours of 4.30 & 5 a.m. the machine gun section supplied by the Batt. Grenadiers	

WAR DIARY
or
INTELLIGENCE SUMMARY

Army Form C. 2118

9th Northumberland Fusiliers

Page 40

Place	Date	Hour	Summary of Events and Information	Remarks and references to Appendices
Trenches P. Sect. Sq 5c 8201.	16th Feb.		under 2nd Lt W Watson received orders to join 7th Batt East Yorkshire Regiment and 1 non-comm. can report in the Canal sector. 2nd Lt W Watson and Lt Huston were wounded in this attack.	See appendices
			The Regt was relieved in the "P" section by the 29th Batt Canadian Infantry. "A" Coy relieved "D" Coy 10th Lancashire Fusiliers and the sector was taken over by O.C. 10th Lancashire Fusiliers. Nº9 + B.C. v D Companies marched to Kettle on DICKEBUSCH. Enemy was within BLUFF and part of our original front line trench of it.	
Dickebusch	17th Feb.		10th Lancashire Fusiliers arrived in left subsection by 10th West Yorks. "A" Coy came under orders of O.C. 10th West Yorks. H.Q. and B.C. v D Companies remained in billets at DICKEBUSCH.	
do	18th Feb.		In the evening of this day "A" Coy was relieved in trenches at 23.24 by a company of 10th West Yorks and rejoined the Batt. at DICKEBUSCH. While attached to 10th Lancashire Fusiliers and 10th West Yorks they supplied fire parties, the companies billeted in DICKEBUSCH were all engaged in carrying fatigues.	See appendices
do	19th Feb.		In reserve billets at DICKEBUSCH. Companies engaged in engineers fatigues	

WAR DIARY or INTELLIGENCE SUMMARY

Army Form C. 2118

9th Yorkshire Regt.
Fusiliers

Page 41

Place	Date	Hour	Summary of Events and Information	Remarks and references to Appendices
DICKEBUSCH	20.2.16		In reserve. On the evening of this day "D" Coy was sent to reinforce the 10th Batt West Yorkshire Reg at Spoilbank, and "B" Coy to reinforce the 9th West Riding Reg at Vormezeele. "A" and "C" Coys went engaged on fatigues.	
do	21.2.16		Batt. received orders to hand over Billets to 6th Dorset Reg and to move to rest Camp at RENINGHELST. Notice received that this Batt. would relieve 2nd Suffolk Reg in right subsection Left Sector (just north of J/M 88 - COMINES Canal) on night of 23/2/16.	
RENINGHELST	22.2.16		Party of officers proceeded to Bully Grenay tomorrow new line and the line of the tacks at RENINGHELST during the afternoon Maj. E.P. Westmacott D.S.O. assumed Command of the Batt. vice Lt. Col. H. Bryan CMG on sick leave	
do	23.2.16		Batt. paraded at 1 p.m. and marched to trenches. Route LA CLYTTE, DICKEBUSCH (where a halt of 2½ hours was made for hot meal tea) CAFE BELGE, KRUISSTRAATHOEK, Road junction I 20 a Centre, to trenches. The dispositions on so taking over right to left :-
"B" Coy minor subgroup Jordan Post.
"D" Coy 30 R 30 S 31 S
"A" Coy 32 S, 33 S, (15 point 44 b. 22.1.)
"C" Coy In barn near Batt. H.Q.	Sufficient trench, W illiams trench

WAR DIARY or INTELLIGENCE SUMMARY

Army Form C. 2118

9th Northumberland Fusiliers

Page 42

Place	Date	Hour	Summary of Events and Information	Remarks and references to Appendices
Armentieres Billets & Trenches	24.2.16		The relief was complete at 10.30 p.m. The 12th Manchester Regiment is on our left, and 10th West Yorkshire Reg. on our right — just south of the Ypres-Comines Canal	
do	25.2.16		A quiet day. Our heavy artillery shelled the Bluff and unnamed trenches north of it. Brig. Gen. H.C. Barton inspected the trenches	
do	26.2.16		Our artillery again heavily shelled enemy positions. A patrol consisting of my Bombfield (2nd Suffolk Reg) Lt. Elton, Pte Caldwell and Pte Baly (9th Northd Fus) examined a new enemy position about New Year Crater.

Our artillery shelled the enemy positions intermittently throughout the day. At 4.30 p.m. the enemy opened a fierce artillery fire on our trenches and positions in rear. They established a complete barrage between Rosan Wood — shortly after 5 p.m. the bombardment of the front line ceased and the enemy opened a heavy rifle and machine gun fire on our trenches. When our men went into enemy trenches were crossed grenades were thrown in large numbers. The retaliation responded. The enemy did not attempt the French probably owing to the support sent to the 12th Manchester Regiment on our left. Lights opened a fire. Enemy fired on the enemy trenches. An estimate 28 casualties. | |

WAR DIARY Army Form C. 2118
or
INTELLIGENCE SUMMARY

9th Northumberland Fusiliers

Page 43

Place	Date	Hour	Summary of Events and Information	Remarks and references to Appendices
Trenches, Right sub-section, Left Sector. N.17/maps Comines Canal	27.2.16		Parties of 1st Gordon Highlanders, 8th King's Liverpool Regiment and 2nd Suffolk Regiment visited the trenches. On the night of the 12th Manchester Regiment on our left was relieved by the 9th Batt. West Riding Reg. Late the previous evening the 10th Lancashire Fus. moved up in support of the 12th Manchester Reg. in the left subsection, left sector.	
do	28.2.16		Heavy artillery work on both sides.	
do	29.2.16		Parties of Regiments manned close visited trenches. Considerable artillery activity. Our heavy guns severely shelled the Bluffs and trenches north of it.	

J T Bryan
Lt Col
Comdg 9th North Fus.

Appendix — L

9th North'd Fusiliers.

13170	Sgt	Graham W. J.	Died of Wounds	1.2.16
4943	Pte	Hayes S.	Killed	9.2.16
11339	"	Todd S. (att'd 132nd R.E.)	Died of Wounds	9.2.16
12301	CSM	Lish J.R.	Wounded	6.2.16
12504	L/Cpl	Burnett C.R.	do	10.2.16
13395	Pte	Richards R.	do	11.2.16
12945	"	Worley	Severely Wounded	12.2.16
1130	L/Cpl	Shaw W.	Wounded } Died of wounds }	14.2.16 15.2.16
	Lieut	R.O.H. Dallas	Slightly Wounded	14.2.16
	do	A.R. Haslam	Wounded	15.2.16
	2 Lt.	W. Watson	do	15.2.16
6267	Pte	Brindley J	Missing - Killed	15.2.16
6234	"	Beavis G.	Wounded	15.2.16
3023	"	Moore M.	do	15.2.16
12925	"	Gascoigne O.	do	15.2.16
12305	"	Newton D.O.	do	15.2.16
12119	"	Batey R.E.	do	15.2.16
10595	"	Young R.	do first reported missing	15.2.16 } 15.2.16
do	"	do		
10460	"	Calvert J.P.	Slightly Wounded	15.2.16
13320	L/Cpl	Mooney P.J.	do	15.2.16
12189	Pte	Barnshaw J.	Wounded	15.2.16
12144	"	Johnson J.L.	do	15.2.16
12937	"	Cook W.B.	do	17.2.16
10570	"	Edwards T.	do	17.2.16
13115	"	Keefe J.	do Died of Wounds	17.2.16 } 18.2.16
10586	CSM	Quigley J.E.	Wounded Died of Wounds	24.2.16 } 25.2.16
10584	L/Cpl	Russell E.	Killed	24.2.16
13019	Pte	Coxford H.	Slightly Wounded	25.2.16
13055	L/Cpl	Draper	Shell Shock	25.2.16
13024	Pte	Nelson	do	25.2.16
13008	"	Culley	do	25.2.16
Capt.		R. Haslehurst	Shell Shock	26.2.16
9035	Pte	Butterwell J.	Wounded	26.2.16
12012	"	Chisholm R.	Died of Wounds	26.2.16 }
12798	"	Routledge	Wounded	26.2.16
15601	L/Cpl	Cox J.B.	do	26.2.16
12933	Pte	Thompson	do	26.2.16
6706	"	Norman	do	26.2.16
12948	"	Cook S.	do	26.2.16
8592	"	Munday R.	do	26.2.16
14905	"	Ord J.	do	27.2.16

Appendix L

9th North'd Fusiliers Continued

22681	Pte Bullough W	Wounded	26.2.16
12304	" Varty J.A.	do	26.2.16
10184	" Long H.	do	26.2.16
11293	Sgt Byrne Jr.	Missing	26.2.16
16132	Pte Sykes E.	Wounded	26.2.16
10612	" Godfrey	do	26.2.16
15716	" Hornsby	do	26.2.16
10469	" Calvert	do	26.2.16
15063	" Foster W.	do	26.2.16
13126	" Harris J.	do	26.2.16
8933	" Corn W.	do	26.2.16
13190	" Hampton R.	do	26.2.16
13205	" Hull A.	do	26.2.16
5217	" Wakelin A.	do	26.2.16
9820	Sgt Nolan F.	do	26.2.16
13206	Pte Sherlock C.J.	do	26.2.16
18696	" Howes R.B.	do	26.2.16
11362	" Smith D.	do	26.2.16
11469	L/Cpl Hoare D.	do	26.2.16
13597	Pte Brady J.	do	28.2.16
19015	" Edge J.	do	28.2.16
16289	L/Cpl Holding J.	do	29.2.16
13002	Pte Morton W.	do	29.2.16
12985	" Sumby J.W.	do	29.2.16
19135	Sgt Davidson	do	29.2.16
13091	Pte Stokoe	do	29.2.16
10769	" Johnson A.	do	29.2.16
13000	" Mills	do	29.2.16
13375	" Greenwood	Shell Shock	29.2.16
13960	" Derrick	Wounded	29.2.16
12928	" Botwright W.H.	Killed	29.2.16
10410	" Oliver J.	do	29.2.16
	" Holland A	do	29.2.16
10507	" Wills R.	do	29.2.16
16407	" Bedford	Wounded	29.2.16
15227	" Cupit J.	do	29.2.16

Missing   1
Killed   7
Died of Wounds   6
Wounded   63
Total   77

17/4

9th Hathumb
Vol 7
———

WAR DIARY or INTELLIGENCE SUMMARY

9th Northumberland Army Form C. 2118
Fusiliers

Place	Date	Hour	Summary of Events and Information	Remarks and references to Appendices
Trenches N of YPRES COMMINES CANAL	1.3.16		During the day, there were heavy artillery bombardments at times the Batt on companion with the 9th Batt West Riding Regiment, and supporting artillery, demonstrated as though about to attack. The enemy's front line trenches were violently bombarded by our heavy artillery and field guns from 4.40 p.m. to 5.5 p.m. At 5.5 p.m. the artillery lifted and we opened a fierce fire and machine gun, rifle and grenade fire. At 6.7 the Batt cheered and made a display with bayonets. The enemy replied by a heavy bombardment establishing two barrages behind our positions. Lt. Newsom was wounded during this bombardment. During the night the Batt was relieved in the trenches as follows, by the 76th Brigade:- 3rd Division - who carried out prior to an attack:- B Coy 2nd Suffolk Reg. 2nd Welsh Fusiliers. D Coy 3rd King's Liverpool. A Coy 1st Gordon Highlanders. C Coy 7th Lancashire Reg. (S.R.Batt) The Batt marched	So app... M.
			The relief was completed by 2 am (2nd March) to rest camp at RENINGHELST.	

Army Form C. 2118

9th Northumberland Fusiliers

Page 4.5

WAR DIARY
or
INTELLIGENCE SUMMARY
(Erase heading not required.)

Instructions regarding War Diaries and Intelligence Summaries are contained in F.S. Regs., Part II. and the Staff Manual respectively. Title Pages will be prepared in manuscript.

Place	Date	Hour	Summary of Events and Information	Remarks and references to Appendices
RENINGHELST	2nd March		At 9 am news was received that attack by 76th Brigade had succeeded. At 11.15 am the Batt. received orders to Stand to arms. At noon the Batt stood down, and the remainder of the day was spent in resting.	
do	3rd March		During the morning the Batt had the use of the baths at RENINGHELST. In the evening the Batt moved into reserve at DICKEBUSCH.	
DICKEBUSCH	4th	"	In reserve.	
do	5th	"	In reserve.	
do	6th	"	The Batt relieved the 7th East Yorkshire Reg. in the ST. ELOI Sector. Paraded 6 pm and marched to trenches via CAFÉ BELGE, KRUISTRAATHOEK, VOORMEZEELE. The relief was completed by 10.40 pm. The dispositions were as follows: A Coy. 92 DUNCANS LANE. B Coy + 1 plat. Q1.a Q1.b. D Coy + 1 plat. C Coy + 1 plat: R1 R3. D Coy. R2.5. D Coy had 2 Platoons The 19th Batt. 2nd Canadian Division was on our right, and 1/2 4/Manchester Reg. on our left.	

1875 Wt. W593/826 1,000,000 4/15 J.B.C. & A. A.D.S.S./Forms/C. 2118.

Army Form C. 2118

WAR DIARY
or
INTELLIGENCE SUMMARY

(Erase heading not required.)

9th Northumberland Fusiliers

Page 46

Place	Date	Hour	Summary of Events and Information	Remarks and references to Appendices
	1916			
ST. ELOI (Trenches)	7th March		A quiet day. A severe snowstorm raged all day, and continued until the following morning.	
do	8th March		The enemy very quiet. Batt sustained one casualty.	See appendix M
do	9th March		Considerable aeroplane activity. One of our machines was brought down between our lines by an enemy machine (Fokker). On this night the Batt. was relieved by the 6th Dorset Reg. and marched to RENINGHELST.	
RENINGHELST	10th March		The day was spent in rest.	
do	11th		The Batt. paraded at 9.30 am and marched to new billets in 2nd Corps area. The billets are situated N of Bailleul OUTTERSTEEN near METEREN. Route - RENINGHELST, LOCRE, BAILLEUL. Billets were reached about 2.30 p.m.	
NEAR METEREN	12th March		At Rest.	
"	13th		At rest. On this day Lt Col H Bryant (Wheaving relieved from sick leave) took over the command of the Batt. from Maj J. P. Westmacott. D.S.O.	
"	14th		At rest. On this day the Batt was reinforced by draft of 5 officers and 106 other ranks.	

WAR DIARY or INTELLIGENCE SUMMARY

(Erase heading not required.)

Army Form C. 2118

9th Northumberland Fusiliers

Page 47

Place	Date	Hour	Summary of Events and Information	Remarks and references to Appendices
METEREN	15.3.16		Company training.	
"	16.3.16		At Rest. The Batt was inspected by the 2nd Corps Commander.	
"	17.3.16		At Rest. Company training.	
"	18.3.16		At Rest. The Batt was inspected by the Brigadier General H.G. Ruggles who said "goodbye" to the Battn on his relinquishing the Command of the 52nd Infantry Brigade.	
"	19.3.16		Batt paraded at 10 a.m and marched to the LA CRECHE area, arriving about 12 noon.	
La Creche area	20.3.16		Batt paraded at 8am and marched to ARMENTIERES arriving at 10.15am.	
ARMENTIERES	21.3.16		The Batt relieved the 13th Batt NORTHUMBERLAND FUSILIERS in the Right Centre Section. The dispositions are as follows:— Right to left:- "D" Coy Trench 79 and part of 80. "C" Coy " 78 and part of 77 with support trenches Nos 79S, and 80S. "B" Coy "G.P.Z" (1 platoon) and VANCOUVER trench "A" Coy Subsidiary line. The relief was completed by 11.15 p.m. The 10th Lancashire Fusiliers are on our right, and the 12th Northumberland Fusiliers on our left.	

Army Form C. 2118

9th Northumberland Fusiliers

WAR DIARY or INTELLIGENCE SUMMARY
(Erase heading not required.)

Page 48.

Place	Date	Hour	Summary of Events and Information	Remarks and references to Appendices
ARMENTIERES	21.3.16 continued		Information was this day received that No. 9775 R.S.M. Thomas Padley had been awarded the Military Cross, and that No. 133 & 6 Sergeant Nolans Fuller and No. 18704 Pte James Liddell had been awarded the Distinguished Conduct Medal.	See Appendix M
Trenches Right	22.3.16		A quiet day. We continued on our usual Northumberland Fusiliers' trenches in our left- and relieved by the 12th Batt. Manchester Regiment.	
do	23.3.16		A quiet day. One party of our patrols which went out early in the morning encountered two enemy enemy patrols.	
do	24.3.16		Work continued improving and cleaning trenches in our sector with extra tool stores.	
do	25.3.16		A S.L.U. Lt Briggs visited trenches. On this day "A" Coy returned from the trenches, the last company going into a keep in our sector and being relieved by "D" Coy.	
do	26.3.16		Our morning and L.S. North artillery shelled a new work in the enemy front line opposite our trenches. The enemy retaliated on our front line with heavy trench mortars and rifle grenades. Exchange, but we had only one casualty.	See Appendix M

Army Form C. 2118

9th Northumberland Fusiliers

Page 49

WAR DIARY
or
INTELLIGENCE SUMMARY
(Erase heading not required.)

Instructions regarding War Diaries and Intelligence Summaries are contained in F.S. Regs., Part II. and the Staff Manual respectively. Title Pages will be prepared in manuscript.

Place	Date	Hour	Summary of Events and Information	Remarks and references to Appendices
Trenches Right Sector Sec. 6	27/3/16		A quiet day. Two of the enemy fell to our snipers.	
do	28/3/16		The dispositions of the Infantry in the line were somewhat in accordance with Brigade Scheme of attacks (shewn on 26.3.16). Our front line is now covered up and "defended localities". The RIGHT front line is being styled as described and so follows:- "A" Coy (Right) Trenches 78 and 79. "B" Coy (Left) " 80 and 81. C. & D. Coy. in Reserve.	
do	29/3/16		A quiet day. Work in Trenches carrying forward.	
do	30/3/16		The Batt. was relieved by the 7th Batt. Yorkshire Reg, and marched to rest billets in ARMENTIÈRES.	
ARMENTIÈRES	31/3/16		At rest. Batt marched by companies to baths at PONT DE NIEPPE	

J V Bryan Lieut. Col.
Commdg.
9th North. Fusiliers

Casualties:- 9th Bn Northd Fusiliers

Regtl No	Rank	Name	Casualty	Date	Remarks
13046	Pte	Hardwick. A.	Wounded	1-3-16	
6823	"	Robinson. G	do	do	
4339	"	Fletcher. J.H	do	do	
15329	"	Cain. J.	do	do	
13210	"	Smith. W	do	do	
13159	"	Rendell. J.	Killed	do	
10454	"	Horner. J.H.	Wounded	do	
5852	"	Curran. C.	do	do	
15070	"	Blaucke. T.	do	do	
15694	"	Hamil W. X	do	do	
13383	"	Robson. A. X	do	do	
14531	"	Godbehere. J	do	do	
18693	"	Lowe. J.	do	do	
16623	"	May. J.D	do	do	
14451	"	Hall. J.	do	do	
14412	"	Gibson. J.E.	do	do	
	2nd Lieut	J. C. Grey	do	do	
	2nd Lieut	W. Watson	do	do	
18708	Pte	Gilston S. L.	do	2-3-16	attd to 10th West Yorks
6472	"	Craig. W.	do	2-2-16	rptd on 4-3-16
13383	"	Robson. A. X	Died of wounds	1-3-16	wounded 1-3-16
15694	"	Hamil W. X	do	1-3-16	do 1-3-16
15262	"	Hall. J.	Killed		
13010	"	Coxford. N.	Wounded	21-3-16	
13006	"	Ferry. J.	do	do	
4207	"	Cook. W.	Killed		
17935	"	Woods. J.	Wounded	25-3-16	
13746	"	Carr. A	do	26-3-16	
13169	"	Johnson. A	do	26-3-16	
15216	"	Riddell J.	do	28-3-16	
15215	"	Elder. W.	do	23-3-16	
11805	"	Bird. E.	do	28-3-16	
3266	Sgt	Young J.A	do	29-3-16	
23816	Pte	Gibb. J	do	29-3-16	
23671	L/Cpl	Bolam. S.	do	29-3-16	

Statement

Killed	3
Died of wounds	2
Wounded	30
Total Casualties	35*

*Includes 2 officers

WAR DIARY or INTELLIGENCE SUMMARY

Army Form C. 2118
9th Northumberland Fusiliers
Page 50

Place	Date	Hour	Summary of Events and Information	Remarks and references to Appendices
ARMENTIERES	1st APRIL 1916.		At rest	
"	2nd April		do. } in Divisional Reserve	
"	3rd April		do.	
"	4th April		do. Brigadier inspected Batt.	
"	5th April		do. Batt. watched by companies 15 baths at PONT DE NIEPPE.	
"	6th April		do. In Divisional Reserve	
"	7th April		In the evening the Batt. relieved the 7th Yorkshire Reg in the trenches (Right Centre Section) Dispositions:— Firing Line (Right Coy) trenches 78 & 79 "C" Coy. (Left Coy) trenches 80 & 81 "D" Coy. S.P.2. & VANCOUVER "B" Coy. Subsidiary Line "A" Coy. The relief was completed by 9.30 p.m.	
Trenches	8th April		A quiet day. The enemy fired a few 77 H.E. shells and a few rifle grenades at trenches 78 & 79. No damage was done. We retaliated.	
"	9th April		Our 4.5 howitzers engaged enemy dug outs in his second line	
"	10th April		A quiet day. Brigadier visited the trenches	

WAR DIARY or INTELLIGENCE SUMMARY

Army Form C. 2118

9th Northumberland Fusiliers

Page 51

Place	Date	Hour	Summary of Events and Information	Remarks and references to Appendices
Trenches	11th April		Our snipers were very active today. Two of the enemy were shot in the head, while two others who appeared themselves for an instant were fired at and are believed to have been hit. In the afternoon "A" Coy relieved "C" Coy in trenches 78 and 79. The latter company going into support in the Subsidiary line while "B" Company relieved "D" Coy in trenches 80 & 81, "D" Coy moving into S.P.2. & VANCOUVER. The relief which commenced at 4 p.m. was completed without incident shortly before 6 p.m.	
do	12th April		A very quiet day. Two men of other enemy fell to our snipers	
do	13th April		The 2nd Corps Commander visited the trenches in the evening. Maj G.P Westmacott DSO assumed Command of the Batt. vice Lt. Col H Bryan C.M.G who went on leave.	
do	14th April		Still another victim fell to our snipers today, making a total of seven hits in seven days	
do	15th April		A quiet day. On this night the Batt. was relieved in the night entire again by the 7th Batt. Yorkshire Reg. The relief was completed by 9.45 p.m. The Batt went into rest billets in ARMENTIERES.	

Army Form C. 2118

WAR DIARY
or
INTELLIGENCE SUMMARY
(Erase heading not required.)

9th Northumberland Fusiliers

Page 52

Place	Date	Hour	Summary of Events and Information	Remarks and references to Appendices
ARMENTIERES	16th April		At rest } In Divisional Reserve.	
do	17th April		At rest }	
do	18th April		At rest }	
do	19th April		Lt Col H Bryan CMG having returned from leave took over the command of the Batt from Major G P Westmacott DSO. Companies marched to the Baths at PONT DE NIEPPE.	
do	20th April		At rest } In Divisional Reserve.	
do	21st April		At rest }	
do	22nd April		At rest. As the Batt is due to go into the trenches tomorrow, St. George's Day was celebrated today in the afternoon a voluntary entertainment was held in the Cinema, which was attended by Officers and men and in the evening the Officers of the Batt dined together, the Divisional General being present.	
do	23rd April		The Batt relieved the 7th Batt Yorkshire Reg in the right Centre Section. The relief was completed by 9.5 pm. Dispositions trenches 78 & 79 "C" Coy, 80 & 81 "D" Coy, Vancouver and S.P.2 "B" Coy, Subsidiary line "A" Coy.	

1875 Wt. W593/826 1,000,000 4/15 J.B.C. & A. A.D.S.S./Forms/C. 2118.

Army Form C. 2118

WAR DIARY or INTELLIGENCE SUMMARY

9th Northumberland Fusiliers
Page 53

(Erase heading not required.)

Place	Date	Hour	Summary of Events and Information	Remarks and references to Appendices
Trenches	23rd April (cont)		The 10th Kent Lancashire Brigade was on our right and the 12th Batt Manchester Reg. on our left.	
do	24th April		The front held by the Batt was heavily bombarded. The trenches shelled were – 79, 79.S, 80, 80.S, 81, The Orchard and Batt HQ. A certain number of shells fell about VANCOUVER, and the Subsidiary line behind the trenches named the bombardment lasted about nine hours. In addition to 77 Shrapnel and H.E. 4.2 H.E., 5.9 Howitzer and trench mortar shells, in shells of heavier calibre than 5.9 were known about our position. The Batt sustained 26 casualties including three officers, Captain C.B.L. Deshurst being mortally wounded.	(see appendix N)
do	25th April		A quiet day.	
do	26th April		During the afternoon our Heavy Artillery, field guns, trench mortars and rifle grenades batteries bombarded with great effect the enemy's salient opposite PONT BALLOT. The enemy's retaliation was weak. At 8.30 pm the enemy opened a fierce bombardment on the	

WAR DIARY

9th = Northumberland Fusiliers

Army Form C. 2118

Page 54

INTELLIGENCE SUMMARY

Place	Date	Hour	Summary of Events and Information	Remarks and references to Appendices
Trenches	26th April (cont)		front of the Batt, during the time between the river LYS and reaches the front-cement trenches an hour and ten minutes. At 7.30pm the enemy recommenced and continued with great intensity until 8.15pm. The "S.O.S." signal was sent up by the Batt immediately S. of the river (9th West Riding Regt). The enemy attacked their trenches but were driven off meanwhile our Batt was standing to arms. The following movements took place on the front held by the Batt. One platoon "B" Coy reinforced trench S.79 and one platoon "A" Coy S.79.6 one platoon moving up from VANCOUVER and from the subsidiary line the 6th Dorset Reg reinforced the subsidiary line as follows One Company PONT BALLOT RD to Cemetery - two Coys. Cemetery to L'EPINETTE HOUPLINES RD.	
do	27th April		The day passed quietly. At 6.20 am the 6th Dorset Reg returned to "Reels" and the platoons of A & B Coy in S.79.6 moved back to their lines. Bells run to Ams and C Coy to A Coy relieved C Coy on the right of our position and "B" Coy relieved D Coy in the left the relay lopin place accordingly.	

1875 Wt. W593/826 1,000,000 4/15 J.B.C. & A. A.D.S.S./Forms/C. 2118.

Army Form C. 2118

9th Northumberland Fusiliers
Page 55

WAR DIARY
or
INTELLIGENCE SUMMARY
(Erase heading not required.)

Place	Date	Hour	Summary of Events and Information	Remarks and references to Appendices
Trenches	28th April		The artillery of both sides fired a few registering shots; beyond this there was very little activity.	
"	29th April		A quiet day. The enemy are working hard on their trenches in the salient opposite PONT BALLOT	
"	30th April		The enemy have been particularly quiet today. Very little movement has been seen either in the front line or about their trenches in rear.	

W. Bryan
Lieut. Col.
Comdg.
9th North'd Fusiliers

Appendix N

Casualties 9th Northumberland Fus.

Reg No	Rank	Name	Date	Casualty	Remarks
19203	Pte	Whiteman A.	9.4.16	Wounded	
23816	"	Jobb J	do	do	
15533	"	Wright Gm.	do	do	
12119	"	Batty R.E.	12.4.16	do	accidentally
15526	"	Wardell A	13.4.16	do	
7738	"	Maguire S	do	do	
13248	Sgt	Fuller	15.4.16	do	
4748	Pte	Crawford J.	9.4.16	do	remained at duty
14804	L/Sgt	Bell	14.4.16	do	do do
23194	Pte	Creighton A.	17.4.16	do	
12820	"	Robson J.	do	do	remained at duty
23784	"	Greenwood S	14.4.16	do	do do
15886	"	Connor G.J.	20.4.16	do	
	Capt	C.B.R. Dashwood	26.4.16	Died of wounds	wounded 24.4.16
	2/Lt	C.J.K. Jupins	24.4.16	wounded	
9775	R.S.M	Poulter F.J.	23.4.16	do	
11336	Pte	Turner J.	do	do	returned to duty
16032	"	Elew P.S.	do	do	
13027	"	Scott A.	24.4.16	do	
14569	L/Cpl	Wankers L.	do	do	
12216	"	Alder R.	do	do	
8786	Pte	Hagg R.H.	do	Killed	
14457	"	Hall J.	do	wounded	
4105	"	Phillps A.	do	do	
10595	"	Needy R.	do	do	
15584	"	Wilson W.	do	do	
9605	CSM	Smith J.W.	do	do	
23611	Pte	Carr R.	do	Killed	
818	Cpl	Bowles E.	do	wounded	
22773	Pte	Illingworth H	do	do	
16359	"	Swinhoe	do	do	
22644	"	Turley A	do	do	remained at duty
13184	"	McElwee J	do	do	
22244	"	Connor C.	do	do	
22972	"	Tait J.A.	do	do	
13196	"	Helm W.	do	do	
18229	"	Hume R.	do	do	remained at duty
14797	"	Robertson Ja	do	do	do
10604	"	Chilton E	do	do	do
14589	"	Fletcher JH	do	do	do
10451	"	Moore	20.4.16	do	
	Capt	Cosby G.S.	24.4.16	do	
23477	Pte	Muff J.	25.4.16	do	
13024	"	Nelson H	do	do	
22809	"	Summer C	do	do	
13223	"	Pocklington J	do	do	accidentally
22720	"	Stevens W.D	26.4.16	do	
28993	"	O'Donnell W	do	do	remained at duty
24028	"	Ingram A.	do	do	do do
18701	Cpl	Graham J	27.4.16	do	
14118	Pte	Moran J	29.4.16	Died of wounds	wounded 28.4.16
13067	"	Hewitson H	28.4.16	Killed	
9588	"	Cook S.	do	do	
4196	"	Collins J.	29.4.16	wounded	
10600	"	Keating J	do	do	
10617	"	Gibbons J.W.H	do	do	
8555	"	Clifford J	do	do	
12984	"	Berkley A	do	do	
4608	"	Spence H	30.4.16	do	

Summary

Killed	4
Died of wounds	2
Accidentally	2
Returned to duty	13
Wounded	38
	59 x

x includes officers

9th Northumb: Fus:
vol: 6

Army Form C. 2118

9th Northumberland Fusiliers
Vol 9
Page 56

WAR DIARY
or
INTELLIGENCE SUMMARY
(Erase heading not required.)

Place	Date	Hour	Summary of Events and Information	Remarks and references to Appendices
Trenches before ARMENTIERES	1st May 1916		The Batt. was relieved in the trenches by the 7th Yorkshire Reg. The relief was completed without incident at 10 p.m.	
ARMENTIERES	2nd	"	In Divisional Reserve	
"	3rd	"	In Divisional Reserve	
"	4th	"	In Divisional Reserve	
"	5th	"	In Divisional Reserve. At 7.30 p.m. the thunderstorm and other gas alarms were sounded. At 8.30 p.m. the Batt. received orders to "stand by". The Batt. was ordered to stand down at 10.4 p.m.	
"	6th	"	In Divisional Reserve	
"	7th	"	In Divisional Reserve	
"	8th	"	In Divisional Reserve	
"	9th	"	The Batt. relieved the 7th Yorkshire Reg. in the right centre sector. Dispositions:— Trenches 78 & 79 & supports 'C' Coy. Trenches 80 & 81 + Orchard "D" Coy. "S.P.2" & VANCOUVER "B" Coy. Subsidiary line "A" Coy. The relief was complete at 9.55 p.m.	
Trenches	10th	"	Party of 2nd Canterbury Batt. (Newzealand expl. force) attached to Batt. for instruction	
"	11th	"	Apart from a certain amount of reciprocal shelling the day passed without special incident	

8 d

WAR DIARY or INTELLIGENCE SUMMARY

Army Form C. 2118

9th Northumberland Fusiliers

Page 57

Place	Date 1916	Hour	Summary of Events and Information	Remarks and references to Appendices
Trenches	12th May		There was considerable artillery activity on both sides during the day. A section of the 19th Jäger Batt gave himself up to our Lewis Gun team in trench 80 at 3.40 am. Between 4 pm and 6 pm "B" Coy relieved "C" Coy in trenches 78, 79 and supports, and "A" Coy relieved "D" Coy in trenches 80, 81, and ORCHARD	
"	13th "		With the exception of a few sniping shots our artillery and that of the enemy remained silent throughout the day. Our snipers shot one of the enemy on the road.	
"	14th "		Our snipers secured another victim today. Our field guns shot three of the enemy force at intervals during the day.	
"	15th "		There was some artillery activity during the afternoon. In the evening the Batt. was relieved by the 2nd Canterbury Regt. (New Zealand Exp. Force.) and marched to billets in ARMENTIÈRES	
ARMENTIÈRES	16th "		The Batt. had the use of the baths at PONT DENIÈPPE during the day. At 10.30 pm the Batt. paraded and commenced march to training area. Starting Point H.G.O. 0.9. (Sheet 36) Time 11.15 pm Order of march: Batt HQ, "A" Coy, "B" Coy, "C" Coy, "D" Coy, 1st line transport	

Army Form C. 2118

1/4 Northumberland Fusiliers
Page 58

WAR DIARY or INTELLIGENCE SUMMARY
(Erase heading not required.)

Place	Date	Hour	Summary of Events and Information	Remarks and references to Appendices
ESTAIRES	17th May		The Batt arrived at ESTAIRES at 2.30 am and went into billets. At 1.15 pm the Batt paraded and marched to MORBECQUES where it arrived at 6.40 pm. The night was spent in camp 2½ miles W. of MORBECQUES. Straight from an arduous and fatiguing journey in the trenches this forced march carried out as it was on an exceedingly hot day, severely tested the endurance of the Batt. The Batt accomplished 25 miles in 19 hours.	
MORBECQUES	18th May	10-30 am	Batt paraded at 7 am and marched to RACQUINGHEM arriving at 10-30 am. Here a halt was made for the night.	
RACQUINGHEM	19th May	10-15 am	Batt paraded at 6 am and marched to ST MARTIN au LAERT arriving at 10.15 am. The Batt will be billeted here during the period of training. At 6 pm the Commanding Officer addressed the officers of the Batt on the scheme laid down for the training of the Batt.	
ST MARTIN au LAERT	20th May		The Batt marched by companies to baths at ST OMER.	
	21st May		Church Parade. Interior economy.	
	22nd May		Company training. Night operations on learning area near CORMETTE	

Army Form C. 2118

9th Northumberland Infantry

Page 59

WAR DIARY
or
INTELLIGENCE SUMMARY
(Erase heading not required.)

Instructions regarding War Diaries and Intelligence Summaries are contained in F.S. Regs., Part II. and the Staff Manual respectively. Title Pages will be prepared in manuscript.

Place	Date	Hour	Summary of Events and Information	Remarks and references to Appendices
ST MARTIN au LAERT	23rd May		Company training	
"	24th May		Company training. The following Officers joined the Batt: 4th Lt J.B. Chand, 2/Lt G.H. Hewitt. In the afternoon 52nd Inf Brigade inspected the Billets	
"	25th May		Batt. training	
"	26th May		Batt. training	
"	27th May		Batt. training. The G.O.C. 17th Div inspected the Billets	
"	28th May		Church Parade	
"	29th May		Batt. training	
"	30th May		Brigade training	
"	31st May		Brigade training	

J.A. Bryan
Lieut. Col.
Comdg
9th North Fusiliers

WAR DIARY or INTELLIGENCE SUMMARY

Army Form C. 2118

9th Northumberland Fusiliers

Vol 10 — Page 60 — June

XVII

Place	Date	Hour	Summary of Events and Information	Remarks and references to Appendices
ST MARTIN AU LAERT	June 1st		Batt marched past G.O.C. 17th Division	
"	2nd		Company training	
"	3rd		The Batt paraded at 3.30 am and took part in a Divisional Scheme	
"	4th		Church parade 10.45 am	
"	5th		The Batt paraded at 8.15 am and took part in a Divisional Scheme	
"	6th		Company training	
"	7th		Company training	
"	8th		Company training	
"	9th		Company training	
"	10th		Interior economy - Cleaning of Billets &c	
"	11th		The Batt paraded at 7.20 pm and marched to ST OMER where it entrained. The train moving out of the station at 9.2 pm	
COISY	12th		The Batt detrained at LONGEAU 4 Kilom S.E. of AMIENS at 5.45 am and marched to billets at COISY where was received at 9.40 am	
"	13th		Interior economy	
"	14th		Interior economy. Inspection of kit &c Route march	
"	15th		Inspection of kits Company training	
"	16th		Coy training. Party of Officers visited the line E. of ALBERT	
"	17th		Company training	
"	18th		Church Parade. Batt practise organisation of a dump. Party of Officers visited the line E. of ALBERT	

WAR DIARY or INTELLIGENCE SUMMARY

9th Northumberland Fusiliers

Army Form C. 2118

Page 61

Place	Date	Hour	Summary of Events and Information	Remarks and references to Appendices
COISY	June 19th		Company training. Draft of 7 Officers and 40 OR joined Batt. for duty.	
"	" 20th		do. Party of Officers visited the line E of ALBERT.	
"	" 21st		Batt. marched by Companies to LONGPRÉ to baths. Draft of	
"	" 22nd		Company training. Party of Officers visited the line E of ALBERT	
"	" 23rd		Batt. paraded at 5 a.m. and marched to BOIS de MAI to practice wood fighting	
"	" 24th		Batt. paraded at 9 a.m. and marched to BOIS de MAI for exercises in wood fighting.	
"	" 25th		Church Parade. After the parade the General Officer Commanding the 17th Division addressed the Batt. The Batt. paraded at 7.45 P.M. for night-march exercises.	
"	" 26th		Company training.	
COISY HEILLY	" 27th		Batt. paraded at 10.40 a.m. and marched to HEILLY (10 miles), arriving at 3.15 p.m. On arrival the Batt. went into the 52nd Inf. Bde. Camp situated on the R. Ancre, 500 yds S.E. of HEILLY. A draft of 3 Officers joined the Batt. for duty.	
HEILLY	" 28th		At rest.	

Army Form C. 2118

9th Northumberland Fusiliers
Page 62.

WAR DIARY
or
INTELLIGENCE SUMMARY

(Erase heading not required.)

Instructions regarding War Diaries and Intelligence Summaries are contained in F.S. Regs., Part II. and the Staff Manual respectively. Title Pages will be prepared in manuscript.

Place	Date	Hour	Summary of Events and Information	Remarks and references to Appendices
HEILLY	June 29th	9 am – 12 noon.	Route March by Coys. 2 p.m. – 5 p.m. Bathing under Coy arrangements	
"	" 30th		Battn. paraded at 8 p.m. & marched to BOIS DES TAILLES (8 miles) where I bivouacked. A reconnoitring party left at 2 p.m. rejoined at 12 M.N.	

J. Bryan
Lieut. Col.
Comdg.
9th North'd Fusiliers.

9.7.16.

52nd Inf.Bde.
17th Div.

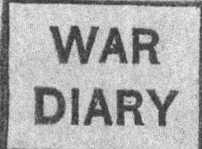

9th BATTN. THE NORTHUMBERLAND FUSILIERS.

J U L Y

1 9 1 6

Attached:

Appendices.
Casualty Returns.

CONFIDENTIAL

July
17
Vol 10

WAR DIARY
OF
9th Service Bn Northumberland Fus: Officers N. Fus

From 1st July 1916 To 31st July 1916.

WAR DIARY
or
INTELLIGENCE SUMMARY

(Erase heading not required.)

Army Form C. 2118

9th Northumberland Fusiliers

Page 63.

Place	Date	Hour	Summary of Events and Information	Remarks and references to Appendices
In Bivouac at BOIS DES TAILLES	July 1st		At 7.30 a.m. our artillery commenced an intense bombardment of the enemy front, which was followed at 6 a.m. by an infantry assault, made by the leading divisions of the 4th Army in co-operation with the French on our right. By 8 p.m. reports reached the battalion that MONTAUBAN and MAMETZ had been captured. About 1190 German prisoners were seen to pass through the camp during the course of the day. 52nd Inf. Bde. in Divisional Reserve.	MSR
MORLANCOURT	"	2nd	Batt. paraded at 5.45 a.m. & marched to MORLANCOURT (2 miles), where it remained in billets ready to move at half an hour's notice. 52nd Inf. Bde. in Divisional Reserve.	cbSR
MORLANCOURT	"	3rd	During the afternoon it was reported that the 51st Inf. Bde. had entered FRICOURT at noon, & proceeded to mount, but halted on the N. edge of FRICOURT WOOD. 52nd Inf. Bde. in Divisional Reserve. A reconnoitring party left MORLANCOURT at 12 noon, & proceeded via FRICOURT along the Sunken road leading to CONTALMAISON, & returned via BÉCOURT WOOD. The Batt paraded at 4.15 p.m. & marched to MÉAULTE (3 miles), where it halted till 12 M.N.	cbSR
In Bivouac E. of BÉCOURT Château	"	4th	52nd Inf. Bde. relieved 21st Div. on the line SHELTER WOOD – ROUND WOOD ALLEY. The Batt. left MÉAULTE at 12 M.N. on the night of the 3rd/4th & marched via BÉCORDEL – BÉCOURT – BÉCOURT WOOD valley to our original support line, reaches 700 yds. E. of BÉCOURT CHÂTEAU. The Batt. was in position by 4. a.m., and remained in Bde. reserve during the rest of the day.	cbSR

Army Form C. 2118

9th Northumberland Fusiliers

Page 64.

WAR DIARY
or
INTELLIGENCE SUMMARY
(Erase heading not required.)

Place	Date	Hour	Summary of Events and Information	Remarks and references to Appendices
2 Trenches E. of BÉCOURT Château	July 4th	4 —	At 5 p.m. preliminary orders were received that Batt. should assault QUADRANGLE TRENCH between BOTTOM ALLEY (inclusive) and a point 250 yds. S.S.W. of the junction of SHELTER ALLEY with QUADRANGLE TRENCH. A reconnoitring party was accordingly sent out at 7 p.m. under the 2nd in Command to select an assembly position. At 9.30 p.m. the Battn. proceeded via FRICOURT, FRICOURT WOOD, FRICOURT FARM to RAILWAY COPSE, where Battn. H.Q. were established. At 10.30 p.m. the Battn. relieved the 8th Batt. S. Staff. Regt. & the 10th Batt. Sherwood Foresters in trenches running along the help line between BOTTOM WOOD & SHELTER WOOD. The relief was completed by 11.45 p.m. The Battn. sustained the following casualties during the day:- Wounded: 1 Officer (Capt. O.E. Watford Brown - mortally) O.R. 2.	see Appdx. 9ii closp.
2 Trenches July 5th	5 —	At 12.15. a.m. the 15th 60 p.s artillery opened an intense bombardment on the German QUADRANGLE TRENCH, lifting gradually so as to allow line of assault to reach objective at 12.45. a.m. The assault was made on a front of about 1500 yds. by the two battalions of the 22nd Bde. (7th Div.) and two battalions of the 52nd Bde.	

WAR DIARY or INTELLIGENCE SUMMARY

Army Form C. 2118
Page 65

7th Northumberland Fusiliers

Place	Date	Hour	Summary of Events and Information	Remarks and references to Appendices
2 Trenches	July	5ᵃᵐ	Dispositions for the assault were as follows:- 1st Line – fighting patrols of 'A' & 'D' Coys. 2nd Line – 6 platoons of 'A' & 'D' Coys. 3rd Line – 'B' Coy. 4th Line (reserve) – 'C' Coy. Dispositions of neighbouring troops:- In support – 8th Battn. S. Staffs. Regt. (51st Inf. Bde) In reserve – 12th Battn. Manchester Regt. (52nd Inf. Bde) Right flank – 1st Battn. Royal West Kent Regt. (assaulting) } 22nd Inf. Bde 7th Divn 2nd Battn. Royal Warwick Regt. (in reserve) Left flank – 10th Battn. Lancs. Fusiliers (assaulting) } 52nd Inf. Bde 9th Battn. Duke of Wellington's Regt. (in reserve) Our assault, made across the open, was entirely successful. The enemy, who held the line with a Battn. of the 163rd Regt. & 2 machine guns, opened to be taken by surprise, & no severe rifle, machine gun, or artillery fire was encountered. A considerable number of the enemy were found to have been killed in the trench by our preliminary bombardment. Those that remained in the trench were immediately pursued by our rifle & Lewis Gun fire. Both enemy machine guns were captured.	

WAR DIARY or INTELLIGENCE SUMMARY

Army Form C. 2118

Page 66

Northumberland Division

Place	Date	Hour	Summary of Events and Information	Remarks and references to Appendices
2 Inches	July	5th	A large number of documents taken from the dead were transmitted to Bde H.Q., together with shoulder straps & Schilder. The reserve Coy was not employed. The work of consolidation was begun at once & continued intermittently to Machine guns of the 52nd Inf Bde M.G. Coy were in position by 3.30 a.m. After consolidation "B" Coy was withdrawn to the support line. The wounds on our wounded right & left flanks also caused the enemy's objection. Our artillery co-operation on our immediate front was good & kept up intermittent & occasionally severe hostile shelling which caused numerous casualties. In the left half sector ("D" Coy), splendid work was done during the day in consolidating the captured position. Major G.P. Westmacott D.S.O. was wounded while working the support line. At 9 p.m. the 9th Battn S. Staffs Regt was relieved by the 7th Battn S. Yorks Regt. (50th Inf Bde). On the right of the 5/6th July the 38th Div. relieved the 7th Div on the Left & the 23rd Div relieved the 19th Div on the left of our Bde sector. The casualties sustained by the Battn during the attack & subsequently during the day were as follows :-	

WAR DIARY or INTELLIGENCE SUMMARY

Army Form C. 2118

9th Northumberland Fusiliers

Page 67

Place	Date	Hour	Summary of Events and Information	Remarks and references to Appendices
In Trenches	July	5th	Officers — 2/Lieut. F. Drummond — Killed in the attack. 2/Lieut. J.G. Brady — wounded in the attack. Capt. J.S. Allan — do. do. {A Coy / D Coy} 2/Lieut. G.H. Hewitt — wounded during the day. O.R. In the attack 38. Subsequently during the day 41.	See Appendix
QUADRANGLE & HEDGE LINE Trenches	July	6th	The Batt. remained in the captured position during the day. The enemy attempted no counter-attack, contenting himself with subjecting our positions, including Batt. H.Q., to an intermittent and occasionally severe bombardment. At a conference held at Bde HQ at 5 p.m. it was intimated that the 52nd Inf Bde would assault QUADRANGLE SUPPORT TRENCH at 2 a.m. on the 7th. Detailed orders were received at 9.25 p.m. The enemy shelling throughout the evening of the 6th was intense. Casualties O.R. 42.	MSP
QUADRANGLE & HEDGELINE Trenches	July	7th	At 12 M.N. 6th/7th July the Two Coys ("B" & "C") in support were moved up to relieve the 14th Batt. Royal Dublin Fusiliers to hold line to QUADRANGLE TRENCH, when, after taking over the whole of QUADRANGLE ALLEY to its junction with QUADRANGLE TRENCH, the Battalion awaited the assault.	MSP

Army Form C. 2118

Page 68

WAR DIARY 7th N. Thunderland Fusiliers
or
INTELLIGENCE SUMMARY

(Erase heading not required.)

Place	Date	Hour	Summary of Events and Information	Remarks and references to Appendices
QUADRANGLE & HEDGE LINE Trenches	July 7th	7—	Dispositions for the attack — as on morning of 5th July. 'B' & 'C' Coys interchanging with 'A' & 'D' Coys. 'D' Coy (in support) was ordered to form a defensive flank in QUADRANGLE ALLEY & was allotted 2 Stokes Guns from 52nd Inf Bde T.M.B. & 1 Flammenwerfer for this purpose. Dispositions of neighbouring troops. On right — 14th Batt. Royal Welsh Fusiliers } 113th Inf Bde. On left — 10th Batt. Lancs Fusiliers — co-operating in assault (38th Div) In Support — 9th Batt. Duke of Wellington's Regt } 52nd Inf Bde In reserve — 12th Batt. Manchester Regt The attack, which was essentially local in character, being made by two battalions of the 52nd Inf Bde only, was preceded by a bombardment lasting 35 min, for which the List 10 min were intensive. The assaulting Coys were ordered to reach their objective — QUADRANGLE SUPPORT — at 2 a.m. At 1.10 a.m all communication between the front line Batt. H.Q. & Bde H.Q. was cut by artillery fire. At 3.15 a.m a runner reported that they first waves of the attack had failed to reach their objective. This report was followed by a lamp signal message from 'A' Coy that the attack had been held up by m.gun fire.	

Army Form C. 2118

WAR DIARY or INTELLIGENCE SUMMARY

(Erase heading not required.)

9th Northumberland Fusiliers

Page 69

Place	Date	Hour	Summary of Events and Information	Remarks and references to Appendices
QUADRANGLE TRENCH LINE	July 7th		At 3.45 a.m. Capt. J.S. Allen reported by runner that reorganisation was being effected with a view to a second attack, 2 Coys of 9th Battn Duke of Wellington's Regt. having come up in support. At 4.20 a.m. orders were received from 52nd Inf. Bde. to send up the 2nd in command & reorganise on the line of QUADRANGLE TRENCH, & that no further attack was to be made by the Battn. At 4.25 a.m. Major G.R. Westmacott D.S.O. was sent forward with these orders. It was subsequently learnt that the assaulting lines had met with severe opposition, the trench being strongly held by the enemy, probably in preparation for a counter attack. It was also reported that, in addition to intense rifle & M.G. fire, a heavy artillery barrage was opened, as soon as our troops appeared on the skyline, about 300 yds from their objective. The enemy of the attack was faulty, Bde time having been altered 3 times between 6.30 p.m. on 6th & 1 a.m. on 7th, with a maximum variation of 20 min. The artillery preparation was inadequate, the heavy artillery being very short. The assaulting lines were withdrawn & reorganised with coolness & judgment by Capt. J.S. Allen, who showed conspicuous bravery & ability throughout. Tho' already wounded in the action on the morning of the 5th, he was again wounded twice during the course of the second attack, but continued to carry on until	

WAR DIARY or **INTELLIGENCE SUMMARY**

Army Form C. 2118

9th Northumberland Fusiliers

Page 70.

(Erase heading not required.)

Place	Date	Hour	Summary of Events and Information	Remarks and references to Appendices
QUADRANGLE & HEDGE LINE Trenches	July 7th	7-	relieved by the 2nd in Command. His last report was written at 4.45 a.m. During this action the Batt. sustained the following officer casualties :— **Killed**: Lieut. P.D. Robinson, Lieut W.E. Ward, 2/Lieut J.G. Cornell, 2/Lieut J.H. Winter. **Wounded**: Capt. J.C. Allen, Capt. R.B. Garrard, 2/Lieut S.D. Clark, 2/Lieut S.I. Deeds, 2/Lieut E.B.L. Pigott. At 7. a.m, in accordance with instructions received from 52nd Inf. Bde., the 10th Batt. Lanc. Fusiliers on our left were relieved by the 9th Batt. D. of Wellington's Regt, preparatory to the latter making a fresh attack at 8. a.m on PEARL ALLEY & QUADRANGLE SUPPORT. After being relieved the 10th Batt Lanc. Fus. withdrew to FRICOURT WOOD. At the same time the 12th Batt. Manchester Regt. received orders to relieve us in QUADRANGLE TRENCH T Co. operated with the 9th D. of Wellington's Regt in the attack on QUADRANGLE SUPPORT. At 7.45. a.m. the 12th Batt. Manchester Regt. passed through the hedge line, on reaching QUADRANGLE TRENCH a few minutes later, crossed it without pausing & advanced towards the objective. The Batt. then withdrew by platoons to the hedge line. By 9 a.m. 2 Coys. had been withdrawn, and by 9.20.a.m the whole Batt. was in line At 10. a.m a verbal message from 52nd Inf. Bde. was received through the liaison officer, 2/Lieut M.G. Fallon, ordering the Batt. to move up from the hedge line & reoccupy QUADRANGLE TRENCH. The move began at 10.5. a.m, & was carried out unopposed. At 11.7. a.m the Batt. was in position with 4 Machine Guns	see Appendix

WAR DIARY or INTELLIGENCE SUMMARY

Army Form C. 2118

5th Northumberland Fusiliers
Page 71.

Place	Date	Hour	Summary of Events and Information	Remarks and references to Appendices
QUADRANGLE & HEDGE LINE French	July 7th		About midday it was known that the attack made by the 12th Batt. Manchester Regt. & the 9th Batt. D. of Wellington's Regt. had failed. At 12.20.p.m Lt Col E. G. Harrison C.B., D.S.O. 12th Batt. Manchester Regt. was ordered by the Brigadier to take command of all troops in QUADRANGLE TRENCH to organize a fresh attack on QUADRANGLE SUPPORT. At 1.30 p.m. Lt Col. Harrison was wounded & Lt Col. H. Bryan 6.M.G. was placed in command of the troops in QUADRANGLE TRENCH with orders to organize an attack as soon as possible with the 9th Batt. Northumberland Fusiliers & any other details of the 52nd Inf Bde that could be collected. After conferring with Lt. Col. Elair M.P., 6.6.7th Batt. S. Yorks Regt., & Capt. Du Val 6.6. 12th Batt. Manchester Regt., Lt Col. Bryan reported the situation verbally to the Bde at 2 p.m. On receipt of this report, the orders previously given to launch the third attack were cancelled. At 4.15. p.m. the following orders were received from the 52nd Inf Bde; (1) Units of 52nd Bde. to withdraw immediately; (2) 10th Batt. Sherwood Foresters (51st Inf Bde) to take over line held by 52nd Bde; (3) Units to reorganize at FRICOURT after withdrawal. In accordance with these orders the Batt. was gradually relieved by the 10th Batt. Sherwood Foresters, the relief being completed by 6. p.m.	

Army Form C. 2118

WAR DIARY or INTELLIGENCE SUMMARY

(Erase heading not required.)

8th Northumberland Fusiliers

Page 72

Place	Date	Hour	Summary of Events and Information	Remarks and references to Appendices
QUADRANGLE HEDGE LINE Trench	July	7th	The Battn. assembled near the cross roads S.W. of FRICOURT & reorganised. Water rations having been issued, the Battn. paraded at 8.45 p.m. & marched in pouring rain to MÉAULTE (3 miles) when it went into billets. The casualties amongst O.R. sustained by the Battn. during the day were 176. The casualty lists for the 4 days from 4th – 7th July show that during this period the Battn. lost, in killed, wounded & missing, 14 Officers & 297 O.R.	cop.
MÉAULTE	July	8th	The Battn. paraded at 4.45 p.m. & marched to VILLE-SOUS-CORBIE (2½ miles) where it went into billets.	105P.
VILLE-SOUS-CORBIE	July	9th	Interior economy & reorganisation. The following Special Order was issued by G.O.C. 52nd Inf. Bde. "The Brigadier General Commanding desires to place on record his appreciation and gratitude for the magnificent conduct of all ranks and units of the Brigade during the operations of the past week. The traditions of the famous Regiments to which the New Army Battalions belong were most nobly maintained. He congratulates the 9th Northumberland Fusiliers and 10th Lancashire Fusiliers on their successful attack which resulted in the capture of QUADRANGLE TRENCH. Nothing could have exceeded the gallantry of the 9th Duke of Wellington's Regiment and 12th Manchester Regiment in their attack in broad daylight over the open on the QUADRANGLE SUPPORT TRENCH. The co-operation of the Brigade Machine Gun Company & Brigade Trench Mortar	

WAR DIARY or **INTELLIGENCE SUMMARY**
(Erase heading not required.)

Army Form C. 2118

7th Northumberland Fusiliers

Page 73

Place	Date	Hour	Summary of Events and Information	Remarks and references to Appendices
VILLE-SOUS-CORBIE	July 9th		Battery with the Infantry was carried out with marked success. Whilst deploying the loss of so many horses and leaders officers man. The Brigadier desires to record afresh that the initiative to necessary for success as was rewarded with us, and to the fact merely we have not been much altogether in vain.	copy
VILLE-SOUS-CORBIE	July 10th		The Battn. paraded at 6.45 a.m. marched to MERICOURT Station (3 miles), where, after a delay of 4 hours, it entrained at 12.10 p.m. for AILLY-SUR-SOMME, the train moving off at 12.35 p.m. On arrival at AILLY at 2.45 a.m. the Battn. detrained & marched via PICQUIGNY – CAVILLON – OISSY to RIENCOURT (10 miles), which was reached about 8 p.m. shortly after arrival the Battn. went into billets.	copy
RIENCOURT	July 11th		Bathing under Bay arrangements. Electrical inspection by M.O.	copy
RIENCOURT	July 12th		Morning – Interior economy reorganisation. Afternoon – Company drill with arms.	copy

Army Form C. 2118

1st / 7th Northumberland Fusiliers

Page 74

WAR DIARY or INTELLIGENCE SUMMARY

(Erase heading not required.)

Place	Date	Hour	Summary of Events and Information	Remarks and references to Appendices
RIENCOURT	July	12th	The following wire was received from the 52nd Inf Bde. Wire from 17th Div: begins AAA Following message has been received from GOC 15th Corps AAA Begins AAA The Corps Commander desires to convey to all ranks of 17th Div his high appreciation of the efforts made & the tenacity & endurance displayed during the past 10 days of hard fighting AAA He recognises to the full that the wet weather added enormously to the hardships endured & to the difficulties overcome AAA He hopes that the Div will have a few days rest & then return shortly to the front line to continue their good work AAA The Divisional Commander is proud of the way in which the Div. he trusts has fought AAA Major General P.R. Philkin C.B. bade farewell to the Battn. in relinquishing the command of the 17th Div.	Appx. Appx. Appx.
do.	"	13th	At Vrest. Company & Specialist training	
do.	"	14th	At rest. Company training.	
do.	"	15th	Battn. paraded at 6.20 a.m. & marched via HANGEST-CONDÉ-L'ÉTOILE to VAUCHELLES-LES-DOMARTS (12 miles), which was reached about 12.20 p.m. On arrival the Battn. went into billets & rested during the remainder of the day	A draft of 60 O.R. joined the Battn. Appx.
VAUCHELLES LES-DOMARTS	"	16th	At rest. The Battn. paraded at 10 a.m. for Divine Service	Appx.
do.	"	17th	Company & Specialist Training	Appx.

WAR DIARY or INTELLIGENCE SUMMARY

(Erase heading not required.)

Army Form C. 2118

3rd Northumberland Fusiliers

Page 75

Place	Date	Hour	Summary of Events and Information	Remarks and references to Appendices
VAUCHELLES	July	18th	Company Training. A draft of 27 O.R. joined the Battn. for duty.	c1659
do.	"	19th	Company + Specialist Training.	c1659
do.	"	20th	Company Training. A draft of 59 O.R. joined the Battn for duty.	c1659
do.	"	21st	Company Training. A draft of 2 Officers + 200 O.R. (all of the Manchester Regt D) joined the Battn for duty	c1659
do.	"	22nd	During the morning the Battn. carried out an Outpost Scheme.	c1659
do.	"	23rd	The Battn. paraded at 9 a.m. + marched to HANGEST-SUR-SOMME (7 miles), arriving at 12 noon. At 5.30 p.m. it proceeded by train to MERICOURT, where it detrained on arrival at 11.30 p.m. + marched to a field 1½ miles N.W. of DERNANCOURT. Concentration was reported complete at 1.15 a.m. on the 24th. Battn. ordered to be ready to move at 3 hours notice.	c1659
L Guerinne near DERNANCOURT	"	24th	At rest. A draft of 3 Officers joined the Battn. for duty. Battn. held itself in readiness to move at 2 hours notice.	c1659
do	"	25th	Company Training	c1659
do	"	26th	Lt. Col. N. Bryan C.M.G. vacated the command of the Battn. on proceeding to take over command of the 19th Battn Cheshire Regt. Before leaving Lt. Col. Bryan bade farewell to the Battn. on a special parade held at 10 a.m., + expressed his regret at advancing age has compelled	

WAR DIARY *or* **INTELLIGENCE SUMMARY**

Army Form C. 2118

9th Northumberland Fusiliers

Page 76

Place	Date	Hour	Summary of Events and Information	Remarks and references to Appendices
In Bivouac near DERNANCOURT.	July 26th		him to relinquish the command of the Battn. for which he had always been so proud, & calling for cheers for Lt. Col. Bryan and Major G.P. Wedgwood D.S.O. around the Colonel of the soldiers in which he had always been held of the highest which all ranks felt at his departure. The following Special Order of the Day was issued by Lt. Col. Bryan "Today I hand over the command of the 9th Battn. Northumberland Fusiliers. In so doing I wish all ranks 'God Speed'. This Battalion, which I leave with very great regret, has always striven hard to earn success, & so has achieved & deserved it. I know that the high standard of duty which animates us today will carry the 9th Battalion through all trials to victory. I trust it fully to maintain the high tradition of the "Fighting Fifth." (sd) Lt. Col. Bryan's departure Major G.P. Wedgwood D.S.O. assumed command of the Battn. Until 12 noon the Battn. remained under orders to hold itself in readiness to move at 2 hours notice. During the afternoon the Battn. had the use of the baths at DERNANCOURT. From 7 a.m. the Battn. was under orders to be ready to move at 1/2 hours notice.	
do.	July 27th			1659

WAR DIARY or INTELLIGENCE SUMMARY

Army Form C. 2118
9th Northumberland Fusiliers
Page 77

Place	Date	Hour	Summary of Events and Information	Remarks and references to Appendices
Lizerne in BERNANCOURT	July 27th	4 p.m.	At 4 p.m. the Battn. paraded & marched to a neighbouring field, when it took part in a Divisional Parade for the Presentation of Military Medals. In the absence of the Bde. Commander, Major Gen. P.R. Robertson C.M.G., G.O.C. 17th Div, decorated the recipients of the medals, amongst whom were included the following N.C.O.'s & men of the Battn:— 14801 Sgt. F. Bell, 14501 Sgt. E. McConnell, 5222 L/Cpl. T. Jowsey, 5207 Pte. W. Beanland, 12281 Pte. J.B. Long, 10651 Pte. D.C. Forster. In the evening a successful concert was held.	See appendix
do.	28th		Until 12 noon Battn. was under orders to be ready to move at 1½ hours notice. During the afternoon Companies marched to R. ANCRE & bathed. A cwf of 1 Offr. joined the Battn. for duty.	USP
do.	29th		Company training. In the afternoon a boxing competition was held in the lines of the 12th Battn. Manchester Regt. & in the evening a combined concert.	USP
do.	30th	9.30 a.m.	Church Parade was held at 9.30 a.m. in our lines. From 12 noon Battn. was under orders to be prepared to move at 2 hours' notice. After 4.30 p.m. Battn. remained in readiness to move at 1 hour's notice.	USP
do.	31st	7.30 a.m.	Until 7.30 a.m. Battn. remained under 1 hour's notice to move. Between 7.30 a.m. & 12.45 p.m. all instructions were removed. After 12.45 p.m. Battn. was under orders to be prepared to move at 1½ hours' notice.	USP

WAR DIARY
or
INTELLIGENCE SUMMARY

Army Form C. 2118

9th Northumberland Fusiliers

Page 78

(Erase heading not required.)

Place	Date	Hour	Summary of Events and Information	Remarks and references to Appendices
In Bivouac nr BERNANCOURT	July	31st	A draft of 1 Officer joined the Battn. for duty.	A61P.
	31.7.16.		Geo P. Holcroft Major.	
			Cmdg 9th Northumberland Fusiliers	

A P P E N D I C E S .

"A" Form.　　　　　　　　　　　　　　Army Form C. 2121.
MESSAGES AND SIGNALS.　　　　　No. of Message............

Prefix........ Code.........m. Office of Origin and Service Instructions.	Words	Charge	This message is on a/c of:	Recd. at........m.
	Sent At...........m. To......... By.........		..................Service. (Signature of "Franking Officer.")	Date......... From......... By.........

TO	LOIN	LOOT	LOVE	LORD
	LUCK	LUNG		

* Sender's Number	Day of Month	In reply to Number	AAA
BM 2	12		

Wire from 17 Div begins aaa Following message has been received from G.O.C. 15 Corps begins aaa The Corps Comdr hereby desires to convey to all ranks of 17 Div his high appreciation of the efforts made and tenacity and endurance displayed during the past 10 days of hard fighting aaa He recognises to the full that the wet weather added enormously to the hardships endured and to the difficulties overcome aaa He hopes that the Div will have a good rest and be ready to return shortly to the firing line to continue their doubtless deeds aaa Ends aaa The Divisional Commander is proud of the way in which the Div he commands has fought

From LOCK
Place
Time 2.30 p.m.

The above may be forwarded as now corrected.　(Z)

Censor.　Signature of Addressee or person authorised to telegraph in his name.

* This line should be erased if not required.

War Diary

FOURTH ARMY.

SPECIAL ORDER OF THE DAY.

The Commander-in-Chief desires that the following may be made known at once to all the troops:—

"The Russians are attacking in great force and with success on many parts of their front and have captured many thousands of prisoners and much war material in the last few days.

The Italians have pressed the Austrians back a considerable distance and are following up their advantage vigorously.

The French troops on our right have already gained brilliant successes and captured a large number of prisoners, guns, etc. They are pressing on steadily; their left flank co-operating closely with our right.

On the main front of attack our troops have broken, on a front of 12,000 yards, right through systems of defence which the enemy has done his utmost for nearly two years to render impregnable. We have inflicted heavy loss on him, capturing 8,000 prisoners and many guns, mortars, machine guns and other war material.

The enemy has already used up most of his reserves and has very few now available.

The defences which remain to be broken through are not nearly so deep, so strong, or so well prepared as those already captured, and the enemy's troops, exhausted and demoralized, are far less capable of defending them than they were ten days ago.

The battle is, in fact, already more than half won. What remains to be done is easier than what has been done already and is well within our power.

Let every attack be pushed home to its allotted objective with the same bravery and resolution as on the 1st July.

Let all objectives gained be held against all comers as British soldiers have always known how to hold them.

There is no room for doubt that steady, determined, united, and unrelenting effort for a few days more will definitely turn the scale in our favour and open up the road to further successes which will bring final and complete victory within sight."

Headquarters, Fourth Army.
12th July, 1916.

H. Rawlinson, General,
Commanding Fourth Army.

1st Printing Co., R.E. 4th Army Section. 458

SPECIAL ORDER OF THE DAY
BY
GENERAL SIR DOUGLAS HAIG,
G.C.B., K.C.I.E., K.C.V.O., A.D.C.
Commander-in-Chief, British Armies in France.

The following telegrams are published for the information of all ranks:—

I. GENERAL SIR DOUGLAS HAIG, COMMANDER-IN-CHIEF, BRITISH ARMIES IN FRANCE.

16th July.

The continued successful advance of my troops fills me with admiration, and I send my best wishes to all ranks. The Emperor of Russia has asked me to convey his warm congratulations to the troops upon the great success they have achieved.

GEORGE, R.I.

II. HIS MAJESTY THE KING,
BUCKINGHAM PALACE, LONDON.

17th July.

The British Armies in France offer most respectful and grateful thanks for this further mark of your Majesty's gracious appreciation of what they have achieved.

They also respectfully beg that their grateful acknowledgment may be conveyed to the Emperor of Russia for His Majesty's congratulations.

SIR DOUGLAS HAIG.

III. GENERAL SIR D. HAIG, COMMANDER-IN-CHIEF, BRITISH ARMIES IN FRANCE.

14th July, 1916.

I have heard with great joy of the new successes just won by the British Army. The French Armies applaud the progress which is effected every day by our gallant comrades. I am glad to voice their feelings in offering to the Commanders and soldiers of your armies, and in particular to you, my dear General, my very cordial felicitations.

GENERAL JOFFRE.

IV. GENERAL JOFFRE, COMMANDER-IN-CHIEF OF THE FRENCH ARMIES.

15th July.

Sincere thanks from myself and all ranks under my command for your very kind telegram.

We cordially appreciate the felicitations of our brave Allies whose steadfast courage and endurance in the long struggle at Verdun gave us time to prepare for the combined offensive which has begun so well on both sides of the Somme. Your splendid artillery continues to give us valuable assistance.

GENERAL HAIG.

V. GENERAL SIR D. HAIG, COMMANDER-IN-CHIEF, BRITISH ARMIES IN FRANCE.

(Translation.)

14th July.

The unbroken success of the offensive of the British Armies under your command confirms our unshakeable faith in the power and genius of the British people.

All honour to England in her greatness, to her King, her Armies and her Fleet! They have won immortality in a heroic contest.

PRESIDENT OF THE ASSEMBLY OF ZEMSTVOS
OF THE GOVERNMENT OF SAMARA.

VI. PRESIDENT OF THE ASSEMBLY OF ZEMSTVOS, SAMARA, RUSSIA.

14th July.

I beg you to convey to the Zemstvos of Samara on behalf of the British Army under my command our warm appreciation of your inspiriting message. On our side we have watched with admiration the great feats of the Russian Armies and Navy and the heroic determination of the Russian Emperor and his people. United in a great cause we shall march together with unshakeable confidence to the final triumph.

SIR DOUGLAS HAIG.

General Headquarters,
17th July, 1916.

Commanding-in-Chief,
British Armies in France.

War Diary

SPECIAL ORDER OF THE DAY
BY
GENERAL SIR DOUGLAS HAIG,
G.C.B., K.C.I.E., K.C.V.O., A.D.C.
Commander-in-Chief, British Armies in France.

The following telegrams, sent on the occasion of the celebration of the Belgian National Fête, are published for information:—

I. HIS MAJESTY THE KING OF THE BELGIANS.

July 21st.

On the occasion of this great anniversary I respectfully beg on behalf of the British Army under my command to offer to Your Majesty and the Belgian nation the expression of our admiration and sympathy. Fighting as we are side by side with your gallant soldiers for the same ideal we feel thoroughly confident that by the united efforts of all the Allies victory cannot fail at no distant date to be ours.

DOUGLAS HAIG.

II. GENERAL SIR D. HAIG.

July 22nd.

I thank you heartily for the good wishes you send me on behalf of the British Army and I express you my sincere admiration for the great bravery displayed by your gallant troops.

ALBERT.

General Headquarters,
27th July, 1916.

*Commanding-in-Chief,
British Armies in France.*

ARMY PRINTING AND STATIONERY SERVICES A—7/16.

17th DIVISION.

S P E C I A L O R D E R.   13th July 1916.
****

On giving up command of the 17th Division Major General T.D.Pilcher, wishes to thank all ranks for the invariable support they have given him and for the magnificent work which they have always done.

He wishes the Division every good fortune and hopes that it will add laurels to the fame it has already gained.

Address by Major General P.R. Robertson, C.M.G. to
the 17th. Division on the occasion of presentation of
Military Medals, 27th. July 1916.

Officers, N.C.O's. and men of the 17th. Division, the Corps Commander had hoped to be here himself to-day, to present the Military Medals to the N.C.O's. and men of the Division, but he was very sorry that owing to press of work he was unable to come. Therefore the honour of doing so has devolved on me.

As this is the first opportunity I have had of speaking to you on parade, I would like to tell you all how very proud I am at finding myself in command of such a fine Division; a Division whose reputation stands very high in the British Army. I have heard from many how well the Division has always fought, and especially how splendidly they did during the first ten or twelve days of the present battle, and it is with the fullest confidence that I look forward to the time when you will again meet the enemy, and am certain that you will then add to the laurels already gained by the 17th. Division. The N.C.O's and men who are now to receive decorations, have been brought to notice for special acts of gallantry and devotion to duty, and the names of others have been forwarded for rewards to Higher Authority, but besides all these I know that there are many Officers and men who have done most gallantly, but whose deeds are unrecorded. In every big battle this must be so, but every one of you, whether rewarded or not, has the satisfaction of knowing that it is your individual efforts which combined, all go to build up the fine reputation of the Division, and also that each one of you has done his duty well, for the British Empire and a great and just cause.

SPECIAL ORDER OF THE DAY
BY
GENERAL SIR DOUGLAS HAIG,
G.C.B., K.C.I.E., K.C.V.O., A.D.C.
Commander-in-Chief, British Armies in France.

The following telegrams, sent on the occasion of the celebration of the French National Fête on July 14th, are published for the information of all ranks :—

I. MONSIEUR POINCARÉ, PRESIDENT OF THE FRENCH REPUBLIC.
14th July.
The British Army, fighting by the side of the brave soldiers of France in the bitter struggle now proceeding, expresses on the occasion of this great anniversary its admiration for the results achieved by the French Army and its unshakeable confidence in the speedy realization of our common hopes.

SIR DOUGLAS HAIG.

II. GENERAL SIR D. HAIG, COMMANDER-IN-CHIEF, BRITISH ARMIES IN FRANCE.
14th July.
I thank you, my dear General, for the good wishes which you have expressed towards France, and beg you to convey to the brave British Army my lively admiration of the fine successes which it has just achieved and which only this morning have been so brilliantly extended. They have produced a deep impression on the hearts of all Frenchmen. Those of your magnificent troops who have to-day paraded in the streets of Paris, in company with those of our Allies, received throughout their march a striking proof of the public sentiment. I am glad to have this opportunity of sending you—to you personally and to your troops—my warm congratulations.

POINCARÉ.

D. Haig. Genl.

General Headquarters,
18th July, 1916.

Commanding-in-Chief,
British Armies in France

SPECIAL ORDER OF THE DAY

BY

GENERAL SIR DOUGLAS HAIG,
G.C.B., K.C.I.E., K.C.V.O., A.D.C.
Commander-in-Chief, British Armies in France.

The following message has been received from His Majesty the King :—

GENERAL SIR DOUGLAS HAIG,
COMMANDER-IN-CHIEF,
BRITISH ARMIES IN FRANCE.

6th July.

Please convey to the Army under your command my sincere congratulations on the results achieved in the recent fighting. I am proud of my troops. None could have fought more bravely.

GEORGE, R.I.

The following reply has been sent :—

HIS MAJESTY THE KING,
BUCKINGHAM PALACE, LONDON.

7th July.

Your Majesty's gracious message has been conveyed to the Army, on whose behalf I return most respectful and grateful thanks. All ranks will do their utmost to continue to deserve Your Majesty's confidence and praise.

SIR DOUGLAS HAIG.

D. Haig, Genl.
Commanding-in-Chief,
British Armies in France.

General Headquarters,
7th July, 1916.

ARMY PRINTING AND STATIONERY SERVICES A 7/16.

Order of the Day
by
Lieut.-Col. H. Bryan C.M.G.
Comm'g 9th North'd Fusiliers   26.7.16

Today I hand over the command of the 9th Batt'n Northumberland Fusiliers. In so doing I wish all ranks "God Speed".

This Battalion, which I leave with very great regret, has always striven hard to earn success, and so has achieved and deserved it.

I know that the high standard of duty which animates us today will carry the 9th Battalion through all trials to victory, and enable it to fully maintain the high traditions of the "Fighting Fifth".

(Sgd) H. Bryan
Lieut.-Col
26.7.16   Comm'g 9th B'n North'd Fusiliers

CASUALTY RETURNS.

x = Remained at Duty

Regt Number	Rank	Name	Coy	Date	Casualty
12514	Pte	Blair J.E.	B	10.7.16	Died of wounds. Previously reported wounded in No. 102 list.
8451	"	Cockburn J.C. x	B	7.7.16	Shrapnel Head.
12179	"	Grant W.C. x	B	do	Wounded S.W. Head
16835	"	Sandy x	A	do	do
13207	"	Sanderson C.J. x	D	do	do
20659	"	Storey J. x	D	do	do
12895	Sgt	Swinburne M. x	A	do	do
5516	Cpl	Hunter C. x	D	5.7.16	do
23263	Pte	Elliot J.H.	A	do	do
	Lieut	Dexter E.J.	D	7.7.16	do
10435	Pte	Rooks P.	C	13.7.16	Previously reported missing now repd Wounded & not missing
23697	"	Hedley J.	B	do	do
22205	L/Cpl	Carr J. x	C	7.7.16	Wounded
13244	Pte	Gavin J.M. x	C	do	do
15544	"	Thompson R.W. x	C	do	do
10618	"	Gilfillan R. x	C	do	do
12443	"	Noble D. x	C	do	do
23720	"	Russell J.W. x	C	do	do
10744	"	Allan J. x	C	do	do
14918	"	Yaxley D. x	C	do	do
10619	"	Fallow J. x	C	do	do
	Capt	Penney H.G.			Wounded while attached to 6" Dorset Regt
13177	Pte	Towns D.	D		Wounded Shell Shock
22940	"	Pearson W.	D		do do
12326	"	Badsey B.	B	25.7.16	Previously reported missing now reported as slightly wounded
23700	"	Johnstone J.	A	25.7.16	Accidently wounded while practicing bombing
12937	"	Gibson W.	C	7.7.16	Killed attached 52nd M.G.C
17988	"	Richardson J.		do	Wounded do
13183	"	Laidler A.		do	do do
	Lieut	Howes E.	B	2.8.16	Killed
12884	Sgt	Silverton J.S.	A	do	Killed
5211	Pte	Hargreaves R.	C	do	Killed
20675	"	Ryder J.	A	do	Killed
8/10048	"	Bell A.J. x	A	do	Wounded
13356	"	Hunter R.	A	do	do
11415	"	McGuiness J.	C	do	do
12972	"	Cook J.	A	do	do Shell Shock

To War Diary. / Appendix Q. No 102

Herewith Casualty Return

Regtl No	Rank & Name		Coy	date	Casualty
12924	Pte	Hutchinson H.E.	A	7-7-16	Killed
13093	"	Morris. R.	A	6-7-16	do
12978	"	Taylor. A.	A	7-7-16	do
12267	Cpl	Laidler F.C.	B	do	do
12247	Pte	Easten G.J.	B	do	do
9884	Cpl	Cram. J.	B	6-do	do
12314	Pte	Blair J.E.	B	7-7-16	Wounded
12233	"	Porteous A.S.	B	do	Killed
12822	"	Robson. J.	B	do	do
12112	Sgt	Peebles J.A.	B	6-7-16	do
22847	Pte	Cuadell. B.	B	7-7-16	do
8518	L/Cpl	Mack. E.	B	do	do
14635	Pte	Mellonberg. A.	B	do	do
12345	"	Thorpe F.	B	do	do
12357	"	Watson J.S.	B	6-7-16	do
12258	"	Douglas E.W.	B	6 do	do
12978	"	Fozzard R.J.	B	6 do	do
9960	L/Cpl	Lindsay J.	A	6 do	do
14918	Pte	Scott F.G.	C	7-7-16	do
22993	"	Birtles. W.	C	do	do
23663	"	Kelly. W.	C	do	do
16016	"	Kay. R.	C	do	do
19119	"	Singleton A.	C	do	do
15609	"	Needham. A.	C	do	do

24.
23 K. 1 W.

102 Cont⁴

Regt No	Rank	Name	Coy	Date	Casualty
14756	Pte	McKenzie. W.	C	7-7-16	Killed
8345	"	Craik. W.	C	5 do	do
13201	Lp̄l	Scott J.G.	D	6-7-16	do
11476	Pte	Hoare G.J.	D	do	do
5119	"	Woodhall J.	D	do	do
13255	L/Cpl	Darlington. H.	D	7-7-16	do
16322	"	Haines. J.	D	6 do	do
15585	Pte	Pearson. R.	A	5-7-16	Died of Wounds.
6068	"	Woodward	A	do	do
5901	L/Cpl	Hawdon J.B.	C	7-7-16	do
18715	Pte	Elder. W.	C	do	do
15275	"	Lievers. H.	A	do	Missing
14145	"	Robson. R.	A	do	do
12234	L/Cpl	Paston. G.	B	do	do
479	Pte	Ramsay. J.	B	6-7-16	do
12148	L/Cpl	Goldthorpe S.J.	B	7-7-16	do
12303	"	Truttman A.O.	B	do	do
12268	Pte	Atkinson J.P.	B	do	do
12326	"	Badsey. B.	B	do	do
15327	"	Cammidge A.Co.	B	5 do	do
8457	"	Cockburn J.C.	B	7 do	do
28144	"	Aixon. S.	B	do	do
18160	"	Keeley J.H.	B	do	do
12332	"	Lamb C.J.	B	do	do
12303	"	Moor W.R.	B	do	do
~~	~~~~	~~Loader G.~~	~~~~	~~do~~	~~do~~
12256	"	Stephenson Jno.	A	do	do

26 - 11 - K
15 M

102 Con⁰

Regt No	Rank	Name	Coy	date	Casualty
9265	Dmr	Strickland. W. ✓	B	6.7.16	Missing
23340	Pte	Venus. W. ✓	B	7.7.16	do
23982	"	Irwin. A. ✓	B	do	do
	"	Welford. C. ✓	B	do	do
16629	"	Alderson H.E. ✓	B	do	do
12147	"	Blackie W.W. ✓	B	do	do
1576	"	Baker W.A. ✓	B	do	do
23697	"	Hedley. T. ✓	B	do	do
18161	"	Speight. C. ✓	B	do	do
	Sgt	Young. T. D. ✓	C	7.7.16	Wounded & Missing
13164	"	Ickes. H. ✓	C	do	Missing
10568	"	Taylor. W. ✓	C	do	do
10572	L/Sgt	Wood. C. ✓	C	do	do
855	L/Cpl	Sproat. R. ✓	C	do	do
16489	"	Holding. J. ✓	C	do	do
9254	"	Moody. T. ✓	C	do	do
10535	"	Balmbra. T. ✓	C	do	do
18068	Pte	Smith. J. ✓	C	do	do
14777	"	Lalor. R. ✓	C	do	do
10578	"	O'Neil. J. ✓	C	do	do
4634	"	Richardson. J. ✓	C	do	do
11267	"	Bell. J. ✓	C	do	do
25560	"	McAllister. J. ✓	C	do	do
18113	"	Audley. S. ✓	C	do	do
10617	"	Gibbon J.W.H. ✓	C	do	do
19045	"	Kennedy. J. ✓	C	do	do
10438	"	Rock. P. ✓	C	do	do

10th Cont?

Regt. No	Rank & Name	Coy	Date	Casualty
22639	Pte Locke J.	C	7-7-16	Missing
14560	" Sands G.H.	C	do	do
3080	" ~~Eydes~~ Edgill	C	do	do
~~12961~~	~~" Turnbull T.~~	~~A~~	~~do~~	~~do~~
10598	" Lyall J.	A	do	do
8096	Pte Illingworth A.	A	do	do
13370	" Himsworth A.	D	do	do
13241	" Barker A.	D	do	do
5498	" Ellis G.H.	D	6-7-16	do
10290	" Clark J.	D	7-7-16	do ? (10276)
13107	" Eadie R.	D	6-7-16	do
14813	" McDonald R.	D	6-7-16	~~do~~ Died of Wounds
57648	" Pearson C.	D	do	do
16180	" Goss A.	A	do	Wounded & Missing Believed Dead.
11448	" Rooney W.	C	7-7-16	Wounded & Missing
13031	" Young J.	C	do	do
736	" Hutton J.	C	do	Missing believed killed.
15456	" Little W.H.	C	do	do do
2719	" Rush C.	C	do	Wounded & Missing
12910	" Allen E.	A	8-7-16	Died of Heart Failure after returning from action.
13994	L/Cpl Hunter T.R.	A	7- -16	Wounded
12919	" Winfield A.G.	A	5-7-16	do now rejoined
15188	L/Cpl Bastow W	A	7-7-16	do
6700	" Clark J.	A	5-7-16	do ?
13005	" Draper J.	A	do	do now rejoined
6268	" Hunter J.	A	do	do
~~	" ~~~~			

10? Cont?

Regtl No	Rank & Name	Coy	Date	Casualty
13086	Sgt Scott W.A.	✓A	5-7-16	Wounded
3351	" Walton. R.	✓A	do	do
13090	Pte Bagnall. A.	✓A	do	do
15280	" Bryden J.F.	✓A	7-7-16	do
11273	" Burns J.	✓A	do	do
12087	" Charlton J.	✓A	do	do
15886	" Corner G.T.	✓A	6-7-16	do
23974	" Craven G.P.	✓A	7-7-16	do
10467	" Draper J.	✓A	5-7-16	do
12978	" Fitzsimmonds J.	✓A	7-7-16	do
9/7197	" Forster J.J.	✓A	5-7-16	do
23927	" Foster W.	✓A	7-7-16	do
14881	" Gibson W.S.	✓A	do	do 14811
13064	" Gladstone W.	✓A	do	do
23920	" Grieves H.	✓A	do	do non rejoined
19401	" Griffin G.	✓A	do	do
14549	" Hollan J.	✓A	do	do
9897	" Hughes D.	✓A	do	do
9/13128	Pte James D.	✓A	do	do
13283	" Johnstone G.	✓A	6-7-16	do
13103	" McGee S.E.	✓A	7-7-16	do
15227	" Maloney E.	✓A	do	do
15408	" Mole W.H.	✓A	do	do
13823	" Moore M.	✓A	do	do
23348	" Morrey G.	✓A	5-7-16	do
8472	" Neal E.	✓A	do	do
5796	" Otway C.N.	✓A	do	do

102 cont:

Reg No	Rank & Name	Coy	Date	Casualty	
22636	Pte Partridge J.	A	5-7-16	Wounded	
18515	" Reaney M.	A	7-7-16	do	
25784	" Taylor W.	A	do	do	
16325	" Theaker E.	A	do	do	
12932	" Thompson W.	A	do	do	
1383	" Trueman J.	A	5-7-16	do	
12920	" Wagg C.	A	7-7-16	do	
10423	" Walker J.R.	A	5-7-16	do	
14440	" White Co.	A	do	do	
16098	" White W.	A	do	do	
19203	" Whiteman D.	A	7-7-16	do	
13922	" Wilkinson E.	A	do	do	
12895	Sgt Swinburne M.	A	do	do	Remained at duty.
13104	" Ray J.C.	A	do	do	do
12254	Pte Fairlam J.	B	do	do	
12240	" Melville W.J.	B	do	do	
12107	" Tarbit J.	B	do	do	
9/12236	Sgt Snowball H	B	do	do	
13225	Pte Aggio R.A.	B	6-7-16	do	
23592	" Carr R.	B	5 do	do	
2935	" Patient H.W.	B	5-7-16	do	
12261	Cpl Allan W.D.	B	7-7-16	do	
23953	Pte Hardy C.	A	do	do	
15111	" Noble J.T.	B	6-7-16	do	
7696	" Moffett J.J.	B	7 do	do	
13259	" Philip R.P.	B	6 do	do	
22988	" Towns R.	B	6 do	do	

103 cont?

Regt N°	Rank	Name	Coy	Date	Casualty
12349	Pte	Wilson R.K.	B	7-7-16	Wounded
12356	L/Cpl	Milne C.D.	B	do	do
12290	Pte	Taylor H.	B	do	do
12323	L/Cpl	Humble J.	B	5-7-16	do
12280	Pte	Brown J.W.	B	4-7-16	do
22147	"	Culpan H.	B	5 do	do
17754	"	Dodds E.	B	5 do	do
6662	"	Graham J.S.	B	7 do	do & Missing
10769	"	Johnson A.	B	5 do	do
16654	"	Jackson J.T.	B	7 do	do
12124	"	Lumsden J.W.	B	7 do	do
12219	"	Mitchell R.W.	B	7 do	do
16710	"	Welford H.	B	7-7-16	do
12285	Sgt	Hardcastle J.	B	7-7-16	do
12961	L/Cpl	Harper D.	B	do	do
12141	"	Stephenson J.R.	B	do	do
12197	Pte	Anderson W.	B	do	do
22211	"	Brown A.	B	5-7-16	do
12287	"	Child S.R.	B	4 do	do
6469	"	Chandler H.	B	7-7-16	do
12181	"	Cook W.	B	6-7-16	do
12264	"	Dixon R.H.	B	5 do	do
23990	"	Forster J.H.	B	7-7-16	do
12226	"	Forster R.W.	B	6-7-16	do
13138	"	Garrity J.	B	5-7-16	do
19404	"	Kitching J.	B	7 do	do
11470	"	Lord O.	B	5 do	do

27.

102 Cont?

Reg.No	Rank & Name	Co	Date	Casualty
12230	Pte Price W.S.	B	5-7-16	Wounded (Died 5th from wounds 6/7/16)
18960	" Rhodes. J.	B	6-7-16	do
13867	" Strong. R.	B	do	do
12915	" Sumby. J. W.	B	do	do
12150	Sgt Hall. N.	B	7-7-16	do
9969	Sgt Smith. R.	C	7-7-16	do
15726	L/Sgt Colvin. J.	C	do	do
12058	Cpl Taylor. W.	C	do	do
1542	" Barratt. H.	C	do	do
16783	L/Cpl McTernan	C	do	do
13136	Pte Davis. S.	C	do	do
13335	" Simpson H.	C	do	do
15664	" Hill. R.	C	do	do
23993	" Drysdale. S.	C	6-7-16	do
14794	" Ayre. R.	C	do	do
23960	" McLaughlin. W.	C	do	do
16574	" Warren. J.	C	do	do
21476	" Armitage. G.	C	do	do
13168	" McKenna. J.	C	do	do
16131	" Senior. W.	C	do	do
8648	" McGonnigal. J.	C	do	do
16548	" Brown. C.	C	do	do
13373	" Robinson J.M.	C	do	do (ShellShock)
12140	" Bolam. J.	C	do	do
13323	" Townrow. L.	C	do	do
23265	" Greenwood. J.	C	do	do
8944	" Smith. J.	C	do	do

102 cont?

Rgtl	Rank & Name	Coy	Date	Casualty
4105	Pte Phillips. A.	C	6-7-16	Wounded
13046	" Hardwick A	C	7-7-16	do
10594	" Hayburn. J.	C	do	do
12807	" Boyle. P.	C	do	do
10826	" Conroy. J.	C	do	do
16946	" Bailey. J.	C	do	do
13156	" Dykes D.S.	C	do	do
23632	" Richardson. O.	C	do	do
8904	" Dunnill A.K.	C	do	do (Shell Shock)
13232	" Brown. G.	C	do	do
15292	" Haslehurst. F.	C	do	do
23715	" Coxon. H.	C	do	do
13051	" Sanson. G.	C	do	do
22602	" Lyman. W.	C	do	do
15716	" Hornsby J.	C	do	do
10577	" Oram. S.	C	do	do
13156	" Eyre. A.	C	do	do
15411	" Reed. J.	C	do	do
13167	" Pillatt E.	C	do	do
13235	" Spencer. W.	C	do	do
21912	" Paxton. W	C	do	do
13321	" Crane G.W.	C	do	do
15539	" Drew W.J.	C	do	do
~~17756~~	~~" Conroy J~~	~~C~~	~~do~~	~~do~~ Error.
11458	" Elliot J.	D	6-7-16	do
10481	L/cpl McQueen W.	D	do	do
11306	" Watson J.	D	7-7-16	do

10% Cont'd

Reg't No	Rank & Name	Coy	Date	Casualty
10581	L/Cpl Scott J.H.	D	7-7-16	Wounded
15948	Pte Millward A.	D	6-7-16	do
17213	" King J.	D	6-7-16	do
22972	" Tait F.A.	D	6-7-16	do
13294	" Bruce J.	D	6-7-16	do
7233	" Douglass J.	D	7-7-16	do
13799	" Hardy J.	D	6-7-16	do
16442	" Mills W.	D	7-7-16	do
23791	" Potts H.	D	6-7-16	do
13229	" Hume R.	D	7-7-16	do
8470	" Quinn J.P.	D	do	do
13205	" Hull A.	D	6-7-16	do
2886	" Maxwell R.	D	6/7	do (Shell Shock)
5298	Cpl Baglensh J.	D	6-7-16	do
13285	" Lane Jno	D	7-7-16	do
44180	L/Cpl Reed J.D.	D	do	do
14457	Pte Anderson J.P.	D	6-7-16	do
14607	" Burns J.	D	do	do
11162	" Dodds A.	D	do	do
5216	" Fennon J.	D	do	do
18028	" Cassidy A.	D	7-7-16	do
13780	" Hampton R.	D	6-7-16	do
10771	" Hall E.	D	6-7-16	do
13216	" Livermore J.J.	D	7-7-16	do
5210	" Lambard S.	D	7-7-16	do
16064	" Pearce G.	D	6-7-16	do
22108	" Reed J.R.	D	5/6	do

102 Cont:

Reg No	Rank & Name	By	Date	Casualty
1520	Pte Stobbart G.S.	D	5-7-16	Wounded
2884	- Epud J.	D	5th	do
18704	- Wall J.	D	6-7-16	do
13185	- Burnham A.	D	7-7-16	Missing
12935	- Cowvery J.	D	do	Wounded
13196	- Helm W.	D	do	do (Shell Shock)
13226	Scott R.	D	7-7-16	do
18705	Pte Smith W.	D	5-7-16	do
10456	- Henaghan P.	D	5-7-16	do
18701	- Charles W.	D	6-7-16	do
23708	- Askwith O.	D	5th	do
14348	- Herron G.J.	D	7-7-16	do
10496	- Haram J.	D	do	do
14677	- Lines W.	D	5th	do
5215	- Lambard W.	D	7th	do
5219	- Bradley A.	D	7th	do
1399	- Draper E.	D	6th	do
10484	- Bearis G.	D	5th	do
662	- Read S.	D	5-7-16	do
15906	- Dove M.	D	5-7-16	do
10461	Sgt Edred W.	D	do	do
13218	Cpl Selby A.	D	do	do
13235	L Simpson D.	D	do	do
1323	Pte Bonner C.	D	do	do
13261	- Dearden W.	D	do	do
	- Donaldson J.	D	do	do
10606	- Downey C.	D	5-7-16	do

102 cont'd

Reg No	Rank & Name	Coy	Date	Casualty
4298	Pte Davison. F.	D	5-7-16	Wounded
1762	" Feakes. E.	S	5-7-16	do
39501	" Garnett. W.	S	7-7-16	do
6441	" Hall. E.	D	do	do
16033	" Procter. A.W.	S	5-7-16	do
12984	" Robson. J.H.	S	7-7-16	do
16025	" Roberts. E.	D	do	do
13204	" Railton. J.	S	5 do	do
2261	" Turley. A.	S	4-7-16	do Sick
13088	" Wood. P.	S	5-7-16	do
	Capt. O.E. Wreford Brown	B	4-7-16	Wounded
			7-7-16	Died of Wounds
	2 Lieut F. Drummond	A	5-7-16	Killed
	Lieut L.G.C. Brady	A	5 do	Wounded
	Lieut G.H. Hewitt	S	5 do	Wounded
	Lieut P.S. Robinson	B	7-7-16	Killed
	do W.E. Waus	B	do	do
	2 Lieut A.G. Cornell	B	do	do
	do J.H. Winton	C	do	Missing believed Killed
	Major G.P. Westmacott		5-7-16	Wounded remained at duty
	Capt R.B. Garrard	C	7-7-16	Wounded
	Lieut S.D. Chard	C	do	do
	Capt J.S. Allen	A	do	do
	Lieut E.J. Dexter	A	do	do remained
	Lieut E.B.L. Piggott	A	do	do at duty
17879	Pte Hall. J.	D	5 do	do
23993	" O'Donnell. O	D	5 do	Missing
1640	" Bush. J	B	7-7-16	Wounded

52nd Brigade.
17th Division.

1/9th BATTALION

NORTHUMBERLAND FUSILIERS

AUGUST 1 9 1 6

Appendices attached:-

    Casualty Returns.
    Special Orders
    Rewards.

Vol 12

WAR DIARY
9th NORTHUMBERLAND Fusiliers
August 1916

Army Form C. 2118

WAR DIARY
or
INTELLIGENCE SUMMARY

(Erase heading not required.)

9th Northumberland Fusiliers

Pages 65.

Place	Date	Hour	Summary of Events and Information	Remarks and references to Appendices
Bivouac near Fricourt	Aug 1st		At 11.30pm on 31st July orders were received that the 52nd Infy Bde would relieve the 15th Infy Bde as the front Brigade of the Right Division of the 15th Corps. Accordingly the Battalion left the bivouac at 5am and marched to the neighbourhood near FRICOURT. From here an advance party went forward and reconnoitred the PEAR STREET Sector of trenches. At 5pm the Battalion moved to the neighbourhood of PONMIER REDOUBT and from there proceeded to relieve the 15th ROYAL WARWICKS. Relief was reported complete at 1.5am 2nd August.

Dispositions:
    A Coy   PEAR STREET
    B Coy   PONT STREET
    C Coy   In Reserve
    D Coy   (On left of A Coy to right of 5th SEAFORTHS in reserve with C Coy.)

The Battn Bombers were in reserve.

4 Vickers guns of 52nd M.G.C were in the line and 2 Stokes guns of 52nd T.M.B. in reserve.

Casualties: 3 O.R. wounded
               1 O.R. were accidentally wounded by explosion of a [trench?] mortar detonator. | MWH |

WAR DIARY
or
INTELLIGENCE SUMMARY

9th Northumberland Fusiliers

Army Form C. 2118

Page 80

Place	Date	Hour	Summary of Events and Information	Remarks and references to Appendices
In trenches	Aug 2nd		Our trenches were subjected to intermittent bombardment by the enemy but on the whole everything was fairly quiet. Orders were received by wire about 11:30pm that the Battalion would attack the sector of enemy trenches opposite on the early morning of the 4th and accordingly preliminary arrangements were made. Casualties: 2Lt R.E. RAMSBOTTOM wounded, 2Lt E. HOWES killed. 4 O.R. Casualties. Casualties had been caused by our own shell fire.	M.S.R.
In trenches	Aug 3rd		The majority of the morning was spent in arrangements for attack. The enemy heavily bombarded our trenches from 9pm to 10:20pm and seriously delayed final arrangements for the attack. CAPT E.M. JACKSON who commanded B Coy (the company which was to make the main attack) was wounded along with his acting C.S.M. Our other casualties for this day were very few. Casualties: CAPT R.V.L. DALLAS, CAPT E.M. JACKSON, 2Lt A.D. ROSIE, 20 O.R. Casualties	M.S.R.

Army Form C. 2118

WAR DIARY
or
INTELLIGENCE SUMMARY
(Erase heading not required.)

9th Northumberland Fusiliers

Page 81

Place	Date	Hour	Summary of Events and Information	Remarks and references to Appendices
In trenches	Aug 9	4.0	Dispositions for the assault	

1st line   — Fighting patrols of B Coy
2nd line   — 3 platoons of B Coy
3rd line   — A Coy
In reserve — C Coy

B Coy were to dig a trench from the left of B Coy's objective to the left of their own company sector.

Dispositions of neighbouring troops

In support — Nil
In reserve — Nil
Right Flank — 10th Lancashire Fusiliers
             12th Manchester Regt (assault) } 32nd Bde
             9th West Riding Regt (in support) }
Left Flank — 5th Seaforth Highlanders (in line) 51st Division

The assault was preceded by an intense bombardment by our field guns from 12.35am – 12.40am when the infantry were to deliver the assault. On debouching from the trenches our company met a German barrage in front of his own line. This barrage consisted of shrapnel, machine gun fire. The company could not pass this barrage as barrage & M.G. fire in our original line.

WAR DIARY or INTELLIGENCE SUMMARY

9th Northumberland Fusiliers

Page 82

Army Form C. 2118

Place	Date	Hour	Summary of Events and Information	Remarks and references to Appendices
	Aug 4th (contd)		A significant fact is that as soon as our artillery bombardment slackened the enemy started to retaliate at once with artillery and machine gun fire. As communication between Companies and Batt. HQ. had all been cut no word was received until 3.5 PM when CAPT. TANFIELD reported that the attack had not reached its objective and that he was reorganising. The attack of the 12th MANCHESTER REGT on the right also failed, due to the heavy enemy barrage. The failure of our attack was due to the following reasons (1) Men did not know Officers and 50% of the men had never been under shell fire before. (2) The enemy previous to the assault, emptied getting into position kept up a continuous flare & very lights which showed every movement of our troops while lining up in front. (3) The enemy putting up a strong barrage on our advancing troops combined with M.G. fire. (4) Our right flank being exposed. (5) Party of 12th MANCHESTER REGT having crossed our right flank, retired back over our trenches disorganising the right flank	

WAR DIARY or INTELLIGENCE SUMMARY

9th Northumberland Fusiliers

Page 83

Army Form C. 2118

Place	Date	Hour	Summary of Events and Information	Remarks and references to Appendices
	Aug 4th (contd)		(6) The demoralising effect on the men from our own shell prior to the attack. The remainder of the day was a fairly quiet except for occasional shelling.	MJK
Hendebury	Aug 5th		Casualties 73 O.R. From 9am till 4pm PEAR STREET was evacuated so that the heavy artillery could bombard ORCHARD TRENCH. Several of our shells fell into PEAR STREET. This however was corrected but seemed to show that the F.O.O. did not know the exact position of our trenches. The remainder of the day passed quietly. During the night we were relieved by the 6th DORSET REGT and relief was reported complete at 12.45am 6th.	
Pommier Trench	Aug 6th		On relief the Battn proceed into Divisional Reserve at POMMIER TRENCH. The Company rolls were checked and all deficiencies indented for.	MJK

WAR DIARY or INTELLIGENCE SUMMARY

9th Northumberland Fusiliers

Army Form C. 2118

Page 84

(Erase heading not required.)

Place	Date	Hour	Summary of Events and Information	Remarks and references to Appendices
POMMIER TRENCH	Aug 7th		C Coy supplied fatigue party of 150 men to work under O.C. York & Lancaster Regt. POMMIER TRENCH shelled from 11pm - 3pm 8th. Casualties 12 OR Killed, 17 OR Wounded	
POMMIER TRENCH	Aug 8th		Parades in trench under company arrangements. At 7pm the battalion marched back to bivouac near FRICOURT	
Bivouac near FRICOURT	Aug 9th		Companies bathed in ANCRE near MEAULTE and went to cinematograph exhibition at BELLEVUE FARM during afternoon and 25 men per day during evening. Morning routine for all companies was Physical Drill and "Small helmets Inspection." Specialists being at disposal of Specialist Officers. Orders were received that the 52nd Infantry Bde. would relieve the 53rd Infantry Bde. on the night of the 10th inst.	
Bivouac near FRICOURT	Aug 10th			

Army Form C. 2118

WAR DIARY
or
INTELLIGENCE SUMMARY
(Erase heading not required.)

Place	Date	Hour	Summary of Events and Information	Remarks and references to Appendices

In bivouac near FRICOURT	Aug 10th	(contd)	As the Right Bn. of the Devons & the 7th Lincolns & Left Front Bn. Accordingly the Bn. moved up to the line by the "MAMETZ" road and MONTAUBAN alley to the Green Dump where guides were met to guide the Bn. to "LONGUEVAL" where the relief took place. The relief was completed by 4 am 11th inst.
			
			N.B. The condition in which the relieved Bn. had left the trenches and H.Q. was far from clean especially in the reserve line taken over by "D" Coy. The condition of the trenches was reported by the Company Commanders to the Commanding Officer and by him to the Bde.
			
			Disposition A Coy. 2 platoons front line 2 platoons support
			             B Coy. do
			             C Coy. do
			             D Coy. In reserve. LONGUEVAL
			
			The Bn. Bombers were in reserve with "D" Coy.
			
			Casualties during relief.
			Each Coy receive 10 tins of water before daylight	

Army Form C. 2118

WAR DIARY or INTELLIGENCE SUMMARY
(Erase heading not required.)

Place	Date	Hour	Summary of Events and Information	Remarks and references to Appendices
Trenches	Aug 11th		The Bn. came under the command of the O.C. 10th Lancashires who was ex officio O.C. all troops in Delville wood & LONGUEVAL. Conversation with the 12th Manchester Regt being cut off sent for H.Q. Runners it was desired that the S.O.S. line of field rockets should also be the line for runners from your regiment. (N.B. This was not to success). Dispositions — A.I.Front 10th Lancashire Fusiliers / N. Support 9th West Riding Regt. / W. Front 9th Northumberland Fusiliers / N. Support 12th Manchester Regt.) with whom no direct communication by runner	
		5.15 pm to 8.30 pm	Artillery. The enemy bombed Longueval again their own round the church and H.Q. but not had no casualties.	
		9-10pm	Heavy artillery duel opened on our sector during which LONGUEVAL was again bombed but no casualties. A Request for water from "B" Coy now attached to 13th Lancs.	

WAR DIARY
or
INTELLIGENCE SUMMARY
(Erase heading not required.)

Army Form C. 2118

Place	Date	Hour	Summary of Events and Information	Remarks and references to Appendices
Tondus	Aug	12 noon	Two officers of Army & Corps respectively arrived at H.Q. to learn suspected positions our trenches. Gunner Brown took out a Lewis gun & at S.17.6.5-8. between the hours of 11.45am & 1.15pm. He was able to observe & kill the German in enemy hole S.11.c.5-8. This he believed to be the place from which most of the sniping at our men was done. Since the alarm no further sniping took place. The alarm position S.17.c.8.5- was pointed out & taken up as a new sentinel O.P. for post on Orchard St. Keene Lane. Orders were received that the Bn. would be relieved by the 43rd Infy Bde. on the night of the 12th/13th inst. and that the 10th D.L.I. would relieve the Battalion. The relief commenced at 2 p.m. owing to Lantern platoons being able to steer by daylight and "O" Coy. were sent away by 6 p.m. 10 p.m. The enemy began to shell Longueval and continued to do so intermittently until after the relief was complete which occurred 11.9 slight casualties.	

WAR DIARY
or
INTELLIGENCE SUMMARY
(Erase heading not required.)

Army Form C. 2118

Place	Date	Hour	Summary of Events and Information	Remarks and references to Appendices
Trenches	Aug 12th (Cont'd)		The relief was completed by 7 a.m. and the Btn marched (each platoon respectively on being relieved) to Pommiers Redoubt H.Q's arriving at 11 a.m.	(initials)
Pommiers Redoubt.	Aug 13th		The day passed without incident until time for the Btn to move back to camp near the Albert-Meaulte Road near "DERNANCOURT". The Btn left POMMIERS REDOUT at 7 p.m. and moved by platoons at 50 yards with 100' between companies and later moved by companies. The Btn moved into camp without further incident.	(initials)
Camp Dernancourt.	Aug 14th		TRANSPORT was billeted and moved at 7 p.m. for a two days trek to "CANDAS FIENVILLERS". Btn remained in the and a concert was held in the evening under the direction of the Pandel to which much interest talent was kindly forthcoming. ORDERS were received to the effect that the Btn would move to "FIENVILLERS" by train the following day.	(initials)

WAR DIARY or INTELLIGENCE SUMMARY

Army Form C. 2118

(Erase heading not required.)

Place	Date	Hour	Summary of Events and Information	Remarks and references to Appendices
Dornancourt / Frenvillers	Aug. 15th		In accordance with Bde. orders F.S. officer was sent to MERICOURT as billeting party to prepare for the Bn's arrival. The Bn. arrived at MERICOURT at 5 p.m. but did not leave until 6 p.m. whence it entrained to DANDAS Station and arriving there 8 a.m. arriving in billets at 11 a.m.	(inits)
Frenvillers / Barly	Aug. 16th		Billeting parties having been sent in advance (as) the Bn. moved to the village of BARLY, leaving at 2 p.m. and arriving 6-30 p.m. Packs were carried and the distance approx. 9 miles.	(inits)
Barly / Grouche Luchuel	Aug. 17th		Billeting parties having been sent in advance the Bn. moved to GROUCHE-LUCHUEL where it settled in billets in LUCHUEL 2 miles N.E. of DOULLENS. Arriving 12-30 p.m. the Bn. rested for the remainder of the day	(inits)

Army Form C. 2118

WAR DIARY
or
INTELLIGENCE SUMMARY

(Erase heading not required.)

Instructions regarding War Diaries and Intelligence Summaries are contained in F.S. Regs., Part II. and the Staff Manual respectively. Title Pages will be prepared in manuscript.

Place	Date	Hour	Summary of Events and Information	Remarks and references to Appendices
GROUCHE-LUCHEUL	Aug 18th		Morning Physical Drill. Alexander Games Squad Drill under coy. arrangements.	
do	Aug 19th		Physical Drill & Squad Drill under company arrangements.	
do			In accordance with orders the Bn. moved to the Bde. Reserve at SOUASTRE (Two companies at Chateau de la HAIE.) The Bn. paraded at 5:15 pm (Steel Helmets) and moved via POMMERA - MONDICOURT - PAS - HENU Routes in to SOUASTRE which was entered at 8:45 pm which time was definitely laid down in Bde. orders.	
Souastre + St Amand	Aug 20th		Billeting party had preceded Bn. to destination leaving LUCHEUL at 7am.	
SOUASTRE (2 companies Chat de la HAIE)	Aug 21st		Physical Drill and Squad Drill etc under company arrangements. Various Officers visited Trenches.	

Army Form C. 2118

WAR DIARY
or
INTELLIGENCE SUMMARY
(Erase heading not required.)

Instructions regarding War Diaries and Intelligence Summaries are contained in F.S. Regs., Part II. and the Staff Manual respectively. Title Pages will be prepared in manuscript.

Place	Date	Hour	Summary of Events and Information	Remarks and references to Appendices
Louestoft	Aug 22nd		(Two companies Ch & D in their) Physical Drill and Swedish Helmet Parades other parades under company arrangement	JWP
Louestoft	Aug 23rd		(Two companies C & D in their). 11 a.m. the Sentry of the guard gave the gas alarm but there proving to be no attack, this was quickly suppressed. The two companies at Louestoft dilled during the day. Morning parade "Physical Drill" other parades under company arrangements.	JWP
Louestoft	Aug 24th		Physical Drill and Squad drill &c during day under company arrangements. Roman Catholics paraded 7 a.m. for Services in Louestoft Church	JWP
Louestoft	Aug 25th		Physical Drill and Squad drill under Company arrangements during the day.	JWP
Louestoft	Aug 26th		210 men of the Bn. on fatigue during the day. The remainder were paraded under company arrangements for Physical Drill and Squad drill	JWP

WAR DIARY or INTELLIGENCE SUMMARY

Army Form C. 2118

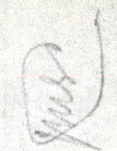

Place	Date	Hour	Summary of Events and Information	Remarks and references to Appendices
SOUASTRE	Aug 27		Church parade during morning at Souastre and Chateau. Orders were received that "A" & "C" Companies would move to FONQUEVILLERS village during the evening and take up the quarters then occupied by Special Coys. R.E. and that they would form the garrison of that portion of the village defences between the lower GOMMECOURT Rd. E.27.c.2.8 to SNIPERS SQUARE. Accordingly they moved to FONQUEVILLERS by platoons at 300 yds interval with 500 yds distance between the first platoon of "A" Coy arriving at FONQUEVILLERS at 6-30 p.m. — Route: BIENVILLERS — SOUASTRE Rd. — "TREK D" WILLOW PATCH — FONQUEVILLERS CEMETARY. Disposition of Bn. "A" & "C" Coys. garrison at FONQUEVILLERS "B" & "D" Coys. Bde. Reserve at CHATEAU de la HAIE. Bn. H.Q. SOUASTRE	

Army Form C. 2118

WAR DIARY
or
INTELLIGENCE SUMMARY
(Erase heading not required.)

Place	Date	Hour	Summary of Events and Information	Remarks and references to Appendices
TRENCHES.	Aug. 28th		After having tried vainly that the Btn. would relieve the 10th Lancashire Fusiliers in the Left Sub-Sector of the 52nd Infantry Bde. It was decided that "B" Coy. should relieve the right sector "A" Coy. —— —— "C" Coy. —— —— "D" Coy. —— —— left While "C" Coy. Should be in support in FONQUEVILLERS "D" & "B" Coys. moved from the CHATEAU de la HAIE by road thro' D.30. D.6.0 – E.25 – 4.3.6 FONQUEVILLERS Rd. The first platoon of "D" Coy. reached the SHRINE at FONQUEVILLERS at 2 p.m.. Bn. HQ. moved up from SOUASTRE during the morning. This is the first relief the Btn. has carried out entirely by day. Disposition. Btn. on right 12th Manchester Regt. " on left 10th Dorsets. A Court of Inquiry was held in Btn. orderly room at SOUASTRE at 9 a.m.	(Inis)

Army Form C. 2118

WAR DIARY
or
INTELLIGENCE SUMMARY
(Erase heading not required.)

Instructions regarding War Diaries and Intelligence Summaries are contained in F.S. Regs., Part II. and the Staff Manual respectively. Title Pages will be prepared in manuscript.

Place	Date	Hour	Summary of Events and Information	Remarks and references to Appendices
TRENCHES	Aug 29th		Trench routine.	(ref)
do	Aug 30th		Trench routine	(ref)
do	Aug 31st		Trench routine	(ref)

Geo. P. Portmeart.
Major
Comdg 9th North'd Fus

1/9/16

20% N.A.I.S.2   107
Base
    Herewith Casualty
return please.

Reg No	Rank & Name	Coy	date	Casualty
	Lieut C Howes	B	2-8-16	Killed
12884	Sgt Silverton J.S.	A	do	do
5211	A/c Hargreaves R	C	do	do
20675	" Ryder J.	D	do	do
9/6048	" Bell A.J.	A	do	Wounded remained at duty
13356	" Hunter R.	A	do	Wounded
11415	" McGuiness	C	do	do
12972	" Cook J.	A	do	Wounded Shock

M. Robertson Lieut 9/1
for O.C. 9 North Fus.

Lichfield
3-8-16

To Officer i/c N.A.I.S.2. Base

No 108

Herewith Casualty Report please.

Regt No	Rank & Name	Coy	Date	Casualty
	Capt Jackson E.M.	B	3.8.16	Wounded.
13176	Sgt Steurmint R	D	do	do Shell Shock
14468	" Holmes J	D	do	do do
14453	Pte Humphries W	D	do	do do
9820	Sgt Nolan F	D	do	do do
18291	Pte McDonald A	D	do	do do
21039	" Jones W	D	2.8.16	do
13145	" McGreigan T	D	3.8.16	do do
10417	" Gibson S	D	do	do do.
21268	" Bain J	C	do	Wounded.
13155	L/Cpl Eales R	C	do	do do
15414	Pte Swinney J	C	do	do do
8399	" Elsender J	C	2.8.16	do
13244	" Gavin J.M.	C	do	do.
23942	" Dougall A	A	do	do
23615	" Moss G	A	3.8.16	Killed
12918	" Knox G	A	do	Wounded.
16356	L/Cpl Holden A	A	do	do
10443	Cpl Sprague T	A	do	do
15881	Pte Harvey V	A	do	Killed

REGT No	RANK AND NAME	COY	DATE	CASUALTY
26790	Pte Atkinson	A	3.8.16	Killed
13029	" Hedley ?	A	do	Wounded Shell Shock
23403	" Pattison G.M.	A	do	do do
17382	" Hood R.J.	A	do	Died of Wounds
13878	" Stevens G.H.	A	do	Wounded
13002	" Nicholson E	A	do	do
14801	Sgt McConnell	A	4.8.16	Killed
14815	Pte Stewart L.J.	A	do	Wounded Shell Shock
13546	" Johnstone W.	A	do	do do
20618	" McKenna H	A	do	do
11374	" Richardson J	A	2.8.16	do
12334	Sgt Poulton J.H.	B	3.8.16	Killed
13042	Pte Morton W.D.	B	4.8.16	Missing
23397	" Wilson W.D.	B	3.8.16	Wounded
13220	Cpl Hardy ?	B	4.8.16	do
24141	Pte Smith R	B	do	do
	Capt R.V.L. Dallas	A	3.8.16	do
	2/Lieut R.E. Ramsbottom	A	2.8.16	do
	Lieut A.D. Rose	D	2.8.16	do

M E Robertson Lieut & Adjt
for O.C. 9th North'd Fusiliers

To Officer i/c N.A.I.S 2.
Base.

No 109.
[stamp: ORDERLY ROOM 5 AUG 1916 9th (SERVICE) BATT. NORTH'D FUSILIERS]

Herewith Casualty Report of men of other regiments attached to 9th North'd Fusiliers

Regt No	Rank and Name	Coy	Date	Regiment	Casualty	
3547	Pte Kirk H	B	4.8.16	11 Manchester	Wounded Shellshock	
2757	" McCabe W	B	do	do	do	do
1792	" Dempsey J	A	do	do	do	S.I.W.
23973	" Knight H	A	2.8.16	do	do	
24776	" Parkinson R	A	3.8.16	do	do	
5459	" Jackson W	A	do	do	do	
3419	" McCann	A	do	do	do	
2429	" Bennett W	A	do	do	do	do
808	" Martell H	B	4.8.16	do	do	
4909	" Hindley J	C	3.8.16	do	Killed	
13344	" Goodwin J	B	4.8.16	do	Wounded	
24703 L/C	Brown J	B	do	do	do	
16634	Pte Bent E	B	do	do	Missing	
798	" Langstaffe W	D	1.8.16	18 D.L.I.	Wounded	
1009	" Wilson O	D	3.8.16	do	do	
254	" Marshall J	C	do	do	Killed	
22450	" Gardiner J	D	do	do	do	
24630	" Bainbridge J	D	1.8.16	do	Missing	
12045	" Shubotham J	B	4.8.16	10 KOYLI	Wounded	
21613	" Sturdage R	B	do	do	do	

W.F. Robertson Lieut
for O.C. 9th North'd Fusiliers

To Officer i/c N.A.I.S 2. No 110.
Base 8

Herewith Casualty Report please

Regt No	Rank and Name	Coy	Date	Casualty
14468	Sgt Holmes J.	D	4.8.16	Previously reported Wounded S.S now reported Died of Wounds
8533	L/C Gibbens M	D	4.8.16	Wounded
28371	Pte Hartley G	D	4.8.16	Do Shell Shock
13248	Sgt Fuller R	C	3.8.16	Wounded
10587	Pte Potter R	C	3.8.16	Do
28363	" Leake F	C	3.8.16	Do
18124	" Purvis S	C	3.8.16	Do Shell Shock
10618	" Gilfillan R	C	3.8.16	Do
10530	" Armstrong J	C	3.8.16	Do
14786	" Smith L	C	3.8.16	Do

W.F. Robertson Lieut & Adjt
for O.C. 9th North'd Fusiliers

To Officer i/c N.A.I.S.2.
Base.

Herewith casualty report of men of other regiments attached to 9" North⁰ Fusiliers

Regᵗ No	Rank and Name	Coy	Date	Regiment	Casualty
13300	Pte Sando F.E.	D	4.8.16	Manchester	Killed
1536	" Hunterman	D	4.8.16	Do	Wounded

W. Robertson Lieut & Adj
for O.C. 9" North⁰ Fus.

To Officer i/c N.R.I.S.2
Base

Herewith Casualty Report please

Reg't No	Rank and Name	Coy	Date	Casualty
24824	Pte Moffatt J	A	8.8.16	Killed
3100	" McAvoy J	A	Do	Wounded
12874	" Mordue G.R.	A	Do	Do
5192	" Turner P.J.	A	2.8.16	Do
23067	" Tweedy J	A	Do	Do
13788	" Gowland W	A	3.8.16	Killed
7045	" Meadows J	A	4.8.16	Wounded
23756	" Lewis N	A	2.8.16	Do
8689	" Turner W.R	A	Do	Do
12898	" Calabrese S	A	Do	Do
12981	" Long J.B.	A	3.8.16	Do
10470	" Crosby W	A	Do	Do
13893	" Saunders F.R	A	Do	Do
~~13871~~	" ~~Truscott N~~	A	Do	Do × Error
12883	" Wright H	A	Do	Do
13062	L/C Butters A	A	4.8.16	Do
12887	Pte Gibson J.W	A	Do	Do
13077	" Green E.W	A	3.8.16	Do
4657	" Hall J	A	Do	Do
13008	" Culley J	A	Do	Do Shell Shock
9240	" Little J	A	Do	Wounded

List 112 Continued

REGT NO	RANK AND NAME		COY	DATE	CASUALTY
13025	Pte	Stoker E	A	3.8.16	Wounded
12972	"	Cook J	A	Do	Do Shell Shock
11898	L/C	Barnes J.T.	B	8.8.16	Killed
18/714	Pte	Gallagher	B	Do	Do
27801	"	Nesbitt G	B	Do	Wounded
14737	L/C	Yearham J	B	4.8.16	Do
12145	Pte	Hamilton S.B.	B	Do	Do
12988	"	Hastings J	B	Do	Do
14800	"	Tickner S	B	Do	Do
12307	"	Henderson J	B	1.9.16	Do Shell Shock
4736	"	Walton H	C	8.8.16	Wounded
13249	L/C	McDonald J	C	1.8.16	Wounded Accidently
10635	"	Morley J	C	Do	Do Do
10747	Pte	Davison J.H.	C	Do	Do Do
8368	"	Fleming W	C	Do	Do Do
14646	"	Jackson W.H.	C	Do	Do Do
13268	"	Riseley E.H.	C	Do	Do Do
14672	"	Smith C	C	Do	Do Do
9739	"	Simpson J	C	6.8.16	Do remd at Duty
12975	"	Holland G.W.	C	Do	Do Do
23605	"	Robson C.E.	C	5.8.16	Wounded
17442	L/C	Barker A	C	4.8.16	Wounded Accidently
15914	Pte	Curry G.W.	C	2.8.16	Wounded
15283	"	Drabble J	C	2.8.16	Do
13157	"	Spencer J	C	4.8.16	Do
15447	"	Graham J	D	8.8.16	Killed
28388	"	Hardy J	D	Do	Do

List 112 Continued

Regt No	Rank	and Name	Coy	Date	Casualty
8628	Sgt	Dawson C	D	8.8.16	Killed
15707	Pte	Dove J	D	do	do
23762	"	Smith W	D	do	do
2225	L/C	Moores W	D	do	Wounded
13160	L/Sgt	Gibson W	D	do	do
13240	L/Cpl	Darlington T	D	do	do
28379	Pte	Messenger S	D	do	do Shell Shock
5220	"	Leslie G.K.	D	4.8.16	do
10551	"	Foster D	D	6.8.16	do
28717	"	Maye S (S)	D	5.8.16	Wounded
13101	"	Coates D	D	4.8.16	do

for Off.

W. F. Robertson Lieut & Capt.
For O.C. 9th North'ns.

To Officer i/c N.A.I.S. 2.
Base.

Herewith Casualty report of men of other regiments attached to 9th North'n Fus.

Regt No	Rank and Name	Coy	Date	Regiment	Casualty
24686	L/C Wood	A	2.8.16	11th Manchester	Wounded
13377	Pte Ayres	A	Do	Do	Do
13620	" Buckley	A	Do	Do	Do
5590	" Healey ?	A	3.8.16	Do	Killed
16374	L/C Ellis J	A	Do	Do	Do
16355	Pte Buxton S.G.	A	Do	Do	Wounded
2647	" Higginson	A	Do	Do	Do
9742	" Fisher B	B	4.8.16	Do	Killed
24012	" Divine E	B	1.8.16	Do	Wounded
24494	" Dawson R	B	4.8.16	Do	Do
16449	" Featherstone	B	5.8.16	Do	Do
24702	" Dunn D	C	9.8.16	Do	Do
2807	" Baxter	C	5.8.16	Do	Wounded
3285	" Shore W	C	1.8.16	Do	Wounded
16351	" Shoreman J	C	1.8.16	Do	Do
24589	" Swift J.	C	2.8.16	Do	Do
10455	" Leather ?	C	4.9.16	Do	Do
23451	" Flanagan ?	D	5.8.16	Do	Do
24400	" Dempsey ?	D	8.9.16	Do	Killed
24494	" Kellet	D	Do	Do	Do

List No 113 Continued

Regt N°	Rank and Name	Coy	Date	Regiment	Casualty
15501	Pte Richardson W	D	8.8.16	11th Manchester	Killed
4385	" Grant H	D	Do	Do	Do
23335	L/C Cunliffe J G	D	Do	Do	Wounded
3593	Pte Duffy M	D	Do	Do	Do
13683	" Graves W	D	Do	Do	Do
27694	" Fairhurst	D	Do	Do	Do S.S
15686	" Irving A	D	Do	Do	Do Do

for Officer

W.F. Robinton Lieut & Adjt
for O.C. 9th North. Fus

To Officer i/c N.A.I.S. No 2.
Base.

Herewith Casualty Report of men of other regiments attached to 9th North'd Fusiliers

Regt No	Rank and Name	Coy	Date	Regiment	Casualty
17475	Pte Vasey J.C.	C	8.8.16	10 KOYLI	Wounded SS
28373	L/Cpl Blakey J	C	6.8.16	16" D.L.I	Acc Wounded
18806	Pte Bousfield RW	C	1.8.16	16" D.L.I	Unwounded at d Acc Wounded
~~1305~~	~~Rooks~~	~~C~~			
1122	" Lannan P	C	1.8.16	15" D.L.I	Do
22836	" Brown RH	D	8.8.16	15" D.L.I	Wounded
25162	" Lowes J	D	4.8.16	14" D.L.I	Do SS

W.F. Robertson
a/Sgt for OC 9/North'd Fus
Lieut

for Off

Orderly Room
9 AUG 1916
No. 114
9th (Service) Batt. North'd Fus

To Officer i/c N.A.I.S No 2.
Base.

Herewith casualty report please

Regt Nº	Rank and Name	Coy	Date	Casualty
12895	Sgt Swinburn M	A	9.8.16	Wounded
12916	L/C Brecken J.C	A	9.8.16	Do
13383	Cpl Ridding R	B	9.8.16	Do
915	Pte Gillespie W	D	9.8.16	Killed
2631	L/Sgt Croft J.E.	D	9.8.16	Wounded

W.T. Robertson Lieut & Adjt.
for O.C. 9th North'd Fus.

To Officer i/c N.A.I.S No 2.
Base.

Herewith Casualty Report of men of other regiments attached to 9th North⁴ Fusiliers

---

11th Manchester Regiment

No 16666 Pte Balsover "C" Coy 9/8/16 Killed

W.F. Robertson
Lieut & Adjt
9th North⁴ Fusiliers

To. Officer i/c N.A.I.S. 2.
Base.

Horwich Casualty Report please.

Regt No	Rank and Name	Coy	Date	Casualty
50/245	L/C McNamee P.J.	B	13.8.16	Killed
28473	Pte Lingard W	B	Do	Do
2.1160	" Hart W	D	12.8.16	Do
11475	" Johnson C	A	13.8.16	Wounded
11857	" Rowley J	A	Do	Do
10562	" Payne A	C	10.9.16	Wounded S.S. returned to duty 11-8-16
10744	" Allan J	C	Do	Do
14786	" Smith L	C	Do	Wounded
18069	" Keeling J	C	Do	Do
23958	" Black	C	12.8.16	Do
15917	" Young J.P.	D	11.8.16	Do
12179	" Dodds J ✗	B	1.9.16	Do rtd to duty 12
21392	" Pickles J ✗	B	1.8.16	Wounded
				✗ Attached to 52nd Coy M.G.C.
10195	" Lambert F	C	10.8.16	Wounded

W.T. Robertson Lieut & a/Adjt
for O.C. 9th North'd Fusiliers

To Officer i/c N.A.I.S. No 2
Base.

Herewith Casualty Report of men of other regiments attached to 9th North'd Fusiliers

Reg't No	Rank and Name	Coy	Date	Regiment	Casualty
24508	Pte Atkinson G.	B	13.8.16	11th Manchester	Killed
24226	" Thorley J.	B	Do	Do	Do
9424/c	" Robinson W.	B	Do	Do	Wounded
23525	Pte Parker R.B.	C	10.8.16	16th D.L.I.	Killed

W. Robertson Lieut & a/Adjt
for O.C. 9th North'd Fusiliers

To Officer i/c N.A.I.S.
         Base.

Herewith Casualty Report please.

No 13383 a/Sergt Ridding R.
Previously reported "wounded"
now reported "Died of Wounds"

                W F Robertson Lieut + a/Adjt
                 for OC 9th North'd Fusiliers

To Officer i/c N.A.I.S. 2
            Base

Herewith Casualty Report please

REGT No	RANK AND NAME	COY	DATE	CASUALTY
12334	Sgt Poulton J.H.	B	16.8.16	Previously reported "Wounded" now reported "Died of Wounds"
12991	Pte Colson W	B	4.8.16	Wounded while attached to 52nd T.M.B. Remained at duty
12799	" Routledge ?	A	11.8.16	Wounded and remained at duty

W. Robertson Lieut & Adjt:
for O.C. 9th North Fus:

[Stamp: ORDERLY ROOM 19 AUG. 1916 No 120 9TH (SERVICE) BATT. NORTHD FUSILIERS]

Lot A.S.202   121
    Base
                    Herewith Casualty
    return please.

Reg No	Rank & Name	Coy	Date	Casualty
2250	Pte Brown A.	C	1-8-16	Wounded (acc)
9/11378	" Richardson J.	A	8-8-16	Previously reptd
2621	L/cpl Croft G.	D	14-8-16	Wounded now Died of Wounds per O1810 No 32.

                          W. Rybuton
                          Lieut & Adjt.
                          For O.C. 9 North'n Fus.
In the Field
21-8-16

O i/c
3rd Army Ink Base 2.
Base

**ORDERLY ROOM
31 AUG 1916
No. 124
9th (SERVICE) BATT. NORTH'D FUSILIERS**

Adm to Casualty Report

Reg.t No	Rank	Name	Coy	Date	Casualty
23926	P/e	Charleston (M Manchester R)	A	Aug 8	Wounded
16268	"	Bloomfield O	A	" 6	W. Shell Shc. Abrasion legs
24001	"	Berry W	B	July 9	Wounded

Not previously reported.

W.T Robertson Lieut &
Adjutant.
for O.C 9th (Ser) Batt. North Fusiliers

Army Form ...
New Army ... A.Z.

Herewith Casualty Report

No	Rank & Name	Date	Coy	Casualty
16659	Pte Lawrence G. (att. to 11th Manchesters)	Aug 20	B	Wounded
3800	Pte Ricks T.S.	Aug 24	A	Wounded

M.T. Robertson
Lieut & Adjutant,
In the Field
for O.C. 9th (Service) Batt. North'n Fusiliers

Stamp: ORDERLY ROOM 25 AUG 1916 No. 122 9TH (SERVICE) BATT. NORTH'N FUSILIERS

Sheard's
Two Army Pnl Section
Base

**ORDERLY ROOM
26 AUG. 1916
No.
9TH (SERVICE) BATT. NORTH⁴ FUSILIERS**

Herewith Casualty Report

to	Rank & Name	Coy	date	
23/52	P/e Sheard C	D	Aug 25ᵗʰ Wounded	

W F Robertson
Lieut &
Adjutant.
for O C 9th (Ser) Batt. North⁴ Fusiliers.

Sent to
New Army Inf Cop 2.
Base

**ORDERLY ROOM
31 AUG. 1916
No. 125
9th (SERVICE) BATT. NORTH⁴ FUSILIERS**

Nominal Casualty Report

Regt No	Rank & Name	Co	date	Casualty
15402	Pte	Thomas J	A	Aug 29	Wounded
14674	Pte	Taylor W	A	" 30	Wounded

W.G. Robertson
Lieut & Adjutant.
for O.C. 9th (Ser) Batt. North⁴ Fusiliers.

SPECIAL ORDER OF THE DAY

BY

GENERAL SIR DOUGLAS HAIG,
G.C.B., K.C.I.E., K.C.V.O., A.D.C.
Commander-in-Chief, British Armies in France.

It is two years since the British Army entered on the greatest struggle in the history of the world against the most formidable fighting machine that has ever been created—a machine fashioned by the unceasing effort of many generations for the deliberate purpose of imposing on all nations the will of one, regardless of justice and of the sufferings to be imposed on humanity.

Originally small in numbers but constant in purpose our Army has fought on during these two strenuous years determined to play a part worthy of our race in the achievement of final and complete victory.

For two years the utmost efforts of a skilful, determined and well-prepared foe have been foiled by the great fighting qualities so freely displayed, of discipline and pluck, tenacity in defence and vigour in attack, steady and patient effort in training for a new and most trying style of warfare, and endurance and cheerfulness in all circumstances however difficult.

By these means time has been gained for forming great new armies during the progress of a great War, a task to which the united efforts of the British Empire have been devoted.

The fighting value of these new armies has been displayed to the enemy and to the world during the last few weeks in which the enemy's front has been pierced and he has been driven from two of his most carefully prepared systems of defence.

The third year of the War opens brightly for us.

With his self-confidence rudely shaken, forced to defend himself on every side against the simultaneous and vigorous offensive of all the allied armies, suffering reverses on every front, the enemy though he still fights strongly fights no longer with the belief of two years ago in his power to impose his will on the human race, but in a desperate effort to save himself from utter defeat and from the punishment he has merited.

However severe the efforts that still lie before us our worst difficulties have already been overcome.

Strong in numbers, well provided with munitions and reserves of all kinds, confident in the justice of our quarrel, and strengthened by the consciousness of what has already been accomplished and by the war experience gained, our fight now is not for time but for victory.

The qualities that have brought us through the past two difficult years successfully will enable us to accomplish what still remains to be done and to take our full share in securing the ultimate complete triumph of the allied cause.

D. Haig. Genl.

General Headquarters,
4th August, 1916.

*Commanding-in-Chief,
British Armies in France.*

War Diary

SPECIAL ORDER OF THE DAY
BY
GENERAL SIR DOUGLAS HAIG,
G.C.B., K.C.I.E., K.C.V.O., A.D.C.
Commander-in-Chief, British Armies in France.

The following telegrams are published for the information of all ranks:—

I. GENERAL SIR DOUGLAS HAIG.
4th August.

On the anniversary of our declaration of war on Germany because of her outrage of the principles of justice and right, the members of the Coal and Shipping Exchange at Cardiff wish to express to you and to the officers and men under your command their great admiration of the noble courage and devotion to duty shown by all. In sending our deep appreciation we feel unbounded confidence in the final victory and the triumph of right and justice over might and outrage.

CHAIRMAN OF THE CARDIFF COAL AND SHIPPING EXCHANGE.

II. CHAIRMAN OF THE CARDIFF COAL AND SHIPPING EXCHANGE.
4th August.

On behalf of the officers and men under my command I heartily thank you and the members of the Coal and Shipping Exchange at Cardiff for your kind telegram which we all deeply appreciate. It is another proof that the nation is now throwing its whole energy into the fight for liberty and justice. After two years of bitter warfare we are more united than ever in our inflexible determination not to relax our efforts until we have emerged triumphant from this titanic struggle.

DOUGLAS HAIG.

III. GENERAL SIR DOUGLAS HAIG.
4th August.

On this, the second anniversary of the outbreak of war, I desire on behalf of the citizens of Glasgow to congratulate you and your brave Army upon your brilliant offensive and to assure you that our workmen will do all they can to keep you supplied with shells and guns so that before long an overwhelming victory may be ours.

LORD PROVOST OF GLASGOW.

IV. LORD PROVOST OF GLASGOW.
4th August.

All thanks to you and to the citizens of Glasgow for your inspiring message. The British Army is well aware how much it owes to the untiring efforts and cheerful endurance of the British men and women workers for the successes achieved. Glasgow may well be proud of the part she has played both in the workshops and in the trenches. Unfaltering in our resolution we are starting on the third year of this great war in which the destiny of our Empire of our race and indeed of the civilised world is involved with absolute confidence in final victory.

DOUGLAS HAIG.

D. Haig. Genl.

General Headquarters,
5th August, 1916.

*Commanding-in-Chief,
British Armies in France.*

SPECIAL ORDER.

August 5th 1916.

The following decorations have been awarded to Officers and men of the 17th Division for gallantry in the field during the recent operations.

The G.O.C., wishes to congratulate the recipients on their well earned rewards.

DISTINGUISHED SERVICE ORDER.

Captain D.V.Hunter, R.A.M.C., att'd 10th West Yorkshire Regt.
Lieut. D.A.Jones, 7th Lincolnshire Regiment.

BAR TO MILITARY CROSS.

Captain E.M.Wood, 8th South Staffordshire Regiment.

MILITARY CROSS.

Captain C.V.Roe, R.A.M.C., att'd 9th Northumberland Fusiliers
" W.Barclay, 51st Field Ambulance, R.A.M.C.
2/Lieut. F.M.Pastour, 51st Company Machine Gun Corps.
" G.E.Gilbert, " " " " "
" J.K.Mitchell, 52nd " " " "
" R.D'Albert Anson, 6th Dorsetshire Regiment.
Lieut. G.L.Davidson, " " "
Captain G.O'Hanlon, " " "
Captain W.Gibson,   8th South Staffordshire Regiment.
2/Lieut. V.H.Clay, 10th Lancashire Fusiliers.
Captain G.W.Thacker " "
2/Lieut. E.V.Speakman, 11th Manchester Regiment.
No. 1015 C.S.Major W.Coleshill " "
Lieut. P.Howe,   10th West Yorkshire Regiment.
No. 10682 C.S.Maj. F.Green   "   "
Lieut. C.W.Lamb,   7th Yorkshire Regiment.
2/Lieut. V.D.Wilkinson, " "
" G.S.R.Roper, " "
" J.A.A.Duncan " "
Captain R.V.L.Dallas, 9th Northumberland Fusiliers.
2/Lieut. J.Potty,   9th West Riding Regiment.
No. 14454 C.S.Major R.V.Shore, " "
No. 8520 C.S.Major H.Jarman, " "

THE DISTINGUISHED CONDUCT MEDAL.

No. 31150 Staff Sgt. G.Simons, 53rd Field Amb., R.A.M.C.
No. 3775 Private H.Cocks, 52nd Coy. Machine Gun Corps.
No. 10992 C.S.Maj. F.Franklin, 6th Dorset Regiment.
No. 10019 C.S.Maj. P.Adams,   "   "
No. 8/12858 Private S.Lee,   8th South Staffs. Regiment.
No. 13072 Private H.Hollingshead, 10th Lancashire Fusiliers.
No. 9844 A/C.S.Maj. B.Harris, " "
No. 5704 Sergeant R.Fitchings, " "

No. 12727 L/Cpl. J.G.Frost,   7th East Yorkshire Regiment.
No. 13184 Private C.L.ness,   7th Lincolnshire Regiment
No. 15406 Private H.Ingley,   6th West Riding Regiment.

MILITARY CROSS.

Lieut. C.D.Morgan, R.F.A. (S.R.) attd. Y/17 T.M. Batty.
Captain J.F.Richardson, 7th Border Regiment.
2/Lieut. E.Langer, "   "   "
Lieut. A.J.M.Lander, 10th Notts & Derby Regiment.

DISTINGUISHED CONDUCT MEDAL.

No. 7/985 C.S.Maj. (A/R.S.Maj.) E.Whiting, 7th Lincoln Regt.
No. 12924 Private, H.R.Hutchinson, 9th Northumberland Fusilier

B.D.—

MILITARY CROSS.

No. 18699 C.S.Maj. W.Trevill, 9th Northumberland Fusiliers.

B.D.—

Special Order.

July 26th 1916.

Award of Military Medal.

The following N.C.O's and men have been awarded the Military Medal by the Corps Commander for gallantry in the field.
The ribbons will be presented at a parade in the immediate future.

50th Infantry Brigade.

10th West Yorkshire Regiment.

12260 Corporal Walter Fallon, 15037 Private Joseph Oliver, 12430 Private Arthur Lester, 11916 Lance Corporal Ernest Taylor, 11666 Corporal Charles Slyfield, 18576 Pte. Francis W. Greavett, 11664 Pte. Ernest Cussons.

7th East Yorkshire Regiment.

12196 Lance Corporal Frank Tanfield, 11950 Private James Bradley att'd. 50th Bde. H.Q., 10308 Pte. Leonard Galey, 9055 Cpl. (L/Sgt) George Edward Briggs, 5079 Pte. Albert Kirby, 7233 Pte. Preston Robinson, 12205 Pte. John Frederick Siddall, 12608 Pte. Walter Gleadhill, 14364 Cpl. Samuel Wright.

7th Yorkshire Regiment.

14124 Pte. John Thomson Ramsay, 13007 Pte. John Sutherland, 16108 Pte. Walter Kenning, 11310 Pte. F. Andrews, 12385 Pte. George Patchett, 11701 Pte. Thomas Cruikshanks, 16067 Pte. Herbert George Larke, 18036 Pte. Sidney Tucker, 21089 Pte. Charles Forrester, 11165 Pte. Patrick Devaney, 2236 L/Cpl. Samuel Gatehouse, 12334 Pte. George William Oxberry, 18793 Pte. John Marwood, 12373 Pte. Peter Tiernan, 12474 Pte. John Thomas Gell.

6th Dorsets.

13083 J.Harris, 11453 L/Cpl. W.Routliff, 11964 Pte. S.Hicks, 12125 L/Cpl. J.C.Ennos.

50th M.Gun Co.

26748 Pte. John Pardey.

50th T.M.Bty.

12744 Pte. G.R.Velar, 12511 Pte. E.Thompson.

51st Infantry Brigade.

7th Lincolnshire Regiment.

14935 Lance Corporal Ernest Batterham, 11500 Pte. Edward Allam.

7th Border Regiment.

7/12650 Pte. William Robson, 10/23067 Pte. William Wiseman, 10/12112 Pte. John Atherton, 7/5294 L/Sergt. Francis William Hurd.

8th South Staffordshire Regiment.

8/10088 Sergt. George Brickwell, 8/13684 Sergt. Richard William Cartwright

Page 2.

10th Sherwood Foresters.

20104 Pte. William Wright, 27059 Pte. John William Robinson, 17351 Pte. Tom Sheldon, 14587 Pte. Charles Wood, 19459 Pte. Henry Dalby, 20483 Pte. John Robinson.

51st Machine Gun Co.

3603 Sergt. James Edward Clarke.

52nd Infantry Brigade.
9th Northumberland Fusiliers.

5207 Pte. Walter Beanland, 12281 Pte. John Beer Long, 14501 Sergt. Edward McConnell, 5222 L/Cpl. Thomas Jowsey, 14801 Sergt. Fairley Bell, 10651 Pte. David Crosbie Forster.

10th Lancashire Fusiliers.

15013 Cpl. Herbert Ripley, 5382 Sergt. Joseph Heathcote, 5105 Cpl. Albert Morris.

9th West Riding Regiment.

11675 L/Cpl. William Roberts, 11652 L/Cpl. John Harrison, 12628 L/Cpl. Norman Lockwood, 15078 Private William Richard Webb.

12th Manchester Regiment.

8002 Pte. Harry Young, 4803 Sergt. Charles Hanes, 5538 Sergt. Charles Bebbington, 7924 Sergt. John McDonald, 1678 L/Cpl. Fullerton Steele, 16278 Pte. Robert Johnstone, 7827 Pte. James Smith.

52nd Machine Gun Co.

3849 Pte. H.V.Straffon.

77th Field Co. R.E.

43037 Cpl. Joseph Sine.

78th Field Co. R.E.

68475 L/Cpl. Irvine McKay, 4917 Cpl. John Dumbell, 59234 Sapper William McKenzie.

17th Divl. Signal Co. R.E.

44734 L/Cpl. James Campbell, 46035 2/Cpl. Thomas Mawdsley, 44727 Spr. Donald Fredrick Allen, 50167 Spr. Thomas Alexander Watt, 77149 Spr. Duncan Macaskill, 49274 Cpl. Owen Arthur Gibbs.

Y/17 T.M.Bty. 23177 Cpl. A.Porley, R.G.A.
Y/17   "   "   17780 Sergt. T.Healey, R.G.A.
X/17   "   "   78519 Sergt. S.Morrison, R.F.A.

51st Field Ambulance. 36763 L/Cpl. A.Abel, 30952 Sergt. E.J.Boulton.
52nd Field Ambulance. 51523 Pte. Ernest Alfred Davies, 41542 Pte. Cyril Gluckstien.
53rd Field Ambulance. 39917 L/Cpl. W.Robson.

CONFIDENTIAL

WAR DIARY
of
9th (S) Bn NORTHUMBERLAND FUSILIERS

FROM 1ST SEPTEMBER 1916 TO 30th SEPTEMBER 1916
(VOLUME)

WAR DIARY
or
INTELLIGENCE SUMMARY
(Erase heading not required.)

Army Form C. 2118

Place	Date	Hour	Summary of Events and Information	Remarks and references to Appendices
TRENCHES.	Sept 1st		Trench routine.	
		7-30pm	During the day our observers and snipers observed a relief. It was in full swing in the enemy lines GOMMECOURT at 7-30 p.m., owing to presence of gas cylinders in our front line we were unable to carry out retaliation. Should treat cylinders.	Pub.
TRENCHES.	Sept 2nd		Trench routine.	Pub.
TRENCHES.	Sept 3rd		Trench routine.	Pub.
TRENCHES.	Sept 4th		Trench routine.	Pub.
TRENCHES / SOUASTRE	Sept 5th		Orders received that Bn. would be relieved by 10th Lancashire Fus. in the left sub Sector during the morning of 5th. Relief of right sector to commence at 5-30 a.m. Accordingly "A" & "D" Companies on relief marched back to SOUASTRE by the route ARTILLERY CROSS ROADS — FONQUEVILLERS CEMETERY — "TREED" BIENVILLERS Rd — SOUASTRE. "B" on relief by the Lanc Fus. taken the Right Sector FONQUEVILLERS defences left — — — — — — — — — — — — "C" — — — — — — — — — — Left — — — — — — — — — — — — The two companies were relieved by the 12th Manchester Regt. about 5 p.m. when they marched back to SOUASTRE by above route. Snipers observed gun. H.Q's were relieved at 5 p.m.	Pub.

Army Form C. 2118

WAR DIARY or INTELLIGENCE SUMMARY
(Erase heading not required.)

Instructions regarding War Diaries and Intelligence Summaries are contained in F.S. Regs., Part II. and the Staff Manual respectively. Title Pages will be prepared in manuscript.

Place	Date	Hour	Summary of Events and Information	Remarks and references to Appendices
SOUASTRE	Sept 6th		Btn. now in divisional reserve. Morning Physical drill. A small fatigue party (1 NCO 16 men) supplied daily while in Div. Res.	
do	Sept 7th		Morning Physical drill. Bathing for Btn. during day at Div. Baths.	
do	Sept 8th		Physical drill and Squad drill. Parties sent for instruction in driving to R.E.'s	
do	Sept 9th		Physical & Squad drill. Whole Btn. on fatigue between 6-30pm and 2am (10 NCO's). In parties hostong each endeav offices were sent at intervals to FONQUEVILLE'S SECTOR to remove empty gas cylinders from "Y" Sector front line.	
SOUASTRE / SOUASTRE Camp	Sept 10th		Orders received that Btn. would move to camp at D.27.d. on the morning of the 10th inst. The Bn/p. moved as follows "A" Coy at 10-30am "B" Coy at 10-45am "C" — 11 - 0 am "D" — 11 - 15 am Btn. again detailed to remove gas cylinders to remove gas cylinders from Y Sector front line. 320 NCO & men were detailed for this fatigue which was carried out under similar circumstances to that of the previous night	

Army Form C. 2118

WAR DIARY
or
INTELLIGENCE SUMMARY
(Erase heading not required.)

Instructions regarding War Diaries and Intelligence Summaries are contained in F. S. Regs., Part II. and the Staff Manual respectively. Title Pages will be prepared in manuscript.

Place	Date	Hour	Summary of Events and Information	Remarks and references to Appendices
SOUASTRE Camp.	Sept 11th		Physical and Squad drill (fatigues). 1 Offr + 50 O.R. detailed 9am. for 191st R.E. + 1 Offr + 500 O.R. at 4pm.	Initials
do	Sept 12th		Physical & Squad drill and same fatigue as day previous	Initials
do	Sept 13th		Physical & Squad drill and same fatigue as day previous. A draft of men arrived about 7pm. (100 strong).	Initials
do	Sept 14th		Same fatigues. Further fatigue of 50 men Lewis Sgt. for trenching cable. A further draft arrived about 6pm.	Initials
do	Sept 15th		A Portion of the Btn was inspected by the G.O.C. 52nd Inf. Bde. between 10-15 am & 11 am. viz.	Initials
			10-15 am. Last two drafts in marching order	
			10-40 am. No 6 Platoon in fighting order	
			10-50 am. Lewis Gun Detachment "C" Coy fighting order handcarts loaded	
			11 am. Btn Bombing Platoon in fighting order	
			All available men on fatigues (including new drafts)	Initials

1875 Wt. W593/826 1,000,000 4/15 J.B.C. & A. A.D.S.S./Forms/C. 2118.

Army Form C. 2118

WAR DIARY
or
INTELLIGENCE SUMMARY
(Erase heading not required.)

Instructions regarding War Diaries and Intelligence Summaries are contained in F.S. Regs., Part II. and the Staff Manual respectively. Title Pages will be prepared in manuscript.

Place	Date	Hour	Summary of Events and Information	Remarks and references to Appendices
SOUASTRE (Corps)	Sept	16th	Physical Drill, Squad Drill, Musketry (A.P.) and Revolver practice (Lewis gunners). Every available man on fatigue	Inits
do	Sept	17th	Physical and Squad Drill. Usual fatigue	Inits
do	Sept	18th	Physical Drill. Divine Service Voluntary. Usual fatigues to 15th R.E.	Inits
do	Sept	19th	Physical Drill & Squad Drill. Usual fatigues (R.E.s)	Inits
do	Sept	20th	Physical and Squad Drill. Kit Inspection. (Special attention paid to fitting pack equipment in preparing for marching order)	Inits
do	Sept	21st	Orders having been received the Btn. moved from the SOUASTRE area to the MONDICOURT area by the HENU – PAS road. "C" Company leading. Btn. was billeted over-night at MONDICOURT.	Inits
do MONDICOURT	Sept	22nd	Btn. paraded at 7-15 am. moved to the BARLY (SOMME) area "D" Coy. leading. ROUTE. DOULENS – AUXI LE CHATEAU main road (Same arrangement and Btn. very crowded in the billets in BARLY	Inits
BARLY				

WAR DIARY
or
INTELLIGENCE SUMMARY

(Erase heading not required.)

Army Form C. 2118

Place	Date	Hour	Summary of Events and Information	Remarks and references to Appendices
BARLY / HEIRMONT	Sept 23rd	6-15 am.	Btn. Moved to MONTIGNY are "A" Coy. leading. Paraded at 6.15 am. ROUTE: FROHEN-LEGRANDE – BEAUVOIR – RIVIERE – MAIZICOURT to HEIRMONT where Btn. was billeted but very crowded.	
HEIRMONT / MILLANCOURT	Sept 24th		Btn. moved to MILLANCOURT its final destination i.e. a four days trek. Good billets were obtained generally but crowded and all available space used. ROUTE – YVRENCH, YVRENCHEUX – GAPENNES – AGENVILLERS to MILLANCOURT.	
MILLANCOURT	Sept 25th		N.B. during the whole trek the Btn. Band although only formed on the 18th inst played the Btn. on the march. Physical drill and kit inspection. New drafts paraded under R.S.M.	
do	Sept 26th		Divisional Instruction in Bayonet Fighting at disposal of "A" Coy. 8-30 to 9 am. "B" Coy 9-30 am. "C" Coy. 9-30 –10 am "D" 10 am – 10-30 am. Btn. paraded at 10-35 am for a lecture demonstration in Bayonet fighting by Maj Hanthill.	

WAR DIARY or INTELLIGENCE SUMMARY

Army Form C. 2118

Place	Date	Hour	Summary of Events and Information	Remarks and references to Appendices
Rubempré	Sept 26th (Contd)	1-4.5-6.3 pm.	Coys. paraded for Elementary Musketry and Skirmishing in training area. Bombers worked under Bde. Bombing Instructor. Fatigue Party of 1 Offr + 60 men with Chords reported to O.C. 93rd R.E. for work on new range. Regimental Canteen opened under charge of Sgt Reynolds.	
do	Sept 27th		Running Exercises. Physical Training. Squad & Platoon Drill. General Routine training. Drafts under R.S.M.	
do	Sept 28th		Running Exercises. Company paraded 9-13 am. Bde. Bayonet fighting course. (A,9 & 36). Lecture at 6 pm by C.R.E. for all officers. Commanding Officer left for leave and Capt F.W.R. Ingall took over command (acting).	
do	Sept 29th		Running Exercises. 9-13 am. Btn. paraded and proceeded to A.10 central for instruction in field work under 93rd Field Coy. R.E. & worked between 10am & 1pm.	
		7pm	Btn. paraded and march to A.16 & for night digging under R.E. Supervision. finishing work about 10 pm.	

Army Form C. 2118

WAR DIARY
or
INTELLIGENCE SUMMARY
(Erase heading not required.)

Place	Date	Hour	Summary of Events and Information	Remarks and references to Appendices
HILLANCOURT	Sept 30th	9.15 am	Companies paraded and proceeded to Bois Regnval fighting aeroplane A.9.c.36.	full
		1-1.15 pm	Company Drill (Continued Routine of Training)	

W.R. Shackelhurst. Capt.
Cmdg 9th Northd Fus

War Diary

SPECIAL ORDER OF THE DAY
By
GENERAL SIR DOUGLAS HAIG,
G.C.B., G.C.V.O., K.C.I.E., A.D.C.
Commander-in-Chief, British Armies in France.

The following letters are published for the information of all ranks :—

To GENERAL SIR DOUGLAS HAIG.
(Translation).

G.H.Q. OF FRENCH ARMIES,
17th September, 1916.

MY DEAR GENERAL,

I desire to convey to you my most sincere congratulations on the brilliant successes gained by the British troops under your command during the hard-fought battles of the 15th and 16th of September. Following on the continuous progress made by your armies since the beginning of the Somme offensive, these fresh successes are a sure guarantee of final victory over our common enemy, whose physical and moral forces are already severely shaken.

Permit me, my dear General, to take this opportunity of saying that the combined offensive which we have carried on now for more than two months has, if it were possible, drawn still closer the ties which unite our two Armies—our adversary will find therein proof of our firm determination to combine our efforts until the end, to ensure the complete triumph of our cause.

I bow before those of your soldiers by whose bravery these successes have been achieved, but who have fallen before the completion of our task; and I ask you to convey, in my name and in the name of the whole French Army, to those who stand ready for the fights still to come, a greeting of comradeship and confidence.

(Signed) J. JOFFRE.

To GENERAL JOFFRE.

GENERAL HEADQUARTERS,
BRITISH ARMIES IN FRANCE,
19th September, 1916.

MY DEAR GENERAL,

I thank you most sincerely for the kind message of congratulation and goodwill that you have addressed to me and to the troops under my command on their recent successes. This fresh expression of the good wishes of yourself and of your gallant Army, without whose close co-operation and support those successes could scarcely have been achieved, will be very warmly appreciated by all ranks of the British Armies.

I thank you, too, for your noble tribute to those who have fallen. Our brave dead, whose blood has been shed together on the soil of your great country, will prove a bond to unite our two peoples long after the combined action of our Armies has carried the common cause for which they have fought to its ultimate triumph.

The unremitting efforts of our forces north and south of the Somme, added to the glorious deeds of your Armies unaided at Verdun, have already begun to break down the enemy's powers of resistance; while the energy of our troops and their confidence in each other increases from day to day. Every fresh success that attends our arms brings us nearer to the final victory to which, like you, I look forward with absolute confidence.

Yours very truly,
(Signed) D. HAIG, GENERAL.

D. Haig. Genl.

General Headquarters,
22nd September, 1916.

*Commanding-in-Chief,
British Armies in France.*

ARMY PRINTING AND STATIONERY SERVICES A—9/16.

Vol 14

CONFIDENTIAL.

War Diary.

From 1st to 31st October

9th (S) Bn Northumberland Fusiliers

Volume I.

Army Form C. 2118

WAR DIARY
or
INTELLIGENCE SUMMARY
(Erase heading not required.)

Instructions regarding War Diaries and Intelligence Summaries are contained in F. S. Regs, Part II. and the Staff Manual respectively. Title Pages will be prepared in manuscript.

Place	Date	Hour	Summary of Events and Information	Remarks and references to Appendices
MILLENCOURT	Oct. 1st		*Ordinary Evening.* Church parade. Roman catholics sam. Bn. paraded the village from road for divine service at "Tent of Village." Holy Communion immediately afterwards on the M.H.R.I.S. C.S.M. Khedivon "A" Coy assumed the duties of R.S.M. vice Y.R.S.M. Armitage J. to England on leave. Winter time resumed all clocks back one hour from 11 p.m.	*[initials]*
do.	Oct 2nd		7.0 – 7.30 am Running Exercise. 9.30am Coys paraded & marched to Bn. beyond fighting course (A.9 c 76) Afternoon decided to Specialists. Evening a night marching scheme service out. 173. All companies moved independently to 4.21. to 5-0 from where Btn. moved by different routes (respectively) to pt. generally at 4.15 to 9.0	*[initials]*
do.	Oct 3rd		Ranges X & Y allotted to Bn. for musketry. Morning A Coy ranges X. (A.16 a 4) B Coy " Y (A.Ka 73) C.O. & Coys. reported and ordered moving consolidation of ground afternoon Vieux Vern.	*[initials]*

Army Form C. 2118

WAR DIARY
or
INTELLIGENCE SUMMARY
(Erase heading not required.)

Instructions regarding War Diaries and Intelligence Summaries are contained in F. S. Regs., Part II. and the Staff Manual respectively. Title Pages will be prepared in manuscript.

Place	Date	Hour	Summary of Events and Information	Remarks and references to Appendices
MILLENCOURT	Oct 4th		7-0 to 7-30 am Running Exercises	
			9-0 to 10-am Physical Training & Bayonet fighting	
			10- to 11-30 am Company Drill	
			11-30 to 12-noon Lectures on Patrols & stalking	
			1-4.5 pm Companies carried out rapid consolidation of ground	
			on Trenches at A.21.c.6.9.	
			Translation of a reply from the 3rd Riechehr [?] (Reserve Infantry) to a Court sent by the North was published in	
			orders	
do.	Oct 5th		7-0 - 7-30 am Running Exercises	
			9-10 am Coys paraded & proceeded to the Bayonet fighting Course	
			Rifle Bomb throwers were too large whether these Coys were sent after Bayonet fighting. X Y range details kept	
			Coys kept carried on by Platoon scheme on by trade ground	
do.	Oct 6th		7-0 - 7-30 am Running Exercises	
			9-0 am Battn paraded on ground "Exercises" under E.S.O.	
			10-30 am "	
			10-3 am Classes for Subalterns under Commanding Officer — Adjutant	
			1-15 pm Companies paraded for bayonet fighting course	

WAR DIARY
or
INTELLIGENCE SUMMARY

(Erase heading not required.)

Army Form C. 2118

Place	Date	Hour	Summary of Events and Information	Remarks and references to Appendices
MILLENCOURT	Oct.	7am	Bn paraded ready to 16.C. for make an attack on their lines under creeping barrage. Officers moved in advance of Bn. under phosphogene. Orderly officer spent day afternoon Coys carried out various methods of attack in creeping barrage.	
do.	Oct. 8.		Orders received that Bn. would move but was later cancelled	
MILLENCOURT to CONTEVILLE	Oct. 9.		Orders were received for the Bn. to move to the HERMONT area and in accordance with same the Bn. marched by the ST ROUIER - ONEUX route to CONTEVILLE in which village it billeted for the night	
CONTEVILLE to BARLY	Oct.	10am	The Bn. received orders to move to the MEZEROLLES area continued its march by BENATRE - MAIZICOURT - WAVANS - FROHEN & GRAND - REMAISNIL to BARLY where it billeted. N.B owing to hilly nature of country the transport left the Bn. at the branch roads leading to REMAISNIL & DOULLENS from FROHEN & GRAND & moved to BARLY by MÉZEROLLES & the valley road.	

Army Form C. 2118

WAR DIARY
or
INTELLIGENCE SUMMARY
(Erase heading not required.)

Instructions regarding War Diaries and Intelligence Summaries are contained in F.S. Regs., Part II. and the Staff Manual respectively. Title Pages will be prepared in manuscript.

Place	Date	Hour	Summary of Events and Information	Remarks and references to Appendices
BARLY — MONDICOURT	Oct.	11th	The Bn. moved to the HALLOY AREA and proceeded by the route OECOCHES – DOULLENS – POMMERA to MONDICOURT. This was the Bn's second visit to MONDICOURT being especially noticeable owing to the extremely bad weather conditions.	(illeg.)
MONDICOURT	Oct.	12th	Having settled down for an unknown period the Bn. held a kit inspection whilst during the afternoon practice in attack was carried out by companies.	(illeg.)
MONDICOURT	Oct.	13th	Physical Drill, bayonet fighting, Company drill; during the afternoon further attacking practice by companies	(illeg.)
do	Oct	14th	Physical training, bayonet fighting, Company drill. Afternoon Brigade practised attack on trenches laid out to represent German Trenches in the HEBUTERNE sector. It is notable that in later questionings of prisoners in Intelligence reports that a prisoner's British attack on these trenches was common talk among the Germans who never discover the number of tanks were accurate.	(illeg.)

Army Form C. 2118

WAR DIARY
or
INTELLIGENCE SUMMARY
(Erase heading not required.)

Place	Date	Hour	Summary of Events and Information	Remarks and references to Appendices
MONDICOURT	Oct. 15th		Roman Catholics paraded at 7.30 am and marched to POMMERA for service. Church of England paraded 9am on 20 "reps" ground. Presbyterians paraded at 9.30am theard 4.9% foreman. Remainder today in rest.	
do	Oct. 16th		Physical drill, bayonet fighting & company drill. Afternoon further practice in attack on the training area.	
do	Oct. 17th		Physical drill, bayonet fighting & company drill. Afternoon further practice in attack. (Forming a letter on previous days mistake) Evening lecture by C.O. to all officers warrant officers & senior N.C.O's	
do	Oct. 18th		General training during day. Specialists under respective officers. Regimental canteen again opened.	
do	Oct. 19th		Further drafts to total [illegible] (20 men NC) General training of [illegible] [illegible] the following is [illegible]	

WAR DIARY
or
INTELLIGENCE SUMMARY

Army Form C. 2118

Place	Date	Hour	Summary of Events and Information	Remarks and references to Appendices
MONDICOURT to LE SOUICH	Oct. 19th		In accordance with orders the Btn. moved to LE SOUICH by the route POMMERA - LUCHEUX - BREVILLERS when the billeted.	
			NB The following awarded the Military Medal for gallantry & devotion to duty	
			No 12700 C.S.M. Richardson.	
			No 10566 Sgt. Macher.	
			No 10277 Sgt. Ross.	
			No 13062 Pt. Butler.	
			No 10469 Pte. Calvert JS.	
LE SOUICH	Oct. 20th		General Training rest	
LE SOUICH	Oct. 21st		Physical drill, Bayonet fighting. No 7 Platoon (marching order) afternoon - Btn. Bombers (fighting ") Btn. S.B. (marching ") were inspected by the G.O.C. 52nd Inf. Bde.	
			They were specially complimented by the G.O.C. & also the Col. on the Btn. in general.	

WAR DIARY
or
INTELLIGENCE SUMMARY

Army Form C. 2118

Place	Date	Hour	Summary of Events and Information	Remarks and references to Appendices
Le Souich	Oct. 22nd		Orders were received that the Bn. would move to the Allonville area. The Transport set out and was Brigaded whence it proceeded to Coisy the Bn's destination. The Bn. entrained at 10am at Le Souich & proceeded to Coisy by the route Boquemaison — Doullens — Talmas — Villers-Bocage — Poulainville at which latter it detrained marching to Coisy where it arrived at 11am.	Smith
Coisy				
Coisy	Oct. 23rd		The Bn. moved again at 8-30am and marched by Allonville — Pont Noyelle — Querrieux to Daours. Bn. remained outside Daours 2 hours owing to troops in Daours not having evacuated billets.	Smith
Daours				
Daours	Oct. 24th		Kit & ammunition inspection.	Smith
Daours	Oct. 25th		General training. G.O.C. 62nd Infy. Bde. inspected billets.	Smith

Army Form C. 2118

WAR DIARY
or
INTELLIGENCE SUMMARY
(Erase heading not required.)

Place	Date	Hour	Summary of Events and Information	Remarks and references to Appendices
DAOURS	Oct.	26th	General training	(init.)
DAOURS	Oct.	27th	Btn. Received orders to march to SAND PITS CAMP and moved off in accordance with same moved by the route LA NEUVILLE – CORBIE – MERICOURT – TREUX – VIELLE – MEAULTE – CARCAILLOT FARM. Btn. encamped in Tents	(init.)
SAND PITS CAMP	Oct.	28th	Rest	(init.)
do	Oct.	29th	Church Parades during morning. "A" Stood too all day for a fatigue which they carried out between 4pm & 9pm	(init.)
do	Oct.	30th	Orders received that Btn. would move prior to camp at S.23.c.22. & march off accordingly at 9-30 am. The march was difficult owing to great amount of traffic and Btn. did not commence to arrive at 4pm. Accommodation was both bad and scarce	(init.)

1875 Wt. W593/826 1,000,000 4/15 J.B.C. & A. A.D.S.S./Forms/C. 2118.

WAR DIARY
or
INTELLIGENCE SUMMARY

Army Form C. 2118

Place	Date	Hour	Summary of Events and Information	Remarks and references to Appendices
Camp G23 b 2.2.	Feb. 3rd		Btn. still in camp awaiting orders as to movement.	

Gerald P. Whitmarsh Col.
Comdg. 9th Northd Fus

CONFIDENTIAL.

WAR DIARY.

OF

9TH (S) BN. NORTHUMBERLAND FUSILIERS

From 1st November 1916.
To 30th — do — — do —

Vol 15

WAR DIARY or INTELLIGENCE SUMMARY

Army Form C. 2118

Place	Date	Hour	Summary of Events and Information	Remarks and references to Appendices
TRENCHES.	Nov.	1st.	The Bn. entered the SOMME TRENCHES between GUEDECOURT and LESBOEUFS opposite LE TRANSLOY. Only one division stood between us and the French Corps. The conditions leading to the trenches made it very difficult to relieve and the actual trenches were as bad as any in the experience of the Bn. We relieved the 12th Bn. Y & L. Much difficulty in finding the superior position was caused owing to CURVES being unable to find suitable land marks.	[signature]
do.	Nov.	2nd.	In the trenches. A lot of sniping took place in this area. The bombers on our right took ZENITH TRENCH from the enemy. Water shortage felt.	[signature]
do	Nov	3rd	The Germans bombed & retook ZENITH TRENCH which was now held by Lincolns. In response to an appeal for assistance our "D" Coy Lewis guns rendered considerable help by directing a plunging fire on the enemy. Later a very complimentary letter was received by our C.O. from the C.O. (Lincolns) expressing thanks for the valuable assistance rendered. The Leinsters Inf. attacked a German strong point with our company but failed owing to extremely muddy nature of the ground.	[signature]

Army Form C. 2118

WAR DIARY
or
INTELLIGENCE SUMMARY
(Erase heading not required.)

Place	Date	Hour	Summary of Events and Information	Remarks and references to Appendices
"H" Camp CARNOY.	Nov 4th	4 pm	Btn relieved by the 12th Hants and moved back to "H" Camp CARNOY to rest. Btn was in huts. Much difficulty was experienced in the marching owing to the very bad condition of the men.	
			During our rest every opportunity was taken to have the men's feet rubbed with whale oil. ROUTES FOLLOWED: SUNKEN RD. – DELVILLE WOOD – LONGUEVAL – MONTAUBAN – COSY CORNER. H.	
"H" Camp	Nov 5th		In rest in "H" Camp.	
do	Nov 6th		In rest in "H" Camp.	
TRENCHES	Nov 7th		Btn again moved to the TRENCHES where they relieved the 12th Man. Ryf. The relief took place in heavy rain but positions were taken up without much difficulty and the relief was completed in good time.	
			Whereas last visit the Btn had 3 coys in the front line and one coy in RAINBOW TRENCH with a platoon of each in reserve at NEEDLE TRENCH. It now had two coys in front line and two coys in NEEDLE now being placed in RAINBOW owing to the heavy	

WAR DIARY or INTELLIGENCE SUMMARY

Army Form C. 2118

Place	Date	Hour	Summary of Events and Information	Remarks and references to Appendices
TRENCHES	Nov.	7th (cont)	(cont) Shelling of the Trench. The front line had during (south) by the 3rd Bn. Taking over the position slightly & extending. This left the Bn. without a comm Trench to BUZZER. Still had to be used communication between R.A H.Q & the front line and very difficult owing to the switchboard of the C.T. & day having was almost impassable. The Trenches were in an even worse condition and several men were found held in the mud for as long as 4 hrs. taking as many as four men to get them out.	(sgd)
do	Nov. 8th		In the Trenches. A strong wind came a slight drying of the ground but several to make the trenches more sticky.	(sgd)
do	Nov. 9th		One of our planes was forced to land in our Trenches an intense Bgr. reply took place. Shelling of HEBUTERNE also on Front line. This was made both slow & difficult by a very bright moon. (82,000)	(sgd)
do	Nov. 10th		Bn. relieved by the 12th (Hants.) Regt. and moved back to 10th camp BERNAFAY wood. (Relieved) This was the heaviest relief	

1875 Wt. W393/826 1,000,000 4/15 J.B.C. & A. A.D.S.S./Forms/C. 2118.

WAR DIARY
or
INTELLIGENCE SUMMARY
(Erase heading not required.)

Army Form C. 2118

Instructions regarding War Diaries and Intelligence Summaries are contained in F.S. Regs., Part II. and the Staff Manual respectively. Title Pages will be prepared in manuscript.

Place	Date	Hour	Summary of Events and Information	Remarks and references to Appendices
Trenches "D" Camp	Nov 10th	(cont)	reformed during our visit to the Somme owing to the wire having repeatedly dried the open ground. N.3 The Col. was straight from the trenches to the trenches and kept Allen took over the Coms of the Bn.	
"D" camp "H" camp	Nov. 11th		The Bn. moved in the evening to "H" camp convoy by the route BERNAFAY WOOD - MONTAUBAN - COSY CORNER - H camp	
do				
CITADEL	Nov 12th		Bn. moved at 5 a.m. to the CITADEL CAMP (find) difficulty found in moving owing to great amount of Traffic on the road Route CARNOY - CROSSRDS. F.8.9. - TRICOURT - BRAY - TRICOURT-BRAY RD. Transport separate from Bn. and at same R.C. camp	
CITADEL	Nov 13th		Meeting in camp before moving into rest area.	
do HANGEST	Nov. 14th		Bn. moved to HANGEST when owing to BREILLY billets being occupied the Brigade for the night bivouacked which they available. Route: CITADEL - BECORDEL - MEAULTE - DERNCOURT Entrained to HANGEST	

Army Form C. 2118

WAR DIARY
or
INTELLIGENCE SUMMARY
(Erase heading not required.)

Place	Date	Hour	Summary of Events and Information	Remarks and references to Appendices
HANGEST / BREILLY	Nov.	15th	Btn. Moved to BREILLY in which area they were billeted. The greater portion was found by busses, the remainder marching. Route HANGEST- CROUY- PICQUIGNY - BREILLY.	
BREILLY	Nov 16th		Btn. settled down in billets	
do	Nov 17th		Btn. billeted	
do	Nov 18th		Physical Training. Billets inspected by the C.O. afternoon Inter Coy Matches	
do	Nov 19th		Church Parade. Churchof E. at 11am Chateau courtyard RCatholics at 11 am in village church. No further parades.	
do	Nov 20th		Programme of training for coming week commenced.	
do	Nov 21st		Work as stated in programme of training	
do	Nov 22nd		Usual training. The Brigade Commander Lt.Col. Goodman CMG. paid a visit to the Btn. during afternoon parade.	

WAR DIARY
or
INTELLIGENCE SUMMARY

Army Form C. 2118

(Erase heading not required.)

Instructions regarding War Diaries and Intelligence Summaries are contained in F. S. Regs., Part II. and the Staff Manual respectively. Title Pages will be prepared in manuscript.

Place	Date	Hour	Summary of Events and Information	Remarks and references to Appendices
BREILLY	Nov. 23rd		Musketry according to programme. "C" Coy on range. Brig. Genl. inspected various detachments of the Bn. expressing himself well pleased.	JHB
do	Nov. 24th		Usual training.	JHB
do	Nov. 25th		Usual training. The 19th Divl. Genl. inspected the Bn. in billets and was exceedingly satisfied with the general appearance of Musketeers.	JHB
do	Nov. 26th		Church parade. (Roman Catholics in village church). Remainder of day men rested.	JHB
do	Nov. 27th		General training also football drill. Bn. team played in final league game, beating the Rane. Fus. by 3-0 at home.	JHB
do	Nov. 28th		General training & football drill. Match against 5th Yorks, ended in our favour by 2-0.	JHB

WAR DIARY
or
INTELLIGENCE SUMMARY

Army Form C. 2118

Place	Date	Hour	Summary of Events and Information	Remarks and references to Appendices
BREILLY	Nov. 29th		General Training. League match against [illegible] the Duke of Wellingtons whom we beat by 5-0.	Sgd.
do.	Nov. 30th		General Training. Further match with B.H. ended in Goalless draw. Reverts to end of month 3 events 1 draw 0 loss.	Sgd.

J S Allen Capt
Comdg 9th [Northd Fus?]

SPECIAL ORDER OF THE DAY
By
GENERAL SIR DOUGLAS HAIG,
G.C.B., G.C.V.O., K.C.I.E., A.D.C.
Commander-in-Chief, British Armies in France.

The following telegrams are published for the information of all ranks:—

I. *From* SIR W. H. DUNN, LORD MAYOR OF LONDON.
   16/11/16.
   Will you kindly convey to General Sir Douglas Haig the hearty congratulations of the Citizens of London on the brilliant successes of the British Troops on the ANCRE, which have caused immense satisfaction and pride throughout the country.

II. *From* GENERAL SIR DOUGLAS HAIG TO SIR W. H. DUNN, LORD MAYOR OF LONDON.
    16/11/16.
    All ranks under my command join with me in sincere thanks to you and the Citizens of London for kind appreciation of recent success on the ANCRE. The troops did excellent work there under most difficult conditions, and they greatly value your kind message.

D. Haig. Genl.

General Headquarters,
22nd November, 1916.

Commanding-in-Chief,
British Armies in France.

ARMY PRINTING AND STATIONERY SERVICES A—11/16—S540—9,300.

War Diary. November.
9th Batt. The North'd Fus.

Casualties November.

Appendix S

Officer i/c
Regular Inf Sec 3
Base   131

Herewith Casualty Report please.

Regt No	Rank and Name	Coy	Date	Casualty
	2/Lieut J.M.T. Craven	✓	8.11.16	Wounded (Remained at duty)
41170	Pte Gaskin E	D	9.11.16	Killed
29/169	" Fairlamb J	"	"	Wounded
28381	" Horn E	"	"	Do
9/446	" Davidson J.R	"	8.11.16	Do
29/637	" Robinson L	"	9.11.16	Missing
41240	" Dangh J	"	9.11.16	Do
22656	" Spence J.R	✓	9.11.16	Wounded
28366	" Hardwick B	✓	10.11.16	Do
5210	" Wragg J	✓	9.11.16	Do (Remained at duty)
6079	L/Cpl Carter W.K.	✓	5.11.16	Do (attached 52? M.B)
41120	Pte Armstrong G	✓	9.11.16	Killed
4229	L/C Shaw S	✓	10.11.16	Wounded
5490	" Carrabine E	✓	9.11.16	Do (Remained at duty)
29/652	Pte Burgess B	✓	9.11.16	Wounded
23873	" Cook A	✓	11.11.16	Do (accidentally)
29/244	" Cawthorne C	✓	9.11.16	Wounded
40184	" Dawson H	✓	9.11.16	Do
28322	" Wylie W.K.	✓	9.11.16	Do
29/247	" Sutcliffe H	✓	10.11.16	Do
29/412	" Saxton J	✓	10.11.16	Missing
29/297	" Durrans G	✓	9.11.16	Killed

Casualty report card

No	Rank	Name	Coy	date	Casualty	
9/454	Pte	Hodgson D	B	3.11.16	wounded	✓
23112	"	Archbold H	B	3.11.16	"	✓
29/446	"	Greenwood J	B	3.11.16	"	✓
12260	"	Muett J.A	B	3.11.16	"	✓
29/323	"	Senson A.	C	3.11.16	"	✓
21176	"	Mole M.	C	3.11.16	"	✓
38970	"	Stonehouse T	C	3.11.16	"	✓
38979	"	Willson J.R	C	4.11.16	"	✓
29/1	"	Collinson J	D	3.11.16	"	✓
20533	L/C	Keoghan B	D	3.11.16	"	✓
41192	"	Leech A	D	3.11.16	"	✓
13131	"	Burns T	D	3.11.16	"	✓
41206	Pte	O'Gorman	D	3.11.16	"	✓
1549	"	Gorman J	D	4.11.16	"	✓
~~====~~		~~========~~		X	"	
41212	"	Payne A	B	3.11.16	wounded	✓
12202	"	Trevor J	B	4.11.16	nerve at duty	
~~====~~	"	~~========~~				

D Robertson Lieut for Adjt
9th North'd Fusiliers

Offrs i/c
Regular Infantry Bn
Base

Eleventh Casualty Report

130

No	Rank	Name	Coy	Date	Casualty
41147	Pte	Campbell A	C	4.11.16	Killed
29/433	"	Exon E.J.C	C	"	"
41171	"	Gill J	C	2.11.16	"
4811	"	Johnson B	C	4.11.16	"
29/405	"	Jowett T	C	3.11.16	"
23766	"	Robinson W.A	A	4.11.16	"
29/525	"	Ramsden E	C	4.11.16	"
13168	Cpl	Colvin ?	C	3.11.16	Died of Wds.
4749	Pte	Crawford A	D	3.11.16	Killed
29/534	"	Rawnsley A	A	3.11.16	Missing
4475	"	Blenkinsop ?	B	4.11.16	Wounded & Missing
Lieut	L.A	Walden	A	4.11.16	Wounded
8807	Cpl	Douglas A	A	2.11.16	"
23671	L/C	Bolam A	A	2.11.16	"
41131	Pte	Bradley J.R	A	3.11.16	"
28221	"	Manville D	A	2.11.16	"
12874	"	Mordue G	A	2.11.16	"
2553	"	Roome W.S	A	3.11.16	"
41188	"	James J	A	2.11.16	"
8124	L/C	McArthur G	B	3.11.16	"
41173	Pte	Hastings J	B	3.11.16	"
41157	"	Davies G	B	3.11.16	"
29/486	"	Brannon ?	B	3.11.16	"

Officer i/c
Regular Inf Lent 3.   [ORDERLY ROOM stamp: 23.XI.16, 9th (Service) Batt. Norths Fusiliers]
   Base

— Herewith casualty report —

No 41444 Pte Copestake J. A Coy
   Wounded 7-11-16

Taken from O1810 11047.

M.J. Robertson
Lieut & Adjt
9th North'ho Fus.

Officer i/c
Reg Infantry Sec 3
Base

ORDERLY ROOM
21 NOV. 1916
No. 132
9TH (SERVICE) BATT. NORTH⁰ FUSILIERS

Herewith Casualty Report please

Ret No	Name Rank	Coy	Date	Casualty
29/259	Pte Johnson J	A	10.11.16	Previously reported missing now reported Evacuated
29/637	Pte Robinson L	D	9.11.16	

W. J. Robertson
Lieut & Adjt
9th North⁰ Fus

Casualty Report continued. No 131.

REGT NO	RANK AND NAME	COY	DATE	CASUALTY
13111	Pte Hara J	A ✓		Wounded attached 52 Tm
12891	" Robinson W.S.	" ✓	9.11.16	Killed
5089	Cpl Trainor S	" ✓	9.11.16	Do
17066	Pte Hudson H	" ✓	9.11.16	Do
17197	" McGurk ?	" ✓	9.11.16	Wounded
9/684	" Whitwam H	" ✓	9.11.16	Do
9/462	" Mitchell ?	" ✓	9.11.16	Do
23404	" Bird J	" ✓	10.11.16	Do
9/1836	" Watson ?	" ✓	9.11.16	Killed
9/259	" Johnson J	" ✓	10.11.16	Missing
~~28396~~	~~" Riley J~~			~~Do~~
2267	Sgt Wild W.W.	B ✓	9.11.16	Killed
2189	" Davidson V.E.	" ✓	9.11.16	Do
2326	Pte Badsey B	" ✓	9.11.16	Do
852	" Wrightson ?	" ✓	9.11.16	Do
2177	L/C Grant R.K.	" ✓	9.11.16	Wounded
3515	Pte Hodgson J.J.	" ✓	9.11.16	Do
1843	" Swan J.W.	" ✓	9.11.16	Do
23918	" Sewell G.N.	" ✓	9.11.16	Do
2114	" McQuillen R.J. ✓	" ✓	9.11.16	Do Remained at duty
2190	" Lishman W.J. ✓	" ✓	9.11.16	Do Do
2172	" Soulsby W	" ✓	9.11.16	Do Do
489	" Precious C	✓		Killed attached 52 TmB
7/477	" Thornton H	" ✓	9.11.16	Wounded remained at duty
561	" Sanderson A	C ✓	4.11.16	Wounded

M. Robertson
Lieut & aj

CONFIDENTIAL.

Vol 16

WAR DIARY

of the

9TH (S) BN NORTHUMBERLAND FUSILIERS.

From 1ST DECEMBER 1916.
To 31ST DECEMBER 1916.

VOLUMN XVIII

14 d-2

Army Form C. 2118

Appendix T.

WAR DIARY
or
INTELLIGENCE SUMMARY

(Erase heading not required.)

9th (S) Batt. Northumberland Fus.

Instructions regarding War Diaries and Intelligence Summaries are contained in F. S. Regs., Part II. and the Staff Manual respectively. Title Pages will be prepared in manuscript.

Place	Date	Hour	Summary of Events and Information	Remarks and references to Appendices
BREILLY	Dec. 1st		Bn. was inspected by the Brigadier General at 9-30am. Battalion on the football field. The General expressed himself as pleased with the turnout. This was followed by the programme of training for remainder of day.	initials
do.	Dec. 2nd		General training. (Bayonet & musketry drills)	initials
do.	Dec. 3rd		Church Parades. C. of E. Chaline 11am. (holy comm celebrated) R.C. 9am in village church. N.C. 9-15am Hotel de Ville Regimey. Remainder of day resting	initials
do.	Dec. 4th		General training as per programme.	initials
do.	Dec. 5th		General training. Rapid consolidation of ground.	initials
do.	Dec. 6th		A+B coy. drills 10-15am & 12-30pm Regimey respectively. General training. Consolidation of ground	initials
do.	Dec. 7th		C+D coy. drills 8-30am & 10-15am Regimey respectively. General training. Four platoon drills.	initials

Army Form C. 2118

WAR DIARY
or
INTELLIGENCE SUMMARY
(Erase heading not required.)

 1/1(S) Batt Nutt Fus

Place	Date	Hour	Summary of Events and Information	Remarks and references to Appendices
BREILLY	Dec 8th		A battalion toilet day was arranged but owing to heavy rain it was postponed and lectures and interior economy carried out in the billets. Lt Col G.P. Westmacott D.S.O. rejoined from hospital and assumed command of the Battalion. Capt J.S. Allen reassumed the duties of 2nd in Command. Transport was inspected by Brig Gen. Goodman.	W.J.R.
BREILLY	Dec 9th		Programme was again upset by heavy rain and lectures and economy were again carried.	W.J.R.
BREILLY	Dec 10th		Voluntary services were held during the morning.	W.J.R.
BREILLY	Dec 11th		A draft of 1 Officer (Capt R.W.L.DALLAS) MC and 137 O.R. arrived. There men had had 5-7 months training in England. Many had been transferred from the A.S.C. Transport left for forward area.	W.J.R.
BREILLY	Dec 12th		Battalion left BREILLY at 1.30pm and marched to LONGPRÉ arriving there about 4pm and went into billets. Route PICQUIGNY - CROUY - HANGEST - CONDE - LONGPRÉ	W.J.R.
Onto Move	Dec 13th		Entrained at LONGPRÉ at 8am and proceeded to EDGEHILL STN arriving there at 12.30pm. Battalion then marched to MEAULTE and arrived there at 3pm. into billets.	W.J.R.

WAR DIARY
or
INTELLIGENCE SUMMARY
(Erase heading not required.)

Army Form C. 2118

9th (S) Batt. Northumberland Fusiliers

Place	Date	Hour	Summary of Events and Information	Remarks and references to Appendices
MEAULTE	Dec	14th	In billets. Training under company arrangements	WR
MEAULTE	Dec	15th	In billets. Brigadier General Commanding 52nd Infy Bde inspected the new draft and one representative platoon. The platoon selected was No 4 platoon of A Coy who presented a very smart appearance. Company training was carried out	WR
MEAULTE	Dec	16th	In billets. Company training was carried out	WR
MEAULTE	Dec	17th	In billets. The customary Church Parades were held. Brigadier General Goodman C.M.G. inspected the men's billets and expressed satisfaction with their cleanliness. Draft of 14 Officers arrived	WR
MEAULTE	Dec	18th	In billets. Fatigue party of 100 men out. Companies carried out two rapid firing practices. Warning orders received to be ready to move on 22nd inst. Draft of 28 OR arrived.	WR
MEAULTE	Dec	19th	A proportion of Officers attended a lecture by Lt Col Collins DSO GSO I 17th Division on "Late Initiative." Coy hand remainder under company arrangements.	WR
MEAULTE	Dec	20th	In billets. Parades under company commanders	WR
MEAULTE	Dec	21st	As above	WR

Army Form C. 2118

WAR DIARY
or
INTELLIGENCE SUMMARY
(Erase heading not required.)

Instructions regarding War Diaries and Intelligence Summaries are contained in F. S. Regs., Part II. and the Staff Manual respectively. Title Pages will be prepared in manuscript.

Place	Date	Hour	Summary of Events and Information	Remarks and references to Appendices
MEAULTE	Dec 22nd		Battalion moved from MEAULTE at 9.30am and reached Camp 17 on CARNOY–MONTAUBAN road arriving there at 2pm and going into huts	WJR
Camp	Dec 23rd		Battalion moved from Camp 17 to Guillemont leaving camp at 11pm and arriving there at 4pm	WJR
Camp	Dec 24th		Battalion relieved the 10th KRRC in the right subsector of the right group relief being reported complete at 11.30pm. Trenches between headland and MORVAL front line :- B Coy, 1st Platoon B Coy, 2 Battn Bombing Dispositions Squads, 3 Lds B Coy. 2 Lds A Coy. Support (THUNDER TRENCH) B&W R C Coy. Reserve (BOVRIL TRENCH) A Coy and remainder of J.B.	WJR
Trenches	Dec 25th		The day was fairly quiet and few casualties sustained. The enemy's wire and sylphomely heard. During the morning two bombardments were carried out by our field Artillery.	WJR
Trenches	Dec 26th		A few hours bombardment was carried out by our siege Artillery from 12 noon – 4pm. The Bombardment was very effective. In its evening the Battalion was relieved by the 10th Lancashire Fus, relief being reported complete at 1.45am on 27/12.	WJR

1875 Wt. W593/326 1,000,000 4/15 J.B.C. & A. A.D.S.S./Forms/C. 2118.

Army Form C. 2118

WAR DIARY
or
INTELLIGENCE SUMMARY
(Erase heading not required.)

Instructions regarding War Diaries and Intelligence Summaries are contained in F. S. Regs., Part II. and the Staff Manual respectively. Title Pages will be prepared in manuscript.

Place	Date	Hour	Summary of Events and Information	Remarks and references to Appendices
Camp	Dec 27th		In Camp 19 on CARNOY – MONTAUBAN Road. The day was spent in cleaning up after the time in the trenches. Only one case of "trench feet" was reported. Casualties were 1 killed & 1 wounded.	W.F.R.
Camp	Dec 28th		In Camp 19. The day was spent in kit inspection and smoke helmet drill for drafts. The baths were also allotted to the Battn.	W.F.R.
Camp	Dec 29th		The Battn. moved to GUILLEMONT camp leaving Camp 19 at 2 pm arriving at GUILLEMONT at 4 pm	W.F.R.
Camp	Dec 30th		The Battn. left GUILLEMONT at 2.45 pm and relieved the 7 LINCOLN REGT in the right subsector in the right Brigade group. Relief was completed at 9 pm	W.F.R.
Trenches	Dec 31st		A quiet day was spent. Our artillery bombarded the enemy at 11 pm. Dispositions:– front line:– C Coy, 1 Stokes Mort., 2 squads R Bombers and 6 Lewis guns. Support trench:– B Coy, 1 Platoon A Coy Bomb trench:– D Coy & 3 Platoons A Coy	W.F.R.

Gen¹ P. Movement

Leaving 9th Battalion

APPENDIX T.
War Diary.
Officer i/c
Regular Infantry
Base

ORDERLY ROOM 28 DEC. 1916 9TH (SERVICE) SIXTEENTH NORTH'D FUSILIERS

Herewith Casualty Report please

No	Rank	and Name	Coy	Date	Casualty
44647	Pte	Tayton C.B.	A	25/12/16	Killed
12242	L/C	Woods R	B	24/12/16	Wounded
41160	Pte	Edwards E	B	26/12/16	Died of Wounds
29/464	"	Marshall P	B	"	Killed
41158	"	Durrans G	B	"	Wounded
24801	"	Butterworth C	D	27/12/16	Died of Exposure
15257	"	Stott J	D	26/12/16	Wounded
13059	Sgt	Taylor H	D	24/12/16	"
41152	Pte	Childs E	D	"	"
32870	L/C	Crawford O	D	"	"
11274	Pte	Barkley A	D	25/12/16	"
29/557	"	Peake C	D	26/12/16	"

W.J. Robertson
Lieut & Adjt
9th North'd Fus

SPECIAL ORDER OF THE DAY
By
GENERAL SIR DOUGLAS HAIG,
G.C.B., G.C.V.O., K.C.I.E., A.D.C.

Commander-in-Chief, British Armies in France.

CHRISTMAS MESSAGES FROM HIS MAJESTY THE KING.

No. 1.

I send you my sailors and soldiers hearty good wishes for Christmas and the New Year. My grateful thoughts are ever with you for victories gained, for hardships endured, and for your unfailing cheeriness. Another Christmas has come round and we are still at War, but the Empire confident in you remains determined to win.

MAY GOD BLESS AND PROTECT YOU.

GEORGE R.I.

No. 2.

At this Christmastide the Queen and I are thinking more than ever of the sick and wounded among my sailors and soldiers. From our hearts we wish them strength to bear their sufferings, speedy restoration to health, a peaceful Christmas and many happier years to come.

GEORGE R.I.

D. Haig. Genl.

General Headquarters,
24th December, 1916.

Commander-in-Chief,
British Armies in France.

"A" Form.
MESSAGES AND SIGNALS.

TO: 9th North. Fus. 10th Lancs. Fus. 9th West R.R. 12th Manch. Regt. 52nd M.Gun Coy. 52nd T.M. Bty. No.4 Coy. Train. 52nd Fld. Ambce.

Sender's Number: BMX1
Day of Month: 16.

AAA

XIV Corps report French report big success between MEUSE and WOEVRE, German Front System of trenches captured on 10 Km. front to depth of 3 Km. MAUDREMONT FORT LOUVEMONT, and village of VACHERAUVILLE as well as minor works captured. French have advanced up to the line BEZON VAUX 6500 German prisoners already passed through cages besides heavy guns and much meterial. French losses slight.

From: 52nd Inf. Bde.
Time: 11 am

The above may be forwarded as now corrected. (Z)

SPECIAL ORDER OF THE DAY
By
GENERAL SIR DOUGLAS HAIG,
G.C.B., G.C.V.O., K.C.I.E., A.D.C.
Commander-in-Chief, British Armies in France.

I desire to convey to all ranks under my command my hearty good wishes for Christmas and the New Year. It is indeed a privilege to command such officers and such men, and I feel confident that the magnificent qualities they have already shewn in the face of the enemy will carry our arms to ultimate victory.

D. Haig. Genl.

General Headquarters,
25th December, 1916.

Commander-in-Chief,
British Armies in France.

ARMY PRINTING AND STATIONERY SERVICES A—12/16.

Confidential

War
Diary of
2nd (S) Batt: The Northumberland Fus.

From Jany 1st. 1917   to Jany. 31st 1917.

(Volume)

Army Form C. 2118

WAR DIARY
or
INTELLIGENCE SUMMARY
(Erase heading not required.)

9th (S) Bn Northumberland Fus

Place	Date	Hour	Summary of Events and Information	Remarks and references to Appendices
Trenches	Jan 1st 1917		A quiet day was spent. Relieved in the evening by the 10th Hank Fus relief being definited complete at 9pm. Casualties for the tour Nil. On relief companies marched to Camp 19.	MWR
Camp	Jan 2nd		Camp 19. Companies carried out Kit inspection etc	MWR
Camp	Jan 3rd		Camp 19. The following awards appeared in the New Years Honours List. MILITARY CROSS CAPT. J. S. ALLEN 52415 C.S.M. (WRQM) ARMITAGE, J. H. MENTION LIEUT. W. F. ROBERTSON 18700 C.S.M. RICHARDSON, A 11487 Sgt STAFFORD, J.	MWR
Camp	Jan 4th		The Battn moved at 2pm to GUILLEMONT CAMP arriving there at 3.30pm. A fatigue party of 210 men were supplied to carry duck boards	MWR
Camp	Jan 5th		GUILLEMONT CAMP. The Batt proceeded to the trenches and relieved the 7th LINCOLN REGT. Relief complete 7pm Dispositions Frontline :- B Coy, 1 Platoon Sply 2 guns R Bombers 6 LGs A Coy (HUNTER TRENCH :- BOVRIL TRENCH :- 2 Platoons B Coy + C Coy	MWR

Army Form C. 2118

WAR DIARY
or
INTELLIGENCE SUMMARY
(Erase heading not required.)

9th (S) Bn. Northd. Fus.

Place	Date	Hour	Summary of Events and Information	Remarks and references to Appendices
Trenches	Jan 6th		A quiet day was spent.	WJR
Trenches	Jan 7th		Quiet day. Six enemy working parties were seen and hts open on it and inflicted heavy casualties. Identification later showed them to belong to the 121 R.I.R.	WJR
Trenches	Jan 8th		An extra day was spent in the trenches this time and in the evening Bn was relieved by the 7th Yorkshire Regt. Relief completed 8 p.m. Casualties for tour 1 O.R. wounded. On relief companies moved to Camp 19.	WJR
Camp	Jan 9th		Camp 19. During day Company were bathed and kit inspections held. 60 men reinforcements arrived. 2 Lt. I.G.C. BRADY 2 Lt. J.R. GOLDTHORPE	WJR
Camp	Jan 10th		Camp 19. Inspection of huts by Co. Snake Helmets, S.A.A, and Iron Rations were inspected during the day.	WJR
Camp	Jan 11th		Camp 19. Capt R.V.L. DALLAS, M.C. assumed command of the Bn vice Lt. Col. G.P. WESTMACOTT D.S.O. to England on short leave. Men's feet were treated with new trench treatment	WJR

WAR DIARY
or
INTELLIGENCE SUMMARY
(Erase heading not required.)

Army Form C. 2118

Instructions regarding War Diaries and Intelligence Summaries are contained in F.S. Regs., Part II. and the Staff Manual respectively. Title Pages will be prepared in manuscript.

Place	Date	Hour	Summary of Events and Information	Remarks and references to Appendices
Camp	Jan 13th		Bn moved at 2pm to GUILLEMONT CAMP arriving there at 3.30pm. A working party of 3 Officers and 330 OR. were supplied to the R.E. at night.	MJR.
Camp	Jan 13th		In the evening the Bn relieved the 7th LINCOLN REGT in the new right Subsector, immediately E of SAILLY-SAILLISEL. Relief reported complete to Bde at 5pm. DISPOSITIONS FRONT LINE:- 2 platoons B Coy, C Coy, & 2 Coy, A Coy. In Support:- 2 platoons B Coy Bn Hdqts:- Bn Boundaries	MJR.
Trenches	Jan 14th		A quiet day was spent.	MJR.
Trenches	Jan 15th		The Bn was relieved in the evening by the 1st Bn LANCASHIRE FUS. 29th DIVISION. Relief reported complete 10.15pm. Companies then moved to Camp 19 & available for hour 20 & onwards.	MJR.
Camp	Jan 16th		Battalion entrained at PLATEAU STN at 2.50pm arrived at CORBIE at 7.5pm after a long and tedious journey. Billets were overpacked at LA NEUVILLE near CORBIE	MJR.
Billets	Jan 17th		The day was spent resting and cleaning up generally	MJR.
Billets	Jan 18th		Kit inspection. The feet were thoroughly inspected by the Medical Officer	MJR.

Army Form C. 2118

WAR DIARY
or
INTELLIGENCE SUMMARY
(Erase heading not required.)

Instructions regarding War Diaries and Intelligence Summaries are contained in F. S. Regs., Part II. and the Staff Manual respectively. Title Pages will be prepared in manuscript.

Place	Date	Hour	Summary of Events and Information	Remarks and references to Appendices
Billets	Jan 18th		Programme:- 9-10a Physical Drill and Foot Friction Fatigue	MYR
			10.15-10.45am Musketry	
			10.45-11.15am Section Helmet Drill	
			11.30-12.30pm Squad Drill by NCo Retrainees	
			2 - 3pm NCo Instruction under NCo Instructors	
Billets	Jan 19th		As above	MYR
Billets	Jan 20th		Programme:- 9-10a Physical Drill and Foot Friction Fatigue	MYR
			10.15-10.45am Gas Drill	
			11 - 12.30am Instruction in the Attack	
			2 - 3pm Training of Specialists	
Billets	Jan 21st		Church Parade	MYR
Billets	Jan 22nd		Programme:- Commanding Officers Inspection	MYR
			Training of Specialists	
Billets	Jan 23rd LA NEUVILLE		Programme:- Morning :- Rifle Range	MYR
			A.B.C. Cognomme Lewis Gunners in afternoon	
			Physical Drill	
			Organisation in Attack, Rifle Platoon	
			Afternoon :- Training of Specialists	

Army Form C. 2118

WAR DIARY
or
INTELLIGENCE SUMMARY
(Erase heading not required.)

Instructions regarding War Diaries and Intelligence Summaries are contained in F. S. Regs., Part II. and the Staff Manual respectively. Title Pages will be prepared in manuscript.

Place	Date	Hour	Summary of Events and Information	Remarks and references to Appendices
Billets	Jan 24th		LA NEUVILLE. Programme of training. Range allotted to Coys and details of Bayonet fighters. Gas Drill. Organisation of Companies. Training of Specialists. Afternoon :-	MYR
Billets	Jan 25th		LA NEUVILLE. Programme of training. Companies Range allotted to B Coy. Bathed during morning at CURIE BATHS. Gas Drill and Bayonet fighting. Afternoon :- Training of Specialists.	MYR
Billets	Jan 26th		LA NEUVILLE. Programme of training. Commanding Officers Inspection 8.30am. Swimming. Physical Drill and Bayonet fighting and Lewis Company Drill. Afternoon :- Training of Specialists.	MYR
Billets	Jan 27th		LA NEUVILLE. Physical Drill + foot practise fatigue was carried out. A shooting competition between companies was held. Teams of 6 shooting 15 rounds rapid in 1 minute. This contest resulted in a win for B Coy. 1st B Coy 2nd A Coy 3rd D Coy 4th C Coy	MYR

1875 Wt. W593/826 1,000,000 4/15 J.B.C. & A. A.D.S.S./Forms/C. 2118.

Army Form C. 2118

Appendix V.

WAR DIARY
or
INTELLIGENCE SUMMARY
(Erase heading not required.)

Instructions regarding War Diaries and Intelligence Summaries are contained in F.S. Regs., Part II. and the Staff Manual respectively. Title Pages will be prepared in manuscript.

Place	Date	Hour	Summary of Events and Information	Remarks and references to Appendices
Billets	Jan 28th		The Bath left in lorries for BRONFAY CAMP'S leaving LA NEUVILLE at 9 am and arriving at BRONFAY about 11 am. took over Camp 15C which is also Divisional Rest Camp	WYR
Camp Billets	Jan 29th		Physical training, Lecture, fatigues, carried out along with inspection of S.A.A. Rifles and Smoke helmets	WYR
Camp	Jan 30th		Battalion left camp 15C at 1.30 pm and proceeded to BOULEAUX Wood area arriving there at 5.0 pm	WYR
Camp	Jan 31st		Disposition Bn HQ. Sunken Road between BOULEAUX WOOD and COMBLES A Coy N. of BOULEAUX WOOD C Coy INTERMEDIATE LINE A Coy MORVAL DUGOUTS D Coy MUTTON TRENCH. Bath proceeded to relieve the 7th LINCOLN REGT in the right sub-sector of the NORTH COPSE Sector. Relief was reported complete at 6.45 pm	WYR

George McMahon
Capt.

Appendix U

Casualties for January incurred by 9' Batt" North'd Fus:

To Officer i/c
Regular Infantry Section
Base

Herewith Casualty report please.

Reg't No	Rank & Name	Coy	Date	Casualty
13059	Sgt Taylor H	D	29/12/16	Previously reported wounded, now reported Died of Wounds.
30042 / 9992	Pte Donkin A	D	7/1/17	Wounded
10792	A/Sgt Burton A M	B	8/1/17	Missing

W.J. Robertson
Lieut & a/Adjt.
9th North'd Fus

To Officer i/c
Regular Infantry Section
Base.

ORDERLY ROOM 17 JAN. 1917 No 736 9TH (SERVICE) BATT. NORTHD FUSILIERS

Herewith Casualty Report please

Regt No	Rank	Name	Coy	Date	Casualty
10622	Pte	Dunn H	D	14-1-17	Wounded
39982	"	Elliott J.W.	C	13-1-17	Missing
10744	"	Allen ?	C	18-1-17	Wounded (accident)

M. F. Robertson
Lieut & Adjt
9th Northd Fus.

To O/C

Regular Infantry Section 3
Base

Reference Casualty Report
No 136 of 17 January 1917.
No 38982 Pte Elliott JW, has
now rejoined, having been detained
in 53rd Field Ambulance. Please.

W Robertson

Lieut & Adjt
9th Northd Fus

Confidential

Vol 18

17/32

War Diary

of

The 9th (S) Batt: the Norfl: Fusiliers

for the

Month of February 1917.

Volume XX

From 1-2-17
To 28-2-17

WAR DIARY
or
INTELLIGENCE SUMMARY
(Erase heading not required.)

Army Form C. 2118

Place	Date	Hour	Summary of Events and Information	Remarks and references to Appendices
Trenches	1/5/17		Enemy artillery fairly active. We suffered 1 Officer & 3 other ranks wounded.	A.W.
Trenches	2/5/17		Quiet day, no shoot. Battalion was relieved at night by 8th Batln. Lord Strath. Regt, and proceeded to camp. A & D Companies to BOIS D'ORÉ CAMP, B & C " to MALTZHORN CAMP H.Qs " to	A.W.
Camp	3/5/17		Companies proceeded independently to BRONFAY CAMP, the last arriving at 2 P.M.	A.W.
Camp	4/5/17		Baths were allotted in camp & all companies. Physical training and kit inspection etc. were carried out.	A.W.
Camp	5/5/17		Battalion paraded at 1.30 P.M. and proceeded at 5 minute intervals to forward camps. Disposition as follows: "A" Co. MORVAL ROAD DUGOUTS (T.M.D.) "B" Co. Intermediate line near Bde. H.Q. "C" Co. MUTTON TRENCH. H.Q. - BOULEAUX WOOD. "D" Co. Camp N. of BOULEAUX WOOD.	A.W.

WAR DIARY
or
INTELLIGENCE SUMMARY
(Erase heading not required.)

Army Form C. 2118

Place	Date	Hour	Summary of Events and Information	Remarks and references to Appendices
Camp	6/2/17		Battalion proceeded to the trenches and relieved the 7th Battn. Lincoln Regt. in right sub-sector of the NORTH COPSE sector, relief being complete at 7.45 P.M. Disposition of companies as follows:- RIGHT COMPANY "A" Coy CENTRE " "C" Coy LEFT " "B" Coy RESERVE " "D" Coy "A" Coy. Bombing Squad with "A" Coy "B" " " " "C" Coy "C"D" " " " at Bn. H.Q. Considerable artillery activity on both sides. We had no Casualties	
Trench	7/2/17		German line was attacked successfully at 7.30 A.M. by the 7th Battn. YORKS. REGT. operating on our right flank. We rendered assistance by sending supplies of bombs. About mid-day we employed the following casualties:- 1 O.R. killed, 1 O.R. died of wounds, 13 O.R. wounded, and 5 O.R. missing, total. 20	att.
Trench	8/2/17			att.

WAR DIARY
or
INTELLIGENCE SUMMARY
(Erase heading not required.)

Army Form C. 2118

Place	Date	Hour	Summary of Events and Information	Remarks and references to Appendices
Trenches (contd)	8/2/17		Battalion was relieved on night of 8/9th Feby by 8th Bath. St. Staffs and proceeded to COMBLES, moving from the line by platoons. Earlier in the evening of 8th, "D" Coy bombing squad and 1 Lewis Gun of "D" Coy was sent to reinforce right flank of "A" Coy.	Att.
Dugouts (COMBLES)	9/2/17		Battalion moved at midday to camp at BRONFAY.	Att.
Camp	10/2/17		Physical drill & foot drill was carried out in the morning and baths were allotted to all companies during afternoon.	Att.
Camp	11/2/17		Prophylaxis treatment of the feet was carried out during the morning from 7.30 A.M. to 9.30 A.M. Divine service in camp "A" & "D" Coys at 9.30 A.M. "B" Coy & at 10.30 A.M. Presbyterians & Nonconformists in Quiet Room interval at 9.45 A.M. Battalion paraded at 2 P.M. and proceeded at 5 minutes interval to forward camps. Disposition as follows:— H.Q. A & D Coys MALTZHORN CAMP "B" & "C" Coys BOIS DORÉ	Att.

Army Form C. 2118

WAR DIARY
or
INTELLIGENCE SUMMARY
(Erase heading not required.)

Instructions regarding War Diaries and Intelligence Summaries are contained in F. S. Regs., Part II. and the Staff Manual respectively. Title Pages will be prepared in manuscript.

Place	Date	Hour	Summary of Events and Information	Remarks and references to Appendices
Camp	12/7/17		Lt. Colonel Harris DSO took command of the battalion which proceeded to the trenches to relieve the 1st Lincoln Regt in right sub sector of the NORTH COPSE sector. Disposition as follows. Right Coy "B" Coy Centre " "C" Coy Left " "D" Coy Reserve " "A" Coy. One Lewis Gun of "A" coy went into "B" Coy. A working party supplied on the 12/7/17 suffered the following Casualties. 1 O.R. missing, and 7 O.R. wounded.	Art.
Trenches	13/7/17		Quiet day was spent.	
Trenches	14/7/17		Artillery activity during day. We had 1 O.R. wounded. Battalion was relieved by 8th Lth Staffs. and proceeded to forward camps. Relief was completed at 2.45 A.M. on morning of 15th. Disposition of companies as follows. "B" "C" Coys. MALTZHORN CAMP "A" "D" Coys. BOIS DORÉ H.Q. MALTZHORN CAMP Lt. Col. Harris DSO. Hches to take command of 7th Yorks Regt.	Art.

WAR DIARY
or
INTELLIGENCE SUMMARY
(Erase heading not required.)

Army Form C. 2118

Place	Date	Hour	Summary of Events and Information	Remarks and references to Appendices
Camp	15/2/17		Major Allen M.C. assumed command of the Battalion whilst proceeded to BRONFAY CAMP. Extracts from London Gazette 9/2/17 T/Capt J.L. Allen to be Temp. Major (July 25/16) T/Lieut (of Captain whilst comdg a Company) V.H. Thornton to be Temp Capt. (July 25/16) 2/Lt N.J. Hearson to be Temp Lieut (July 25/16) Officers { 2 Lt. O.A. Hodgson taken on strength and posted to 'A' Coy. 10/2/17 taken on { 2 Lt. W. Pellerby " " " " D " 13/2/17 strength Small Box respirators fitted and explained to all ranks. Baths were allotted during afternoon to all Companies. MILITARY MEDAL 3194 L/Sgt W. Taylor. D.Coy. 9th R.F.	Att Att
Camp	16/2/17			

Army Form C. 2118

WAR DIARY
or
INTELLIGENCE SUMMARY
(Erase heading not required.)

Place	Date	Hour	Summary of Events and Information	Remarks and references to Appendices
Camp	17/7/17		Battalion moved to forward camp, heading at 2 P.M. and proceeding at 5 minutes interval. Disposition as follows:- Intermediate line 'B' Coy Front Dug outs 'A' 'D' Coys Printers Street 'C' Coy BOULEAUX WOOD H.Qrs.	Att.
Camp	18/7/17		Battalion proceeded to the trenches and relieved the 1st Lincoln Regt. in right sub. sector of NORTH COPSE sector. Disposition as follows:- Right Company B Coy Centre A Coy Left D Coy Reserve C Coy One Lewis gun of "C" Coy attached to B Coy. for this tour.	Att.
Trenches	19/7/17		Quiet day, was spent, conditions very bad, slow following had set. Battalion was relieved on night of 19th by 2nd Bn. So. Wales Borderers and proceeded to forward camps. Relief was completed at 11 P.M.	Att.

WAR DIARY
or
INTELLIGENCE SUMMARY

(Erase heading not required.)

Army Form C. 2118

Place	Date	Hour	Summary of Events and Information	Remarks and references to Appendices
Trenches 19/20th	Feb 1917		Disposition of companies as follows:- A & C Coys at MALTZHORN. B & D " BOIS DORÉ" H.Q. at MALTZHORN	A.W.
Camp	20/2/17		Battalion proceeded by road to BRONFAY CAMP, where they collected packs and blankets. Later proceeded to PLATEAU Station where they entrained to HEILLY, thence by foot to FRANKVILLERS, arriving about 9 P.M. in billets.	A.W.
Billets	21/2/17		Day devoted to cleaning of clothes & equipment. A.W. BLOCKLEY takes command of battalion, MAJOR ALLEN assumes 2nd in command. MAJOR 2/Lt. E.L. Taylor taken on strength posted to "B" Coy " J. Bennet " " " " " "C" Coy	A.W.
Billets	22/2/17		Day to cleaning of clothing and equipment.	A.W.

WAR DIARY or INTELLIGENCE SUMMARY

Army Form C. 2118

Place	Date	Hour	Summary of Events and Information	Remarks and references to Appendices
Billet	23/5/17		F.G.C.M. held at Batt. H.Q. Physical drill, company drill and platoon drill and bayonet fighting during morning. C.O' inspected battalion at 2.15 P.M. Kit inspection by O.C. Companies. Battalion bombers disbanded and rejoined companies.	R.O.T.
Billet	24/5/17		Physical drill, bayonet fighting, Gas helmet drill and platoon drill. Battalion paraded at 2 P.M. under R.S.M. Specialists under specialist officers.	R.O.T.
Billet	25/5/17		Baths & all companies during the morning. Battalion church parade 3 P.M. Presbyterians 2.15 P.M.	R.O.T.
Billet	26/5/17		"A"+"B" Companies on rifle range. "C"+"D" Physical drill, Gas helmet drill, Demonstration of platoon in attack on strong point. One O.R. Pte. reported wounded. Afternoon — Boxing Football. "now died of wounds"	R.O.T.
Billet	27/5/17		"C"+"D" Companies on rifle range. "A"+"B" P.T., gas helmet drill & musketry. Demonstration of platoon in attack on O.P. Afternoon — Boxing Football.	R.O.T.

Army Form C. 2118

WAR DIARY
or
INTELLIGENCE SUMMARY

(Erase heading not required.)

Instructions regarding War Diaries and Intelligence Summaries are contained in F. S. Regs., Part II. and the Staff Manual respectively. Title Pages will be prepared in manuscript.

Place	Date	Hour	Summary of Events and Information	Remarks and references to Appendices
Billets	28/6/17		Physical Drill. "C" & "D" Companies on rifle range. "A" & "B" Bombing & skirmishing drill. Afternoon. Boxing & football.	Appx

M.M. Thwaites Col.
Comdg 9th Welch Fus

1875 Wt. W593/826 1,000,000 4/15 J.B.C. & A. A.D.S.S./Forms/C.2118.

Appendix V.

Casualties
incurred during
February.

To O/c
Regular Infantry Section
Base.

Herewith Casualty Report, please

No	RANK AND NAME	COY	DATE	CASUALTY
	2/Lt J.R.G.Burdon-Sanderson	A	1.2.17	Wounded
12996	Corpl Brown D	A	1.2.17	Do
29/461	Pte Milner D	A	1.2.17	Do
32666	" Cowan A	A	1.2.17	Do

W.J.Robertson
Lieut & Adjt
9th North'd Fus

3.2.17.

O i/c
Regular Infantry Section
Base.

Herewith Casualty Report please

Regt No	Rank and Name	Coy	Date	Casualty
16268	L/Corp Bloomfield O	A	8.2.17	Died of Wounds
29/256	Pte Francis F	A	8.2.17	Wounded
6265	" Brennen P	A	8.2.17	Wounded
10450	" Hedley J	A	8.2.17	Wounded
41145	" Carroll W	A	8.2.17	Wounded
41169	" Fidler F	A	8.2.17	Wounded
13112	Corpl Perry E.W.	A	8.2.17	Wounded
13118	L/Corpl Woodruff J	A	8.2.17	Missing
11772	L/Corpl Watson G	A	8.2.17	Missing
24/188	Pte Duffy J	A	8.2.17	Missing
41139	" Booth W	A	8.2.17	Missing
41138	" Bradshaw L	A	8.2.17	Wounded
263/12	" Jackson J	A	8.2.17	Wounded
10167	" Reid D	B	8.2.17	Wounded and remained at duty
28980	" Elliott J	B	8.2.17	
31544	" Boggan J.W.	B	7.2.17	Killed
29/486	" Brannon J.F.	B	8.2.17	Missing
10530	" Armstrong T	C	8.2.17	Wounded and remained at duty
14812	" Hara R A	C	7.2.17	Wounded
32241	" Mason M	D	8.2.17	Wounded

10 February 1917.

M.G. Robertson
Lieut & / Adjt
9th Northd Fus

Officer i/c
Regular Infantry Section 3.
Base

Herewith Casualty Report please

Reg' No	Rank and Name	Coy	Date	Casualty
41121	Pte Aspinal J.R.	B	12.2.17	Missing
41150	Sgt Bowie E	B	do	Wounded
41194	Corp. Lewis H	B	do	do
12298	L/Corp Gardner E	B	do	do
29/454	Pte Hodgson P	B	do	do
9490	" Duffield W	B	do	do
29/506	" Kellett J	B	do	do
28840	" Lertoria D	B	do	do
44566	" Abbott P.N.	B	14.2.17	do

15.2.17.

Lieut & Adjt
9th North'd Fus.

To O/C
Regular Infantry ~~Section~~
Base

    Reference my Casualty Report N° 139
  No 41139 Pte Booth W and
✱ No 11772 L/Corp Watson G
previously reported "Missing" are now reported Killed in Action please.

                Lieut & Adjt
                9th North'd

To Officer i/c
Regular Infantry Section No 3
Base.

142

Herewith Casualty Report please

No 32695 Pte Walton H. D. Coy
Died of Wounds 16 Feb 1917.

26.2.17.

Lieut/Adjt
9th North'd Fus

Vol 19

CONFIDENTIAL

War Diary.

of the

9TH (S) BN NORTHUMBERLAND FUSILIERS

VOLUME XXI.

From 1st March 1917.

To 31st March 1917.

To 52nd Bde:

Herewith War Diary of the Battalion under my command for the month of March 1917. Acknowledge receipt hereon please.

Jave Major
Comdg 9 North'n Fus.
for Lieut Col.

In the field
1.4.17

Army Form C. 2118

WAR DIARY
or
INTELLIGENCE SUMMARY
(Erase heading not required.)

Instructions regarding War Diaries and Intelligence Summaries are contained in F. S. Regs., Part II. and the Staff Manual respectively. Title Pages will be prepared in manuscript.

Place	Date	Hour	Summary of Events and Information	Remarks and references to Appendices
Billets	1/3/17		Battalion paraded at 9.55 a.m. marched to CONTAY, via BEHENCOURT, BAVELINCOURT, AGNICOURT. Arriving in billets at 1.0 P.M.	AW1
Billets	2/3/17		Raining during morning. Football during afternoon.	AW2
Billets	3/3/17		Battalion drill training. Lectures in the afternoon.	AW3
Billets	4/3/17		Battn. paraded at 10.45 a.m. for Divine Service.	AW4
Billets	5/3/17		Raining during morning. Bath rota at 3 P.M. Lectures carried on in Battn. Mess 3 contains. Contact patrols.	AW5
Billets	6/3/17		Games during morning. Football (inter platoon competition) during afternoon.	AW6
Billets	7/3/17		Training and drill. 6.30 p.m. circus pulled screen moved out. 10 OBM ditto.	AW7
Billets	8/3/17		Both cloths & all equipment cleaning. 9 P.M. Nucleo Electoria	AW8

1875 Wt. W593/826 1,000,000 4/15 J.B.C. & A. A.D.S.S./Forms/C. 2118.

Army Form C. 2118

WAR DIARY
or
INTELLIGENCE SUMMARY

(Erase heading not required.)

Instructions regarding War Diaries and Intelligence Summaries are contained in F.S. Regs., Part II. and the Staff Manual respectively. Title Pages will be prepared in manuscript.

Place	Date	Hour	Summary of Events and Information	Remarks and references to Appendices
Billets	9/3/17		Training – Practice in Attack.	aw+
Billets	10/3/17		Kit inspection, training, rifle operations under Brigade scheme.	aw+
Billets	11/3/17		Battalion paraded at 11 A.M. for Divine Service.	aw+
Billets	12/3/17		Training. Class for Lewis Gunners commenced. Lewis Gunners carried out fire practice.	aw+
Billets	13/3/17		Battalion paraded at 10.45 A.M. and marched to billets at BEAUVAL.	aw+
Billets	14/3/17		Battalion paraded at 9.30 A.M. and marched to BOUQUEMAISON.	aw+
Billets	15/3/17		Battalion paraded at 9 A.M. and marched to billets in QUŒUX, FONTAINE L'ETALON Area. Disposition – H.Q., "C" & "D" Companies at QUŒUX "A" & "B" Companies at ERQUIÈRES	aw+
Billets	16/3/17		Foot inspection, foot friction, cleaning of equipment etc.	aw+

WAR DIARY
or
INTELLIGENCE SUMMARY

Army Form C. 2118

Place	Date	Hour	Summary of Events and Information	Remarks and references to Appendices
Billeb	17/3/17		Training and musketry	A.W.H.
Billeb	18/3/17		Battalion paraded at 11 A.M. in valley between QUOEUX and ERQUIERES for Divisional Award. Military Medal to Sgr. J.S. Silvester for gallantry in the field (since killed in action)	A.W.H.
Billeb	19/3/17		Training and musketry. Class for Officers commenced.	A.W.H.
Billeb	20/3/17		Route marches were carried out by companies.	A.W.H.
Billeb	21/3/17		Route marches were carried out by companies. Afternoon B Coy in rifle range, D Coy at Baths. Junior N.C.O's under R.S.M.	A.W.H.
Billeb	22/3/17		Battalion paraded at 10.15 a.m. marched to FROHEN LE GRAND, occupying billets there.	A.W.H.
Billeb	23/3/17		Battalion paraded at 8.45 A.M. marched to SUS ST. LEGER, occupying billets there.	A.W.H.
Billeb	24/3/17		Foot inspection, cleaning of equipment etc.	A.W.H.
Billeb	25/3/17		Working party of 8 officers and 500 O.R. proceeded to LUCHEUX WOOD for work under R.E.s	A.W.H.

WAR DIARY or INTELLIGENCE SUMMARY

Army Form C. 2118

Place	Date	Hour	Summary of Events and Information	Remarks and references to Appendices
Billet	25/3/17		contd. — Draft which arrived on 2nd/3/17 inspected by Brigadier at 10.30 A.M. Voluntary Church Parade for remainder of Battalion.	auth
Billet	26/3/17		Training - Lecture on "Gas" by Medical Officer. Afternoon all lewislla officers under R.S.M. for Instruction. Guard Duties. Capt. Hazelhurst and W. Bowen struck off establishment.	auth
			3 & 2 Platoon in Musketry under No. 11 Platoon in Lewis gun. Batt. Signallers in Lewis gun. Batt. Observers in Lighter under. } Instructed by Brigadier.	auth
Billet	27/3/17		Training - Afternoon Lecture to all officers by Commanding Officer.	auth
Billet	28/3/17		Baths allotted to "A" & "B" companies, H.Q. company & Transport. Remainder carried out Company Training.	auth
Billet	29/3/17		Working party of 8 officers and 400 O.R. proceeded to MAISON FORESTIERE for work under R.E. Remainder, Company Training.	auth
Billet	30/3/17		Training, including digging and construction of Strong Points.	auth
Billet	31/3/17		Battalion paraded at 9 A.M. for Contact Patrol and attack under Brigade arrangements. Afternoon, Cross Country Run.	auth

Sgd Major
Comdg 9th [?] Munster Fus

Confidential

War Diary of the

9th (S) Batn. The North'n Fusiliers

From April 1st. 1917
To April 30th 1917

Volume XXII

To 52nd Bde:

> ORDERLY ROOM
> 30 APR. 1917
> No. NF 142
> 9th (SERVICE) BATT. NORTH'N FUSILIERS

Herewith War Diary of the Battalion under my command for the month of April 1917. Acknowledge receipt hereon please.

AM Hockley, Lieut Col:
Comdg. 9(S) B. North'n Fus

In the Field
30.4.17

WAR DIARY or INTELLIGENCE SUMMARY

Army Form C. 2118

Place	Date	Hour	Summary of Events and Information	Remarks and references to Appendices
Billes	1/4/17		Battalion provided a working party of 8 Officers and 400 men for work at MAISON FORESTIERE de la FONTAINE. "C" Company found two parties to the rifle range. Remainder of officers under Commanding Officer for tactical scheme.	aut
Billes	2/4/17		Divine Service Parades at various hours for all denominations. Football Match - Battalion (2) v. 17 Bn. Signals (0) at CAVROY.	aut
Billes	3/4/17		Tactical scheme under Commanding Officer - Bath allotted to 3 Companies	aut
Billes	4/4/17		Tactical scheme under Commanding Officer - Lecture for Officers by Col. when at 2.30 P.M.	aut
Billes	5/4/17		Battalion paraded at 11.30 p.m and proceeded to HOUVIN-HOUVIGNEUL, occupying billets there.	aut
Billes	6/4/17		Inspections carried out under Company arrangements	aut
Billes	7/4/17		Battalion paraded at 9.35 A.M and proceeded to new billets at LIENCOURT.	aut
Billes	8/4/17		Battalion paraded at 9.35 A.M and marched to SIMENCOURT, occupying billets there.	aut

WAR DIARY or INTELLIGENCE SUMMARY

Army Form C. 2118.

Place	Date	Hour	Summary of Events and Information	Remarks and references to Appendices
Billets	9/4/17		Battalion paraded at 4.30 P.M. and marched through ARRAS & near THILLOY with the intention of following up the Cavalry, who got into action following the British Advance on the morning of the 9th inst. 9th Brigade, to which advance guard to 52nd Infy Brigade. The Cavalry not having advanced sufficiently, Battalion was ordered to bivouac where they stood. This was done, companies using old British / German trenches for shelter.	
Bivouac	10/4/17		At 10 A.M. Battalion was ordered to return to ARRAS, where accommodation was found in cellars etc.	
Billets	11/4/17		After staying one night in ARRAS, the Division was transferred to VI th Corps and was ordered to relieve 15th Division in MONCHY Sector.	
Trenches	12/4/17		Battalion occupied reserve trenches E of ORANGE HILL. We suffered following casualties from hostile shell-fire. 1 O.R. Killed. 7 O.R. wounded. Capt Cohn of R.Iny. securing Congratulation from the Lieut Genl (Casualties) 3 O.R. Killed, 3 O.R. wounded.	
Trenches	13/4/17		On same trenches as on 12th inst.	
Trenches	14/4/17		On same trenches as on 12th & 13th inst. Enemy fired many gas shells on our sector and we suffered 9 O.R. wounded or gassed.	
Trenches	15/4/17		Battalion relieved another battalion of same Division in front line N of MONCHY formed new establishing & extra road 2nd W. Riding Casualties 1 Officer wounded 1 O.R. Killed. 1 O.R. wounded. 1 O.R. missing.	

Army Form C. 2118.

WAR DIARY
or
INTELLIGENCE SUMMARY.
(Erase heading not required.)

Instructions regarding War Diaries and Intelligence Summaries are contained in F.S. Regs., Part II. and the Staff Manual respectively. Title pages will be prepared in manuscript.

Place	Date	Hour	Summary of Events and Information	Remarks and references to Appendices
Trenches	16/4/17		Enemy shelled our position heavily and we suffered the following casualties. 2 Officers killed, 9 O.R. killed, 30 O.R. wounded.	A/4
Trenches	17/4/17		Fairly quiet day. Battalion was relieved in evening by 1/2nd Manchester Regt & stayed the night of 17/18 in reserve trenches at FEUCHY. Casualties 1 O.R. killed, 3 O.R. wounded.	A/4
Trenches	18/4/17		Battalion marched into billets at ARRAS.	A/4
Billets	19/4/17		Day devoted to cleaning of kit & reorganization of companies.	A/4
Billets	20/4/17		Battalion marched to reserve trenches E. of ORANGE HILL.	A/4
Trenches	21/4/17		Quiet day. Enemy gun fire was slight but no casualties occurred. Battalion relieved E. YORKS Regt & took part in the evening.	A/4
Trenches	22/4/17		Preparations made for attack in morning of 23rd.	A/4
Trenches	23/4/17		Battalion successfully co-operated with 29th Divn on right & captured enemy trenches N.E. of our position. Casualties 2 Officers killed, 1 officer wounded, 30 O.R. killed, 55 O.R. wounded.	A/4
Trenches	24/4/17		Battalion was relieved by 12th Manchester Regt & proceeded to reserve trenches at FEUCHY. 1 O.R. killed, 1 O.R. wounded. Remainder of day attended to cleaning of kit & other matters. Battalion paraded in Brigade formation & practised the battalion.	A/4

A5834 Wt.W4973/M687 750,000 8/16 D.D.&L.Ltd. Forms/C.2118/13.

Army Form C. 2118.

WAR DIARY
or
INTELLIGENCE SUMMARY.

(Erase heading not required.)

Instructions regarding War Diaries and Intelligence Summaries are contained in F. S. Regs., Part II. and the Staff Manual respectively. Title pages will be prepared in manuscript.

Place	Date	Hour	Summary of Events and Information	Remarks and references to Appendices
Trenches	25/4/17		Battalion marched into "billets at ARRAS.	AWT
Billets	26/4/17		Paraded at 9 A.M and marched to ARRAS station where battalion entrained for SAULTY. thence by road to billets at IVERGNY.	AWT
Billets	27/4/17		Day devoted to cleaning of clothing, kit equipment &c. Special Order of the Day published conveying thanks to Troops from G.O.C. 17th Division for their work in fighting from 9th April to 25th April	AWT
Billets	28/4/17		Inspection of Clothing, feet, equipment etc; under Company arrangements following extract from London Gazette published main cols 13/4/17. Major L.P. Sertorius D.S.O. relinquishes the acting rank of Lieut Col on ceasing to command a Battalion. Feb 9th 1917.	AWT
Billets	29/4/17		Battalion attended CHURCH PARADE in Parade ground at 10 A.M. Baths allotted to all companies. Following published for information. Maj. A.W. Blackley (Connaught Rangers) To be 2/Lieut Col whilst commander a Battalion. (War List No. (29) 20.2.17	AWT
Billets	30/4/17		Bayonet fighting and Company Drill. The following extract from London Gazette is published for information. 2nd Lieut. 2.A.H. Pickerton to be temp Captain 7.10. 4.4. 1917.	AWT

AWT-obsere JPTC

Army Form C. 2118

WAR DIARY
or
INTELLIGENCE SUMMARY
(Erase heading not required.)

Place	Date	Hour	Summary of Events and Information	Remarks and references to Appendices
Billes	1/4/17		Battalion provided a working party of 8 Officers and 400 men for work at MARON FERTESTIEGS and to FONTAINE. Command sent two lorries to Rifle Range. Remainder of troops under Company Officers for Rifle Drill.	a/s
Billes	2/4/17		Divine Service Parade at various hours for all denominations. Battalion B.S. & L.T. Bn. reported to CAUROY. Football Match.	a/s
Billes	3/4/17		Tactical scheme under Commanding Officer. Bn to attack 1 & 3 Companies.	a/s
Billes	4/4/17		Tactical scheme under Company Officers, lectures for Officers & N.C. Officers at 2.30 P.M.	a/s
Billes	5/4/17		Battalion paraded at 11.30 a.m. and proceeded to HOUVIN-HOUVIGNEUL, arriving billets there.	a/s
Billes	6/4/17		Schemes carried out under Company arrangements.	a/s
Billes	7/4/17		Battalion paraded at 9.35 A.M. and proceeded to new billets at LIENCOURT.	a/s
Billes	8/4/17		Battalion paraded at 9.35 A.M. and marched to SIMENCOURT, occupying billets there.	a/s

WAR DIARY or INTELLIGENCE SUMMARY

Army Form C. 2118.

Place	Date	Hour	Summary of Events and Information	Remarks and references to Appendices
Riencourt	9/4/17		Battalion handed at 4.30 a.m. and marched from ARRAS to THILLOY to take the relieve of men in the line, moving to the front line in the evening. Men of the Batts. marched out 525 strong. The ground advanced over had been entirely shelled to ruin by our guns, it was obvious the enemy had lost a number of 0.Rs and a few men. Battn. was 10 Officers & strength. Enemy had evacuated main of Bilses.	
Biencourt	10/4/17		At 10 A.M. Battalion was ordered to return to ARRAS & ARRAS where reinforcements were found in billets etc.	
Riencourt	11/4/17		Batts. staging one night to relieve 15th Queens in MONCHY Sector and were ordered to relieve 15th Queens in MONCHY Sector. Battn. were no Reserve Trenches E. of ARRAS. Weather suffered following casualties from hostile shell fire. 1 O.R. killed, 7 O.R. wounded.	
Trenches	12/4/17		To same trenches 808 in 12th inf. Bde altar, 3 O.R. killed, - O.R. wounded. Special Order of Day conveying congratulations from Sir Douglas Haig	
Trenches	13/4/17		To same trenches no in 12 & 13th inst. Enemy sent many gas shells on our side and no enemy of O.R. wounded or gassed.	
Trenches	14/4/17		Battalion relieved another Battalion of same Division in front line N. of MONCHY spend it established by relief under S.O. Lt. Collidore, Casualties 1 Officer wounded 1 O.R. missing.	

WAR DIARY
or
INTELLIGENCE SUMMARY.
(Erase heading not required.)

Army Form C. 2118.

Place	Date	Hour	Summary of Events and Information	Remarks and references to Appendices
France	16/4/17		Enemy shelled our Ration parties out we suffered no following casualties. 6 O.Rs killed, 9 O.R killed, 21 O.R wounded.	A.H.
Arras	17/4/17		Each Coy of Bn. Battalion was relieved on evening by 12th Manchester Regt. during the relief of relief we were fired at FEUCHY. Casualties, 1 other rank wounded, 1 O.R. killed. 3 O.R wounded.	A.H.
Trenches	18/4/17		Battalion marched into billets at ARRAS.	A.H.
Billets	19/4/17		Day devoted to cleaning of the men organisation of companies.	A.H.
Billets	20/4/17		Battalion marched to Reserve Trench E. of ORANGE HILL	A.H.
Trenches	21/4/17		Quiet Coy. spent. Our Front line shelled but no casualties occurred. Battalion relieved E. YORKs not 2 front line on the evening.	A.H.
Trenches	22/4/17		Preparations made for attack on morning of 23/4/17.	A.H.
Trenches	23/4/17		Battalion successfully co-operated with 29th Div in attack on Eastern Crevasses, 2 officers killed. Enemy Fire (N.R.) on position. Casualties, 2 officers killed, 1 officer wounded. 30 O.R. killed, 55 O.R. wounded.	A.H.
Trenches	24/4/17		Battalion was relieved by 12th Manchester Regt. proceeded to reserve trenches at FEUCHY. 1 O.R killed, 1 O.R wounded. Consequently congratulations on Lord on Corps a Army Commander. Influence.	A.H.

WAR DIARY
or
INTELLIGENCE SUMMARY.
(Erase heading not required.)

Army Form C.

Place	Date	Hour	Summary of Events and Information	Remarks and references to Appendices
[illegible]	25/4/17		Battalion mustered with [illegible] at ANNAS.	A.o.7.
Billets	26/4/17		Parade to R.A.M.C. and moved to ANNAS. Church Parade held at Billets at ANNAS.	A.o.7.
Billets	27/4/17		Inspection of clothing & arms. Band went into billets from 9th April to 25th April.	A.o.7.
			Special Order on the G.O.C. 17th Division ref 25th April.	
Billets	28/4/17		Inspection of clothing, rifles, equipment & inoculations. Battalion attended Church Parade at 10 A.M. Major L.T. Crothwaite D.S.O. assumed command of Battalion 28 am 1917.	A.o.7.
Billets	29/4/17		Battalion attended CHURCH PARADE in morning. Battalion allotted to all companies. Lt. Col. [illegible] commanding Battalion. Maj. A.O. Blackler (second in command) (Vide List No.129) 22.2.17	A.o.7.
Billets	30/4/17		Baumit [illegible] and Company Drill. The following struck off [illegible] as 2nd Lieut & 2nd Captain Feb 25 1917.	A.o.7.

A.W. Moulay
[signature]

Casualties incurred by the 9th (S) Bn. The North'd Fus. during the month of April 1917.

Appendix X

Casualty Report No.145 (Continued)

Regt No	Rank and Name	Coy	Date	Casualty
19149	Pte Varey J.H.	B	23/4/17	Killed
15748	" Youll J.	B	"	Do
41142	A/Cpl Carline J.W.	B	"	Wounded
12179	" Grant W.C.	B	"	Do
17874	" Newby E.	B	"	Do
12126	L/C Ellender S.G.	B	"	Do
29/848	" Derby W.S.	B	"	Do
12202	" Trevor H.J.	B	"	Do
12177	" Grant R.K.	B	"	Do
48462	Pte Aitken S	B	"	Do
290966	" Athey W	B	"	Do
29699	" Boag C	B	"	Do
48469	" Bramwell E.L.	B	"	Do
29/285	" Clough W	B	"	Do
29/432	" Craven R	B	"	Do
48476	" Collinge H	B	"	Do
44587	" Goodison H	B	"	Do
12210	" Hutchinson E	B	"	Do
32672	" Irving D.P.	B	"	Do
48542	" Killick J	B	"	Do
240876	" Longstaffe D	B	"	Do
32788	" Moncrieff E.W.	B	"	Do
44625	" Lyzack R	B	"	Do
48532	" Tiller E	B	"	Do
44757	" Vero G	B	"	Do
14757	Cpl Yearham J	B	"	Missing Believed Killed
48482	Pte Evans E.R.	B	"	Missing
241189	" Moffatt E	B	"	Do
31429	" Turner H.V.	B	"	Do

Casualty Report No 145 (Continued)

REGT No	RANK AND NAME	COY	DATE	CASUALTY
~~290875~~	~~Pte Tait G.W.~~	~~D~~	~~22/4/17~~	~~Missing~~
~~242600~~	~~" Bentley H~~	~~D~~	~~"~~	~~Do~~
13248	Sgt Fuller R	D	23/4/17	Wounded
16043	" Walker G	D	"	Do
27/128	Pte Caffrey ?	D	"	Do
5214	" Lampard S	D	"	Do
24/1062	" Callaghan ?	D	"	Do
290823	" Foster J.E.	D	"	Killed
265650	" Towns J.R.	D	"	Do
31422	" Goode A	D	"	Do
29/359	" Adams ?	D	"	Do
28366	" Hardwick B	D	"	Do
12/4998	" Callishaw G	B	"	Died of Wounds
48473	" Conner P.J.	A	21/4/17	Wounded
12895	Sgt Swinburne M	A	23/4/17	Do Remained at Duty
44628	Pte Teal A	A	"	Do Do
15879	" Colton H	A	"	Do Do
48479	" Delaney J	A	"	Do Do
12798	" Routledge ?	A	"	Do Do
290502	" Wilson M	C	"	Killed
12/18242	" Yates J	C	24/?/?	Do
6645	" Cobain R	C	22/?/?	Do
200201	" McIntyre J.H.	C	23/?/?	Wounded
27792	" Crawford ?	C	"	Do
290350	" Henderson S	C	"	Do
41204	" Mason C.J.H.	C	22/?/?	Do
13250	LC Detchan O	C	23/?/?	Do
41129	Pte Baitenshaw	C	?	Do

To Officer i/c
Regular Infantry (?) chan No 3.

Herewith Casualty
Report No 145 please

REGT NO	RANK AND NAME	Coy	DATE	CASUALTY
	2/Lieut H.E. Woods		23.4.17	~~missing believed~~ Killed
	2/Lieut W.S. Aitkman		23.4.17	Killed
	2/Lieut T. Bennett		23.4.17	Wounded
13226	Sgt Scott R	B	23.4.17	Killed
3/7260	L/Sgt Archbold A	B	23.4.17	Do
12235	L/Cpl Gibbins J.M.	B	"	Do
48461	Pte Dobby F	B	"	Do
41136	" Brown F	B	"	Do
21/503	" Case P.S.	B	"	Do
29811	" Clough H	B	"	Do
44584	" Faulkes H	B	"	Do
31424	" Grundon P	B	"	Do
32180	" Hurst H	B	"	Do
41187	" Jones J	B	"	Do
29/505	" King F	B	"	Do
39127	" Littler J	B	"	Do
48508	" McBeath A	B	"	Do
19096	" Popely E	B	"	Do
12172	" Soulsby W	B	"	Do
41221	" Stone J.P.	B	"	Do
48547	" Usher H.J.	B	"	Do

Casualty Report No 145 (Cont'd)

Reg'T No	Rank	Name	Coy	Date	Casualty
14799	Pte	Yaxley W.J.	C	24/4/17	Wounded
33463	"	Holmes A	C	22/4/17	Do
33452	"	Holmes J	C	"	Do
27/1011	"	Hall P	C	"	Do
15603	"	Spencer S	C	"	Do
6671	"	Tuckwood G	C	23/4/17	Do
27/1227	"	Simpson R	C	"	Do
4120	"	Taylor J.T.	C	"	Do
13052	"	Emery J.L.	C	"	Missing Believed Killed
15914	"	Curry G.W.	C	15-4-17	Previously reported missing now reported Wounded
38197	L/C	Douglas W	D	16-4-17	Wounded
23897	Pte	Newbold W	D	23/4/17	Wounded
13225	Pte	Ward J.T.H	C	"	Do
~~23897~~	~~"~~	~~Newbold W~~			

M.W. Robertson
Lieut and Adjt
9th North'd Fus.

27-4-1917.

SPECIAL ORDER OF THE DAY
BY
MAJOR GENERAL P.R.ROBERTSON, C.B., C.M.G., COMMANDING 17th DIVISION.

27th APRIL, 1917.

The G.O.C. wishes to express to all ranks of the 17th Division his sincere thanks for, and high appreciation of the most excellent manner in which they have carried out the late active operations against the enemy from 9th to 25th April, and in particular in the pitched battle of April 23rd. Where all have done their utmost and so gallantly, he feels that it would be invidious to make any distinction between units by name. The unfailing spirit of cheerfulness in enduring hardships under the most adverse weather conditions, and the way in which attack and defence has been carried out reflects the greatest credit on all, and fully upholds the splendid traditions of the British Army.

The work of the Field Artillery, Field Companies and Field Ambulances was on the same high level as that of the Infantry.

It is the G.O.C's greatest pride to have the honour of Commanding so fine a Division.

Lieutenant Colonel,
A.A. & Q.M.G., 17th Division.

SPECIAL ORDER OF THE DAY
By
FIELD-MARSHAL SIR DOUGLAS HAIG,
G.C.B., G.C.V.O., K.C.I.E.,
Commander-in-Chief, British Armies in France.

The following telegrams are published for the information of all ranks:—

From HER MAJESTY QUEEN ALEXANDRA to FIELD-MARSHAL SIR DOUGLAS HAIG.

11-4-17.

I congratulate you and your magnificent troops with all my heart on your splendid success. Everything was so fine. The wonderful advance so perfectly carried out with such glorious dash and bravery and ending with such grand results. It is indeed something to be proud of.

To HER MAJESTY QUEEN ALEXANDRA from FIELD-MARSHAL SIR DOUGLAS HAIG.

11-4-17.

Your Majesty's gracious and inspiring message of congratulation is a great source of encouragement and gratification to us all. On behalf of all ranks and of myself I would respectfully beg to offer our deepest thanks to Your Majesty for thinking of us.

From FIELD-MARSHAL SIR DOUGLAS HAIG to GENERAL ALEXEIEFF.

15-4-17.

On behalf of all officers and men of the British Armies in France I desire to offer you our warmest congratulations on your appointment to the supreme command of the Armies of Russia. With a lively recollection of all that our Russian comrades-in-arms have already done we look with confidence for further triumphs by the glorious Russian Army under your able leadership. We beg you to convey to all ranks of the forces under your command the assurance of the firm determination of the British Forces under my command to do all that is in our power to assist our Russian Comrades to overthrow our common enemy. I would ask you and all ranks in your Army to accept the success we have lately won as a proof of our ability to defeat the picked troops of the German Army as well as an earnest of our intention to persist in the struggle till the aims of the Allies have been attained and the territories of Russia and of our other Allies been freed from the invader.

To FIELD-MARSHAL SIR DOUGLAS HAIG from GENERAL ALEXEIEFF.

16-4-17.

(Translation.)

I am deeply touched by the congratulations which your Excellency sends me on the occasion of my promotion to be Commander-in-Chief of the Russian Armies and I beg you to be good enough to convey my most cordial thanks to the gallant troops under your command. You can rest assured that in spite of the difficulties consequent upon the change of Regime the Russian Army will not fail in its duty towards its brave Allies and that it will render them all the help in its power by taking the offensive as soon as the climatic conditions permit.

To FIELD-MARSHAL SIR DOUGLAS HAIG FROM GENERAL MAUDE.

13-4-17.

We are all thrilled by the news of your large capture in men and guns and offer you and your brave troops our warmest congratulations.

To GENERAL MAUDE FROM FIELD-MARSHAL SIR DOUGLAS HAIG.

14-4-17.

All ranks of the British Army in France very greatly appreciate the kind telegram of congratulations which you have been good enough to send us on behalf of the Army under your command.

FROM RUSSIAN ARMY IN THE CAUCASUS TO COMMANDER-IN-CHIEF

14-4-17.

Hearty congratulations to the British Army from the Caucasus Army and its Commander.

To RUSSIAN ARMY IN THE CAUCASUS FROM COMMANDER-IN-CHIEF

15-4-17.

All ranks of the British Army under my command send best thanks to the Caucasus Army for their kind wire which has been greatly appreciated.

To FIELD-MARSHAL SIR DOUGLAS HAIG FROM GENERAL MILNE.

11-4-17.

General Sarrail and French Army here send to you and the British Army in France their heartiest congratulations on your recent successes. With these sincere congratulations I and the British Army in Salonica wish to be identified.

FROM FIELD-MARSHAL SIR DOUGLAS HAIG TO GENERAL MILNE.

11-4-17.

Please express to General Sarrail and the French Army of the East our best thanks for the kind wire you have sent me. The British Army in France is also most grateful to you and the Army under your command for their welcome congratulations on the results of their recent fighting.

General Headquarters,
24th April, 1917.

Commander-in-Chief,
British Armies in France.

SPECIAL ORDER OF THE DAY
By
FIELD-MARSHAL SIR DOUGLAS HAIG,
G.C.B., G.C.V.O., K.C.I.E.,
Commander-in-Chief, British Armies in France.

The following telegrams are published for the information of all ranks:—

To FIELD MARSHAL SIR DOUGLAS HAIG FROM GENERAL ALEXEIFF.

(Translation).

19-4-17.

Please accept the warmest congratulations of the Russian Armies on the brilliant successes gained by their British Ally. In my own name and on behalf of the troops under my command, I beg to express our deep admiration and to assure you that we await the moment when we can take our share in these successes.

To GENERAL ALEXEIFF, GENERAL HEADQUARTERS, RUSSIA, FROM FIELD-MARSHAL SIR DOUGLAS HAIG.

19-4-17.

On behalf of all ranks under my command I thank you sincerely for your inspiring telegram. We send our hearty greetings to you personally and to our comrades of the Russian Army and wish you all the best of luck in your forthcoming efforts against our common enemy.

General Headquarters,
20th April, 1917.

Commander-in-Chief
British Armies in France.

B.O. Diary
War Diary

SPECIAL ORDER OF THE DAY
By
FIELD-MARSHAL SIR DOUGLAS HAIG,
G.C.B., G.C.V.O., K.C.I.E.,
Commander-in-Chief, British Armies in France.

THE FIELD-MARSHAL COMMANDING-IN-CHIEF desires to express to all ranks his great satisfaction on the important successes achieved on the 9th instant by the First and Third Armies. The manner in which the operations were prepared and carried out reflects the greatest credit on Commanders, Staffs and troops.

The capture of the renowned Vimy Ridge is an achievement of the highest order of which Canada may well be proud.

The performance of the VI., VII. and XVII. Corps of the Third Army in surmounting the difficulties which confronted them is proof of very great skill and gallantry.

The Royal Artillery, Heavy, Siege and Field, by its untiring efforts and accurate fire prepared the way for and supported the advance of the infantry in the most efficient manner.

The splendid work of the Royal Flying Corps under very adverse weather conditions and in face of most determined opposition has contributed largely to the success of the operations and calls for the highest praise.

The Heavy Branch of the Machine Gun Corps has been of material assistance and has, under difficult circumstances, played a useful part.

The Cavalry Corps and Corps Mounted Troops have taken the fullest advantage of such openings for cavalry action as the course of the operations has so far afforded.

The Royal Engineers, both in the field and in their work behind the line, have carried out their many duties with the thoroughness and efficiency in which they are never found wanting; while all the various special Corps and Services which took part in the battle, as well as the Administrative Services and Departments on which the Armies depend for their maintenance, have taken their full share in bringing within reach the great successes gained.

The Second, Fourth, and Fifth Armies have played their part admirably in keeping the enemy employed on their respective fronts, while to the Fourth and Fifth Armies in particular belongs the credit of having opened the way for these fresh successes by their splendid achievements on the Somme and the Ancre.

The Commander-in-Chief desires to convey his warmest congratulations to all ranks of the Armies which he has the honour to command on the great success already achieved by their untiring and self-sacrificing efforts, and on the prospects of further successes which have been opened.

General Headquarters,
12th April, 1917.

To Officer i/c
Regular Infantry Section No 3

     Herewith Casualty report please.

No 10611 Corp Frazer W. C. Coy.
No 31400 Pte Pringle H. N. B Coy

Wounded (Gassed) 2.4.1917.

M.V. Robertson
Lieut and a/Adjt
9th North'd F.

In the Field
2. 4. 1917.

To Officer i/c
Regular Infantry Section

Report No 144 please   Herewith Casualty

REGT NO	RANK AND NAME	Coy	DATE	CASUALTY
	Lieut P J Harvie	C	16.4.17	~~Killed~~ Died of Wounds
	2/Lieut O.A. Hodgson	A	16.4.17	Killed
	2/Lieut J.R. Goldthorpe	D	15.4.17	Wounded
	2/Lieut T. Oliver	B	17.4.17	Do (Shell Shock)
21328	Sgt Hobson W A	A	15.4.17	Killed
23203	Pte Gilhooley B	A	12.4.17	Do
240181	" Wilson G	A	16.4.17	Do
266164	" Tighe	A	16.4.17	Do
48480	" Devlin P	A	16.4.17	Do
29/568	" Whittaker H	A	12.4.17	Wounded
41231	" Shandley J	A	12.4.17	Do
48485	" Greenwood W	A	17.4.17	Do
44630	" Ward R.E.	A	16.4.17	Do
14342	Sgt Guise W.H.	B	13.4.17	Killed
45774	Cpl Brown H	B	13.4.17	Killed
48503	Pte Hoffman A	B	13.4.17	Killed
44618	" Smith H	B	16.4.17	Killed
45801	" Moorhouse F	B	16.4.17	Killed
201074	" Pleasants J.K.	B	16.4.17	Killed
292173	" McNaulty J	B	17.4.17	Killed
48546	" Kitchener E.E.	B	16.4.17	Died of Wounds

Casualty Report No 1444 (Cont'd)

REGT No	RANK AND NAME	Coy	DATE	CASUALTY
1271	Pte Tighe J	B	13.4.17	Wounded
29/485	" Barraclough H	B	13.4.17	Do
39023	" Bent C	B	14.4.17	Do
29887	" Brayshaw J	B	14.4.17	Do
12111	L/Cpl Brown S	B	16.4.17	Do
272120	Pte Benson H	B	16.4.17	Do
411602	" Metcalfe D	B	16.4.17	Do
48541	" Winters H.C.	B	16.4.17	Do
40185	" Pearson W.E.	C	12.4.17	Do
266/50	" Strong R	C	12.4.17	Do
41201	" McCarthy J	C	12.4.17	Do
16309	" Patchett J	C	12.4.17	Do
15914	" Curry G.W.	C	15.4.17	Missing
291030	" Frazer J	C	16.4.17	Wounded
25/621	" Seymour H	C	17.4.17	Missing
265626	" Gray R	C	17.4.17	Missing
9954	CSM Parish G	D	16.4.17	Wounded
2995	Sgt Payne H	D	16.4.17	Do
38197	L/Cpl Douglas W	D	16.4.17	Missing
33752	Pte Armstrong J.P.	D	14.4.17	Wounded
13172	" Brown R	D	14.4.17	Do (Shell Shock)
4328	" Burford L	D	14.4.17	Do Do
16907	" Cartwright B	D	14.4.17	Do (Gassed)
32258	" Close M	D	16.4.17	Wounded
27821	" Dean A	D	16.4.17	Do (Gassed)
21247	" Dixon J	D	16.4.17	Killed
25385	" Dickinson R	D	16.4.17	Wounded Gassed
10/258	" Guagan J	D	16.4.17	Do Shell Shock

Casualty Report No 144 (Cont'd)

REGT No	RANK AND NAME	Coy	DATE	CASUALTY
15244	Pte Gascoyne, J	D	16.4.17	Wounded
13145	" Gibson J	D	16.4.17	Do
18659	" Hogg W	D	12.4.17	Do
4854	" Powell A	D	14.4.17	Do (Gassed)
45788	" Parkes J	D	16.4.17	Do
29/593	" Pearson G.A	D	16.4.17	Do
37295	" Reed J	D	15.4.17	Missing
48521	" Roberts J	D	14.4.17	Wounded (Gas)
22320	" Rogerson E	D	16.4.17	Wounded
1542	" Reay G	D	13.4.17	Do
24251	" Sewell J	D	14.4.17	Do
29/243	" Stead J.W.	D	16.4.17	Killed
13294	" Todd G.A.	D	16.4.17	Wounded
200885	" Telfer W	D	16.4.17	Do
204039	" Wadey F.J	D	16.4.17	Do

W.J. Robertson
Lieut and Adjutant
9th North'd Fusiliers

20-4-1917.

To Officer i/c
Regular Infantry Section No 3

Herewith Casualty
Report No 146 please.

REG'T N°	RANK AND NAME	COY	DATE	CASUALTY
1563	Pte Armstrong E	A	25/4/17	Missing
44567	" Baroso J ✗	A	24/4/17	Wounded
31/26	" Gaul R	D	24/4/17	D°
21328	" Purcell E	A	23/4/17	Missing
34/385	" Edmondson B	D	21/4/17	Killed
44747	" Offord L.C.	C	23/4/17	Missing

✗ Attached 52nd M.G.C.

W.F. Robertson
Capt and Adjt
9th North'd Fus

SPECIAL ORDER OF THE DAY
By
FIELD-MARSHAL SIR DOUGLAS HAIG,
G.C.B., G.C.V.O., K.C.I.E.,
Commander-in-Chief, British Armies in France.

The following messages are published for the information of all ranks:—

I. From HIS MAJESTY THE KING to FIELD-MARSHAL SIR DOUGLAS HAIG.

10-4-17.

The whole Empire will rejoice at the news of yesterday's successful operations. Canada will be proud that the taking of the coveted Vimy Ridge has fallen to the lot of her troops. I heartily congratulate you and all who have taken part in this splendid achievement.

GEORGE R.I.

II. From FIELD-MARSHAL SIR DOUGLAS HAIG to HIS MAJESTY THE KING.

10-4-17.

On behalf of all who took part in yesterday's battle I respectfully beg to offer our grateful thanks for your Majesty's most gracious and inspiring message of congratulation. It has given the very greatest gratification to all Your Majesty's troops in France.

III. From THE SECRETARY OF STATE FOR WAR to FIELD-MARSHAL SIR DOUGLAS HAIG.

10-4-17.

War Cabinet desire me to convey to you personally, to the Army Commanders, and to all ranks engaged in the operations yesterday, their warmest congratulations on the results achieved, which are a splendid tribute to the efficiency of the Armies under your command and a further proof of the bravery and devotion to duty of the Regimental Officers and men.

IV. FROM FIELD-MARSHAL SIR DOUGLAS HAIG TO THE SECRETARY OF STATE FOR WAR.

10-4-17.

On behalf of the Army Commanders engaged in yesterday's operations I beg to express our warmest thanks for the kind message of congratulation which the War Cabinet have been kind enough to send.

V. FROM GENERAL NIVELLE, COMMANDER-IN-CHIEF OF THE ARMIES OF THE N. AND N.E., TO FIELD-MARSHAL SIR DOUGLAS HAIG.

(Translation).

10-4-17.

It is with very great pleasure that I send you my warmest congratulations on the splendid success of the important operations carried out yesterday by the First and Third Armies.

VI. FROM FIELD-MARSHAL SIR DOUGLAS HAIG TO GENERAL NIVELLE.

10-4-17.

I am most grateful to you for the kind wire you have been good enough to send me. The First and Third Armies are much gratified at the generous appreciation which you have expressed regarding the results of yesterday's battle.

D. Haig. F.M.

Commander-in-Chief,
British Armies in France.

General Headquarters,
12th April, 1917.

CONFIDENTIAL

Vol 21

WAR DIARY
of the
9th (S) Bn. NORTHUMBERLAND FUSILIERS.

FROM 1st MAY 1917.
TO 31st MAY 1917.

Confidential

To 52nd Infy Bde

Herewith War Diary for May 1917.

Please acknowledge receipt hereon

W. Robertson
Capt & Adjt
for O.C. 9th North'd Fus.

Army Form C. 2118.

WAR DIARY
or
INTELLIGENCE SUMMARY.
(Erase heading not required.)

Instructions regarding War Diaries and Intelligence Summaries are contained in F. S. Regs., Part II. and the Staff Manual respectively. Title pages will be prepared in manuscript.

Place	Date 1917	Hour	Summary of Events and Information	Remarks and references to Appendices
Billets	May 1st		Battalion paraded at 5.40 A.M. and embussed at Cross Roads midway between IVERGNY and SUS ST. LEGER (MAP LENS 11. 1/100,000), and proceeded to camp at LARESSET, 5 miles WEST of ARRAS, and 1 mile SOUTH of ARRAS - ST. POL road.	
Camp	2nd		Struck camp at 1.15 P.M. and marched to ST. NICHOLAS, near ARRAS and occupied tents bivouacs there.	
Camp	3rd		Battalion took over reserve trenches in H1 x H7 (Map 51 B N.W.) This line of trench is known as BROWN LINE	
Reserve Trenches	4th		In reserve Line - BROWN	
Reserve Trenches	5th		In reserve line - BROWN	
Reserve Trenches	6th		Battalion left reserve line and withdrew to old German first line in C.6 x C.12 (Map 51 B N.W.) This is known as BLACK LINE	
Reserve line	7th		In reserve line - BLACK	
Reserve line	8th		In reserve line - BLACK	
Reserve line	9th		Battalion moved up to support trench and relieved a battalion of the K.O.S.B. (9th Div.) in H.6. a. 7. 6. c. (Map 51 B N.W.) This line is known as GREEN LINE. The relief was slightly delayed but carried out without mishap.	

Army Form C. 2118.

WAR DIARY
or
INTELLIGENCE SUMMARY.
(Erase heading not required.)

Instructions regarding War Diaries and Intelligence Summaries are contained in F.S. Regs., Part II. and the Staff Manual respectively. Title pages will be prepared in manuscript.

Place	Date 1917	Hour	Summary of Events and Information	Remarks and references to Appendices
Support trench	May 10th		In support line — GREEN.	
Support trench	11th		In support line — GREEN. At night battalion moved into front line and relieved 9th WEST RIDING Regiment. Front occupied is known as CONRAD. Sectors held by battalion from I.1.B.1.9 to I.1.D.1.2. (map PLOUVAIN 1/10,000) (between 51.B.N.W. & 51.B.N.E.) Casualties, 2 O.R. killed and 10 O.R. wounded.	
Front line	12th		10th Battalion of Lancs Fus. on right of this battalion attacked CHARLIE trench in I.4.B. but failed to reach objective and suffered heavy casualties. We suffered the following casualties. 2 Officers wounded (Lieut. J.E. Taylor & 2 Lt. E.J. Butts) 6 O.R. killed. 24 O.R. wounded.	
Front line	13th		Front line trenches. Fairly quiet. Our casualties 1 O.R. killed & O.R. wounded.	
Front line	14th		Quiet day. At night battalion was relieved by 9th WEST RIDING Regt. and moved back to the railway cutting in "H.1.f.H.7 (Ref. 61.13 N.W.) Our casualties 1 O.R. killed and 2 O.R. wounded.	

Army Form C. 2118.

WAR DIARY
or
INTELLIGENCE SUMMARY.
(Erase heading not required.)

Instructions regarding War Diaries and Intelligence Summaries are contained in F.S. Regs., Part II. and the Staff Manual respectively. Title pages will be prepared in manuscript.

Place	Date 1917	Hour	Summary of Events and Information	Remarks and references to Appendices
Reserve	May 15th		In ration baths H.1 x H.9 (Ref 51B N.W.) 1 O.R. wounded	
Reserve	16th		Battalion moved to hew railway cutting to GREEN LINE H.6 x G.6 (51B N.W.) Leave dug pits. Relieving railway cutting as were shelled with 5.9 howitzers and enfiladed. 3 O.R. killed and 6 O.R. wounded.	
Supportline	17th		In GREEN LINE 1 O.R. wounded	
Support line	18th		In GREEN LINE	
Support Line	19th		Moved into front line and relieved 9th WEST RIDINGS in CONRAD TRENCH from T.1.B.1.9 to T.1.D.1.2 (Ref PLOUVAIN 1/10,000) 1 O.R. killed 1 O.R. wounded	
Front line	20th		In CONRAD trench. Quiet day	
Front line	21st		Fairly quiet day. 4 O.R. wounded.	
Front line	22nd		Preparations made for a post to push forward to line running at T.1.B.6.2 and to into WIT trench held by the French at about T.1.B.85.30 (Ref PLOUVAIN 1/10,000) 1 O.R. wounded	

A 5834 Wt. W4973/M687 750,000 8/16 D.D. & L. Ltd. Forms/C.2118/13.

Army Form C. 2118.

WAR DIARY
or
INTELLIGENCE SUMMARY.
(Erase heading not required.)

Instructions regarding War Diaries and Intelligence Summaries are contained in F. S. Regs., Part II. and the Staff Manual respectively. Title pages will be prepared in manuscript.

Place	Date 1917	Hour	Summary of Events and Information	Remarks and references to Appendices
Front line	May 22nd (Contd)		The objects of the raid were: (a) identification (b) to kill Germans (c) capturing or destroying any machine guns or trench mortar emplacements as they had been obtained on night of 21st.	
Front line	23rd	Zero hour	The raid was fired at 1.30 a.m. The raiding party consisting of 20 Other Ranks under 2nd Lt. E.G. Bates & "C" Company, were armed with rifles and bayonets, and each carried 4 Mills Grenades and 2 clips S.A.A. In each arm the men wore a band of white tape. The conditions were very favourable. The barrage was ordered as follows:— At Zero at least two batteries from Group 1 at 4 rounds per minute on WIT TRENCH. Objective is I.1.B.85.3 to I.1.B.76.5 and No gun in its short shower three bursts than 60x. The moment barrage opens raiding party move forward. At ZERO + 5 barrage may slacken and at ZERO + 10 die away to slow. At ZERO hr 15 min the party left CONRAD at I.1.B.6.2 and proceeded forward, taking up position within 50 yds. of point of entry. (contd)	

A5834 Wt.W4973/M687 750,000 8/16 D. D. & L. Ltd. Forms/C.2118/13.

WAR DIARY
or
INTELLIGENCE SUMMARY.

Army Form C. 2118.

Place	Date	Hour	Summary of Events and Information	Remarks and references to Appendices
	May 19/17		(Contd.) 2nd Lt Butler in charge of the party, reported as follows:— "The barrage firmed smooth at ZERO as we were nearing. The smoke shells were thin than in practice opposite our objective. We were unable to locate this owing however, as our shells were bursting between us and our objective. This occurred long in the barrage lasted. I proceeded to left flank and found my bombing party had gone forward and were bombing the enemy trench. I could not find the N.C.O. i/c of bombing party. C.S.M. Crocker, who said he had gallantly assisted to throw along I bomb as our shells were still falling short. The bombers who had entered that trench killed 6 of the enemy. They continue to the front on which no shells were to have fallen received the heaviest barrage." The raiding party returned without casualties, but during the rest of its stay we suffered 3 O.R. killed and 6 O.R. wounded. At night the Battalion was relieved by 12th Manchester Regt and moved back to GREEN line in H.6.A. H.6.C.	
Scarpe	24th		Battalion was relieved in the evening by 2/7th West Riding Regt and moved down to camp at ST. NICHOLAS.	
Camp	25th		Camp at ST. NICHOLAS.	
Camp	26th		Camp at ST. NICHOLAS near ARRAS.	

WAR DIARY
or
INTELLIGENCE SUMMARY.
(Erase heading not required.)

Army Form C. 2118.

Place	Date	Hour	Summary of Events and Information	Remarks and references to Appendices
Camps	May 21st		Battalion moved up to BLACK LINE in G.6 & G.12 from where they supplied fatigue parties for digging.	
Reserve Line	22nd		BLACK LINE. A fatigue party was again found from the battalion for digging at night. The following appeared in Div. Routine Order. Awarded Military Cross. Capt. M.G. PATTEN 2ⁿᵈ Lt. T.E. BENNET } Act. posted to. Awarded D.C.M. Sgt. HARDMAN. 9th posted to. April 1917. These awards were for work at MONCHY & ST. NICHOLAS	
Reserve	29th		Battalion moved back to camp at ST. NICHOLAS. Letter from Brig. Genl. Commanding 5.D. Infy. Bde. read as follows to the Brigadier congratulates the C.O. and all ranks of the Battalion on their exploit (line mentioned in the Field Marshal's despatches" referred to is that of 23rd May).	

WAR DIARY
or
INTELLIGENCE SUMMARY.

Army Form C. 2118.

Place	Date 1917	Hour	Summary of Events and Information	Remarks and references to Appendices
[train]	May 30		Battalion entrained at ARRAS and marched from the to billets at WARLUZEL (Sheet LENS 11. 1/100 000.)	
Billets	31st		Day devoted to cleaning of kit, equipment etc. —	

W. Robertson
Lt/Col
for O.C. 9th Bn North'd Fus.

To O.C. 9.1.F.3 Appendix Y
Base 147.

Herewith Casualty
Report Number 147 please.

Reg No	Rank & Name	Coy	Date	Casualty
16/160	Pte Robinson J.H.	B	3-5-17	Wounded.
2/152	" Brown ?	B	6-5-17	Wounded.
13019	" Liddle ?	A	4-5-17	Wounded Acc A.F.B.117 has been completed & forwarded to Field Ambulance concerned

W.T. Robertson
Capt & Adjt
for O.C. 9th North'd Fusiliers

In the Field
12-5-17

To Officer i/c
Regular Infantry Section No 3.

Herewith Casualty Report No 148 please.

REGT N°	RANK AND NAME	Coy	DATE	CASUALTY
14063	Pte Cook F.W.	A	11·5·17	Killed
41222	" Stott J A	A	"	Do
13994	Sergt Hunter W.R.	A	12·5·17	Wounded
25/254	Pte Humble R.R.	A	"	Do
48535	L/Corp Taylor H	A	"	Do
29/437	Pte Deplidge G	A	"	Do
1012	" Kelly J	A	11·5·17	Do
41155	" Craig W	A	12·5·17	Died of Wounds
265685	" Heslop H	A	"	Wounded
41156	" Cole F	A	"	Killed
22821	" Marvel D	A	11·5·17	Wounded
44578	" Wright J.H.	A	12·5·17	Died of Wounds
22829	" Davidson J.G.	A	"	Wounded
200870	" Simpson W	A	"	Do
44609	L/Corp Pearson T.A	A	13·5·17	Do
13062	Sergt Butters A	A	6·5·17	Killed
48467	Pte Brennan P	A	"	Do
11484	" Connolly J	A	"	Do

REGT No	RANK AND NAME	COY	DATE	CASUALTY
48505	Pte Jefferson J.J.	C	12.5.17	Wounded
265957	" Hardy J	C	"	do
201933	" Thurlbourne C	C	"	do
36965	" Outhwaite J	C	13.5.17	Killed
10571	Cpl Downs M	C	"	Wounded
10645	L/Cpl Whelan D	C	"	do
4940	Pte Eddowes J	C	"	do
36223	" Lamb W	C	"	do remained at duty
13/24	" Carnall J.L.	C	15.5.17	Wounded
29/594	" Rushworth L	C	17.5.17	do
23805	" Duffy D	C	24.5.17	do
10609	Cpl Everitt G.J.	C	17.5.17	do
15274	Pte Robinson	C	23.5.17	do
19117	" Welford 6	B	24.5.17	Wounded Remained at duty
29/441	" England J	B	"	do
46691	L/Cpl Snowdon J	B	"	do
32228	Pte Thompson G	B	"	Rem at Duty
39287	" Winter F W	B	23.5.17	Wounded
49484	" Green H	B	"	do
42448	" Wise 6	B	"	do
514	" Nicholson J	B	12.5.17	Killed
27240	" Bruce L.S.R.	B	19.5.17	do
4338	" Pearson A D	B	23.5.17	do
22/1043	" Stobbart G	B	23.5.17	do
~~16/1801~~	~~Robinson J H~~	B	3.5.17	Wounded
~~22/1552~~	~~Brown J~~	B	6.5.17	do
12887	a/Sgt Gibson JW	B	17.5.17	do

Casualty Report No 128 (contd)

REGT No	RANK AND NAME		Coy	DATE	CASUALTY
29/24	Corpl Young R	✓	A	16.5.17	Wounded
39516	Pte Webb J	✓	A	"	"
48478	" Charlton E	✓	A	"	"
2717	L/Corp Brammer G	✓	A	21.5.17	"
20618	Pte McKenna H	✓	A	16.5.17	"
15670	a/Sergt Doody E	✓	A	12.5.17	"
15601	Corp Cox JW	✓	A	"	"
14140	Pte Daplington	✓	D	22.5.17	Remained at Duty
29224	Pte Docker G.B.	✓	D	12.5.17	Killed
44158	" Eagan J	✓	D	14.5.17	"
48491	" Harrison ??	✓	D	"	Wounded
408515	" Ganning R	✓	D	11.5.17	"
588	" Pringle J	✓	D	"	"
266261	" Budge R	✓	D	"	"
44585	" Good W	✓	D	"	"
82210	" Dawson G.E.	✓	D	"	"
290923	" Douglass W	✓	D	"	"
48532	" Stent H.G	✓	D	"	"
17106	Cpl Walker K.J	✓	D	22.5.17	"
41241	Pte Springer	✓	D	23.5.17	"
5044	" Ashworth B	✓	D	16.5.17	"
200795	" Robson G	✓	D	13.5.17	Remd at duty
14727	L/Cpl Taylor J	✓	A	21.5.17	"
265414	Pte Hart H	✓	C	6.5.17	"
39197	" Johnson ?	✓	C	11.5.17	"
13161	Sgt Henderson J	✓	C	12.5.17	Killed
201087	Pte Turnbull R	✓	C	"	"

REGT No	RANK AND NAME	Cy	DATE	CASUALTY
28289	Sergt Bromage J.W.	B	12.5.17	Wounded
24/273	Pte Armstrong R.Y.	B	"	do
47196	" Holbrooke	B	"	do
41974	" Peel R.B.	B	"	do
12204	" Yarty J	B	"	do
23155	" Carnegie A	B	"	do
20/695	" Wheaton A	B	"	do
24032	" Connell J	B	"	do
41237	" Watson J.M.	B	"	do
44867	" Dickenson C.R.	B	"	do
12198	L/Sergt Smith C.J.	B	14.5.17	do
7291	Pte Hedley K.N.	B	16.5.17	do
29/458	" Kellett C	B	19.5.17	do
24623	" Wright W	B	21.5.17	do
~~86278~~ ~~21244~~	" ~~Watson J.W.~~ Catch J	B	~~23.5.17~~ 23.5.17	do
22174	" Hodgson J	B	23.5.17	missing believed killed
21/1194	" Simpson R	B	21.5.17	Wounded
20/691	" Wade J.G.	B	12.5.17	do
	Lieut Col A.W. Blockley		9.5.17	remained at duty
	2 Lieut F.G. Taylor		12.5.17	Wounded
	2 Lieut E.J. Bilder			do

W.H. Robertson
Capt & Adjt
9 Northd Fus

26.5.1917.

Special Order of the Day

— BY —

General Sir EDMUND ALLENBY, K.C.B.,
COMMANDING THIRD ARMY.

The following message has been received from the Field Marshal, Commander-in-Chief :—

"The fierce fighting yesterday has carried us another step forward. I congratulate you and all under you on the result of it, and on the severe punishment you have inflicted on the enemy."

The Army Commander has replied as follows :—

"Chief's message highly appreciated by all ranks of Third Army, who are proud of and encouraged by his appreciation."

H.Q., Third Army,
25th April, 1917.

A. F. SILLEM, Major-General,
D.A. & Q.M.G., Third Army

3rd Field Survey Co., R.E. 1590 25-4-17

SPECIAL ORDER OF THE DAY
By
FIELD-MARSHAL SIR DOUGLAS HAIG,
G.C.B., G.C.V.O., K.C.I.E.,
Commander-in-Chief, British Armies in France.

The following telegrams are published for the information of all ranks:—

FROM FIELD-MARSHAL SIR DOUGLAS HAIG TO GENERAL CADORNA.

25-5-17.

All ranks under my command join me in offering their heartiest congratulations on the magnificent success won by the gallant Italian troops on the Carso on 23rd May, which cannot fail to contribute most effectively towards the general progress of the Allied Armies on all fronts. The brilliance of the plans and the success with which they have been carried out in the face of strong opposition and over most difficult country have aroused our warmest admiration. And we are proud that our batteries should have the privilege of taking part in your victory. Their presence is a symbol of the united determination of Italy, Great Britain and the Allies to press the war on all fronts to a successful conclusion. I beg you to convey to your gallant troops the warm greeting of all under my command, and to accept my own personal congratulations to yourself and my best wishes for the continuance of your successes.

To FIELD-MARSHAL SIR DOUGLAS HAIG FROM GENERAL CADORNA.

26-5-17.

[*Translation.*]

For myself and in the name of the troops engaged, I thank you for your congratulations on our victory.

I rejoice that amidst the thunder of artillery on the Carso the enemy has heard the powerful voice of the British Guns, which was a sign to him of the indissoluble fraternity in arms of the Allied nations. Italy, remembering the sympathy of the British for the cause of her independence even from the beginning, rejoices that in this hour, in which she is fighting her greatest battle for the fulfilment of her unity and for the liberty of all peoples, she should have this token of a co-operation which is an assurance of victory.

General Headquarters,
28th May, 1917.

Commander-in-Chief
British Armies in France.

SPECIAL ORDER OF THE DAY
By
FIELD-MARSHAL SIR DOUGLAS HAIG.
G.C.B., G.C.V.O., K.C.I.E.,
Commander-in-Chief, British Armies in France.

To FIELD-MARSHAL SIR DOUGLAS HAIG from THE LORD MAYOR OF LONDON.

24.5.17.

The school children of the City of London assembled in Guildhall on Empire Day respectfully ask you to convey to the brave soldiers under your command their heartfelt thanks for the splendid manner in which they are upholding the cause of Freedom, Liberty and Justice on the battlefield.

From FIELD-MARSHAL SIR DOUGLAS HAIG to THE LORD MAYOR OF LONDON.

27.5.17.

Please give the school children of London my special thanks for their message sent from the Guildhall on Empire Day. Their good wishes are especially valued by all of us, because they are the heirs of everything that we are fighting to preserve.

To FIELD-MARSHAL SIR DOUGLAS HAIG from THE PRESIDENT, OLDHAM BOY SCOUTS.

25.5.17.

One thousand Oldham Boy Scouts send greeting on Empire Day. Congratulations to Army on glorious achievements under your leadership.

From FIELD-MARSHAL SIR DOUGLAS HAIG to THE PRESIDENT, OLDHAM BOY SCOUTS.

27.5.17.

All ranks under my command join with me in thanking you for your message sent on Empire Day.

To FIELD-MARSHAL SIR DOUGLAS HAIG from THE MODERATOR OF ASSEMBLY, FREE CHURCH OF SCOTLAND, EDINBURGH.

25.5.17.

Free Church of Scotland in general assembly sends greeting to all Scottish soldiers under you, as also to those other fronts, bidding them be strong in the Lord.

From FIELD-MARSHAL SIR DOUGLAS HAIG to THE MODERATOR OF ASSEMBLY, FREE CHURCH OF SCOTLAND, EDINBURGH.

27.5.17.

Thank you for your telegram, which will hearten the Scotsmen who are fighting in France.

D. Haig. F.M.
Commander-in-Chief,
British Armies in France.

General Headquarters,
28th May, 1917.

9th (S) Bn North'd Fus. Vol 22

War Diary

1st June 1917
30th June 1917

From
To

20-a

Confidential

Confidential   NFC121

To   52nd Infy Bde

   Herewith War Diary for the
month of June 1917
      Please acknowledge receipt
hereon

                           D.R. Bourne
1/7/17   Comdg North'd Fus
                              Major

WAR DIARY
or
INTELLIGENCE SUMMARY.

(Erase heading not required.)

Army Form C. 2118.

Place	Date	Hour	Summary of Events and Information	Remarks and references to Appendices
L Billes	1/6		Day devoted to cleaning of equipment inspection of rifles, S.A.A. & gas helmets. The a/m officers joined and were taken on strength of battalion. Posted as follows:	Art
			/Lieut M. W. Drysdale "C" Coy	Art
			/Lieut L Adams "C" Coy	
			/Lieut W.H. Barnes "B" Coy	
Billes	2/6		Special Order of Day issued by F.M. Sir Douglas Haig. Battalion paraded at 11 am for Divine Service & in the afternoon all officers attended a conference by B.G. Commanding 52nd Inf "Bde".	Art
Billes	3/6		8 am to 10.30 am devoted to training, special attacks being practised musketry. Bath inspected by Brig. Gen. Como 52nd Bde at 11:30 am. Special training in afternoon. Special Order of Day issued by F.M. Sir Douglas Haig, on occasion of the birthday of His Majesty the King. Officers attend C.O. for tactical scheme in afternoon. Training during morning.	Art
Billes	4/6		Training – Special attacks being practised & musketry close order drill.	Art
Billes	5/6			Art
Billes	6/6		Baths allotted to all companies. Remainder of a.m. training men coys arrangements. Special Order of Day issued by F.M. Sir Douglas Haig.	Art
Billes	7/6		Training – Scheme for officers during afternoon.	Art

Army Form C. 2118.

WAR DIARY
or
INTELLIGENCE SUMMARY.
(Erase heading not required.)

Instructions regarding War Diaries and Intelligence Summaries are contained in F.S. Regs., Part II. and the Staff Manual respectively. Title pages will be prepared in manuscript.

Place	Date	Hour	Summary of Events and Information	Remarks and references to Appendices
Billib	8/6		Training from 9am to 12.30pm. Junior NCO's under RSM from 2pm to 3pm. Junior officers under CO for tactical scheme during afternoon. Special Order of Day issued by F.M. Sir Douglas Haig on complete success of operations carried out on 16/7 by the Second Army. Award No 11468 Sgt D. Haves awarded Distinguished Conduct Medal for gallantry in the field.	AWD
Billib	9/6		Training from 9am to 12.30pm. Battalion sports held, commencing at 6.30pm. Special Order of Day issued by F.M. Sir Douglas Haig, publishing message received from His Majesty the King on success achieved by Second Army. Major DR Osborn rejoined - assumed command.	AWD
Billib	10/6		Battalion paraded at 11am for Divine Service - All ranks inoculated who had not been done since Nov. 1916. Following extracts from London Gazette published for information. To be 2/Lieutenants:- Lieut 2Lt JAC Beaty 2.11.16 Lieut Lt Jas Lords 6.11.16 Serj 252 CLa Walsh 4.2.17.	AWD
Billib	11/6		C.D. Coys. paraded at 4.30 am and proceeded to ranges T.9.D (Sheet 51c) A.B. 10.0 am 2/Lieut N.S. Allen joined Bn & posted to "A" Coy.	AWD

A 5834 Wt. W4973/M687 750,000 8/16 D. D. & L. Ltd. Forms/C.2118/13.

Army Form C. 2118.

WAR DIARY
or
INTELLIGENCE SUMMARY.

(Erase heading not required.)

Instructions regarding War Diaries and Intelligence Summaries are contained in F. S. Regs., Part II. and the Staff Manual respectively. Title pages will be prepared in manuscript.

Place	Date	Hour	Summary of Events and Information	Remarks and references to Appendices
Billsh	12/6		Baths allotted to all companies. Remainder of day devoted to training. Tactical scheme for Junior Officers under C.O. 2 - 2.30 pm. 2/Lieut E.Moore joined Battn. posted to "B" Coy.	acty
Billsh	13/6		Battalion paraded at 9.45 am & proceeded to training area E (nr LUCHEUX) others carried out training of platoons for the competition.	acty
Billsh	14/6		Battn paraded at 7.45 am & marched to "D" area (nr LUCHEUX), where Pack Company training was carried out.	Ditto
Billsh	15/6		'A' & 'B' Coys paraded 3.45 am & proceeded to training at LUCHEUX. 'B' & 'C' " " 7.45 am " to training near D1 & D2 (nr LUCHEUX)	ditto
Billsh	16/6		During morning companies carried out Interior Economy. Lecture to officers by Lt. Col Bird C.M.G. D.S.O. G.S.O.1 of 17th Divn at 9.30 am	acty
Billsh	17/6		C of E. Service held at 5 pm. The f/m men awarded Holiday leave to Salonica. 14242 Pte [illegible] 'C' Coy. 13232 Pte Nown 'C' Coy. 88980 Pte McMinn 'B' Coy. H3635 Pte A McGown R.A.M.C. attach'd 41132 L/C H Bennett 'B' Coy. (L.G. North [illegible])	acty

WAR DIARY or INTELLIGENCE SUMMARY

Army Form C. 2118

Place	Date	Hour	Summary of Events and Information	Remarks and references to Appendices
Billets	18/6 1917		Batt. paraded at 7.15 am proceeded to training area "G" (Chez LUCHEUX) where training for "open warfare" and "trench to trench" attack was carried out. Batts allotted to all companies	att.
Billets	19/6		All officers attended conference by C.O. at 10 am - 11 am. Lecture by Coy Commanders to Platoon Sections Commanders.	att.
Billets	20/6		Battalion paraded at 7.30 am proceeded by bus to camp at ST. NICHOLAS arriving there at 1 p.m.	att.
Camp	21/6		Battalion marched to trenches and relieved 25th Batt. North line in "GREENLAND" AILL" sector of the line, east of ARRAS. During relief no suffered 1 O.R. wounded	att.
Trenches	22/6		Our line was shelled fairly heavily following casualties were caused 3 O.R. killed 16 O.R. wounded	att.
Trenches	23/6		Quiet day spent	att.
Trenches	24/6		Shelling by both sides. Our casualties 1 O.R. killed 6 O.R. wounded	att.

WAR DIARY
or
INTELLIGENCE SUMMARY

Army Form C. 2118

Place	Date 1917	Hour	Summary of Events and Information	Remarks and references to Appendices
Trenches	25/6		There was again shelling by both sides. Our casualties were 8 O.R. wounded.	acct
Trenches	26/6		A quiet day was spent. In the evening the battalion was relieved by the 7th Batt. Yorks Regt. returned to reserve line at Railway Cuttings, at H.4.D (Map 51B N.W.)	acct
Reserve Line	27/6		Day devoted to cleaning of arms, clothing & equipment	acct
Reserve Line	28/6		Working parties provided at night for work under R.E's	acct
Reserve Line	29/6		Working parties provided at night for work under R.E's	acct
Reserve Line	30/6		Battn. marched to Kinches in evening relieved 10th Batt. Lanc Fusiliers in the "CHEMICAL WORKS" sector of front line (Map 51B N.W.)	acct

D.R. Osborne
Major
Comm.d'g 9th North'd Fus.

To Officer i/c
Regular Infantry Section

ORDERLY ROOM 24 JUN 1917 No. 149

Herewith Casualty Report No 149 please.

Regt No	Rank and Name	Coy	Date	Casualty
23302	Pte Gill J	A	21.6.17	Wounded (at Duty)
29/631	" Bellor G.R.	C	22.6.17	Wounded
48554	" Willoughby	A	"	Do
44615	" Stabler W.	D	"	Gassed (at Duty)
6358	" Spatham D	D	"	Do Do
3445	" Bolam J	D	"	Do Do
22294	" Harber J.H.	D	"	Died of Wounds
240040	" Leightley J	B	"	Wounded
44602	" Riley H	D	"	Gassed (at Duty)
29/476	Sgt Sykes G	B	"	Wounded
36228	Pte Robson W	D	"	Do (at Duty)
5312	" Jones S	B	"	Wounded
33685	" McAlister J	C	"	Do Do
32781	" Daglish W	D	"	Do Do
46643	" Tatterton W	B	"	Do (at Duty)
46192	Sgt Brooks W	B	"	Do Do
40188	Pte Towle E	B	"	Do Do
19633	" Lavery D	B	"	Killed in action
48466	" Bowler R.G.	B	"	Do
27/1	" Armstrong H	C	"	Wounded at Duty

S. Hewson Lieut
for O.C. 9th North Fus.

To Officer i/c
Regular Infantry Section

Herewith Casualty Report No 150 please.

25 JUN. 1917
No. 150.

Reg^t N⁰	Rank and Name	Cy	Date	Casualty
29/397	P/L Clough S	A	24.6.17	Killed in action
20421	" Walker W	A	"	Wounded
200752	" Maughan G	A	"	"
13/5908	" Thompson G	A	"	"
18027	" Middleton S	D	"	"
44607	" Pearce R	D	"	"
48515	" Patterson S	D	"	"
3445	" Bolam J	D	22.6.17	*
6358	" Statham D	D	"	*
44602	" Riley H	D	"	*

* Previously reported "Gassed (at Duty)" now "Gassed" to Hospital.

A. Newson
Lieut
p OC 9° North^d Fus.

To Officer i/c
Regular Infantry Section

Casualty Report No 151 Herewith please

Reg^t No	Rank and Name	Co^y	Date	Casualty
15897	Pte Ingram W.E.	B	25/2/17	Wounded
24290	Sgt Kay E.	6	"	Do
16132	- Sykes E.	6	"	Do
16/1681	Pte Burgess T.C.	6	"	Do
44575	- Cooper A	6	"	Do
1466	- Miller G	6	"	Do
10790	- Williamson G.K.	6	"	Do
25/25525	- Gunby G.	6	"	Do remained at duty

for O.C. 9th North^d Fus. Lieut

SPECIAL ORDER OF THE DAY
By
FIELD-MARSHAL SIR DOUGLAS HAIG,
G.C.B., G.C.V.O., K.C.I.E.,
Commander-in-Chief, British Armies in France.

The following telegrams are published for the information of all ranks:—

FROM FIELD-MARSHAL SIR DOUGLAS HAIG TO HIS MAJESTY THE KING, BUCKINGHAM PALACE.

3-6-17.

On the occasion of Your Majesty's birthday, on behalf of all ranks under my command, I beg leave to offer heartiest congratulations and to wish Your Majesty very many happy returns of the day.

To FIELD-MARSHAL SIR DOUGLAS HAIG, FROM HIS MAJESTY THE KING.

3-6-17.

The good wishes which you have conveyed in your telegram on behalf of all ranks in France on the occasion of my birthday have greatly touched me and remind me more than ever of what we all owe to the pluck, spirit and endurance of the troops under your command.

I thank them from the bottom of my heart.

General Headquarters,
5th June, 1917.

D. Haig. F.M.

Commander-in-Chief,
British Armies in France.

War Diary 1st

SPECIAL ORDER OF THE DAY
By
FIELD-MARSHAL SIR DOUGLAS HAIG.
G.C.B., G.C.V.O., K.C.I.E.,
Commander-in-Chief, British Armies in France.

The following messages are published for the information of all ranks :—

To THE FIELD-MARSHAL COMMANDING-IN-CHIEF, BRITISH ARMIES IN FRANCE.

1-6-1917.

The Secretary of the War Office begs to transmit herewith a copy of a resolution passed by the Triennial Delegate Meeting of the Dock, Wharf, Riverside and General Workers' Union :—

RESOLVED :

This Triennial Conference of the Dock, Wharf, Riverside and General Workers' Union hereby expresses its heartfelt gratitude to the Services: Army, Navy, and Mercantile Marine, and all the brave comrades who are fighting for this country.

We earnestly wish safety and success to our fighting forces.

We pledge ourselves to assist in facilitating transport, to help our comrades in every way possible, and we pray that brains and courage may win for the World an honourable and early peace.

(Signed) W. W. DAVIDSON, CHAIRMAN.
BEN TILLETT, GEN. SECRETARY.

To THE SECRETARY, WAR OFFICE.

7-6-1917.

The Field-Marshal Commanding-in-Chief begs to acknowledge receipt of copy of a Resolution passed by the Triennial Delegate Meeting of the Dock, Wharf, Riverside and General Workers' Union, and requests that the Union may be informed that their Resolution is much appreciated by himself and all ranks serving under his command.

A copy of the resolution will be published in General Orders, and will strengthen the bonds between all serving in the Armies in France and their comrades of the Dock, Wharf, Riverside and General Workers' Union at home.

D. Haig. F.M.

Commander-in-Chief,
British Armies in France.

General Headquarters,
8th June, 1917.

SPECIAL ORDER OF THE DAY
By
FIELD-MARSHAL SIR DOUGLAS HAIG,
G.C.B., G.C.V.O., K.C.I.E.,
Commander-in-Chief, British Armies in France.

The complete success of the attack made yesterday by the Second Army under the command of General Sir Herbert Plumer is an earnest of the eventual final victory of the Allied cause.

The position assaulted was one of very great natural strength, on the defences of which the enemy had laboured incessantly for nearly three years. Its possession overlooking the whole of the Ypres Salient was of the greatest tactical and strategical value to the enemy.

The excellent observation which he had from this position added enormously to the difficulty of our preparations for the attack, and ensured to him ample warning of our intentions. He was therefore fully prepared for our assault and had brought up reinforcements of men and guns to meet it.

He had the further advantage of the experience gained by him from many previous defeats in battles such as the Somme, the Ancre, Arras, and Vimy Ridge. On the lessons to be drawn from these he had issued carefully thought-out instructions.

Despite all these advantages the enemy has been completely defeated. Within the space of a few hours all our objectives were gained, with undoubtedly very severe loss to the Germans. Our own casualties were, for a battle of such magnitude, most gratifyingly light.

The full effect of this victory cannot be estimated yet, but that it will be very great is certain.

Following on the great successes already gained, it affords final and conclusive proof that neither strength of position nor knowledge of and timely preparation to meet impending assault can save the enemy from complete defeat, and that brave and tenacious as the German troops are, it is only a question of how much longer they can endure the repetition of such blows.

Yesterday's victory was due to causes which always have given and always will give success, viz.: the utmost skill, valour and determination in the execution of the attack following on the greatest forethought and thoroughness in preparation for it.

I desire to place on record here my deep appreciation of the splendid work done, above and below ground as well as in the air, by all Arms, Services, and Departments, and by the Commanders and Staffs by whom, under Sir Herbert Plumer's orders, all means at our disposal were combined, both in preparation and in execution, with a skill, devotion and bravery beyond all praise.

The great success gained has brought us a long step nearer to the final, victorious, end of the War, and the Empire will be justly proud of the troops who have added such fresh lustre to its arms.

General Headquarters,
8th June, 1917.

Commander-in-Chief,
British Armies in France.

SPECIAL ORDER OF THE DAY
By
FIELD-MARSHAL SIR DOUGLAS HAIG,
G.C.B., G.C.V.O., K.C.I.E.,
Commander-in-Chief, British Armies in France.

The following telegrams are published for the information of all ranks:—

To FIELD-MARSHAL SIR DOUGLAS HAIG, FROM HIS MAJESTY THE KING.

9.6.17.

I rejoice that, thanks to thorough preparation and splendid co-operation of all Arms the important Messines Ridge, which has been the scene of so many memorable struggles, is again in our hands. Tell General Plumer and the Second Army how proud we are of this achievement by which, in a few hours, the enemy was driven out of strongly entrenched position held by him for two-and-a-half years.

FROM FIELD-MARSHAL SIR DOUGLAS HAIG, TO HIS MAJESTY THE KING.

9-6-17.

Your Majesty's gracious message has been read with intense pride and gratification by all who have taken part in the operations on the Messines Ridge.

In the name of myself and Staff, General Plumer and all ranks of the Second Army, I beg to offer our respectful thanks to Your Majesty.

D. Haig. F.M.

General Headquarters,
11th June, 1917.

Commander-in-Chief,
British Armies in France.

SPECIAL ORDER OF THE DAY
By
FIELD-MARSHAL SIR DOUGLAS HAIG,
G.C.B., G.C.V.O., K.C.I.E.,
Commander-in-Chief, British Armies in France.

The following messages are published for the information of all ranks :—

To FIELD-MARSHAL SIR DOUGLAS HAIG, FROM THE SECRETARY, WAR OFFICE.

9.6.1917.

Following from Lord Mayor London begins " Would you kindly convey to Field-Marshal Sir Douglas Haig the warm congratulations of the Citizens of London on the recent successful operations of the Forces under his command and their profound admiration and pride in the brilliant skill and bravery exhibited by our officers and men in these all important undertakings."

FROM FIELD-MARSHAL SIR DOUGLAS HAIG, TO THE LORD MAYOR OF LONDON.

10.6.1917.

Please accept in the name of the British Army in France our sincere thanks for the congratulations sent by you on behalf of the Citizens of London on the operations resulting in the capture of the Messines Ridge. All ranks who took part in the battle welcome your message and are grateful for the appreciation of their fellow-countrymen.

FORWARDED BY THE SECRETARY, WAR OFFICE, TO FIELD-MARSHAL SIR DOUGLAS HAIG.

6.6.1917.

The President, Officers, Council and Delegates of the United Kingdom Commercial Travellers' Association (Incorporated) in Conference assembled at St. George's Hall, Liverpool, offer to you and to the gallant Armies under your command their sincere and heartfelt gratitude for the great efforts that you are making to secure a decisive victory for the Allied cause.

It is impossible for them to express to you all the pride they feel in your wonderful achievements and in the heroic and self-sacrificing gallantry which is shown day by day by our glorious soldiers. We are happy to know that amongst these heroes are a number of the members of this Association, which is proud of what they have done, and thankful beyond telling for their great sacrifices and noble services in the cause of humanity.

The Association offers to you the tribute of its gratitude, its respectful admiration and esteem, and earnestly prays that it may be granted to you to secure an early and triumphant victory and to see your great labours crowned with that success upon the achievement of which the future of civilization depends.

To THE SECRETARY, WAR OFFICE.

11.6.1917.

The Field-Marshal Commanding-in-Chief presents his compliments to the Secretary, War Office, and requests that he will convey to the President, Officers, Council and Delegates of the United Kingdom Commercial Travellers' Association (Incorporated) in Conference assembled at St. George's Hall, Liverpool, thanks of himself and of all ranks under his command for their inspiring message, forwarded by the Secretary, War Office, on the 6th instant.

It is a great source of encouragement to all those fighting out here to know that they have earned the confidence of their fellow-countrymen at home.

General Headquarters,
12th June, 1917.

D. Haig. F.M.
Commander-in-Chief.
British Armies in France.

ARMY PRINTING AND STATIONERY SERVICES A—6/17.

WAR DIARY
of

9th (S) Bn The Northumberland Fusiliers

1st July 1917 to 31st July 1917

CONFIDENTIAL

Confidential   NFC 155

To   52nd Infy Bde

Herewith War Diary for July 1917. Please acknowledge receipt hereon.

D. R. Osborne
Major
Comdg 9th Northd Fus

WAR DIARY
or
INTELLIGENCE SUMMARY

(Erase heading not required.)

Army Form C. 2118

Place	Date 1917	Hour	Summary of Events and Information	Remarks and references to Appendices
Trenches	July 1st.		Quiet day. Fair amount of hostile air activity, but their machines were driven off by our A.A. guns & Lewis Guns.	A.J.J.
Trenches	2nd.		Enemy shelled CHEMICAL WORKS and ROEUX. Our artillery replying on HAUSA WOOD. (see Map 51B N.W.) Our casualties, 1 O.R. missing, believed killed Webb in patrol and 1 O.R. wounded.	A.J.J.
Trenches	3rd.		There was the usual shelling of CHEMICAL WORKS by the enemy and our retaliation on HAUSA WOOD. Enemy Trench Mortars were active from RAILWAY CUTTING but were silenced by our guns. The Battalion was relieved during night of 3rd/4th July. Bn HQ and "A" & "C" companies took over RAILWAY CUTTING ie. H-8-C. H.16.B.6.3 - H.16.B.4.9. "B" & "D" companies proceeded to PUDDING TRENCH at H.16.B.6.3 - H.16.B.4.9. Bath. was relieved by 10th Lancs too.	A.J.J.
Spffart Lindu	4th		Day devoted to cleaning of equipment. Working parties provided at night	A.J.J.
Spffart Lindu	5th		Working parties provided day and night	A.J.J.
Spffart Lindu	6th		Do Do	A.J.J.

Army Form C. 2118

WAR DIARY
or
INTELLIGENCE SUMMARY
(Erase heading not required.)

Instructions regarding War Diaries and Intelligence Summaries are contained in F. S. Regs., Part II. and the Staff Manual respectively. Title Pages will be prepared in manuscript.

Place	Date 1917	Hour	Summary of Events and Information	Remarks and references to Appendices
Saulzoir Trenches	July 7th		Battalion was relieved by 6th Dorset Regt. Moved back individually to camp at ST. NICHOLAS	AWF
Reserve Camp	8th		We had 3 L.G. teams in Reformed area, for Ant. Aircraft Duties, and also had to mount one in camp. One O.R. wounded. G.O.C. 52nd Bde. saw all senior officers for a conference	AWF
Reserve Camp	9th		Whole Battn. carried out training and while provided large working parties for R.E. One O.R. wounded.	AWF
Reserve Camp	10th/15th		Training and instruction in vicinity of camps. On night of 15th/16th Battn. moved up into front line and relieved 1st Batt. Scottish Rifles in CALEDONIAN ROAD Sector (Maps 51B N.W. & D 17 & Div. Map T.13- PLOUVAIN).	AWF
Trenches	16th		Quiet day. Some shelling by both sides.	AWF
Trenches	17th		Quiet day. Enemy Trench Mortars were active but did no damage to our line	AWF
Trenches	18th		Two of our Snipers laid out in NO MAN'S LAND from dawn to dusk, killed 3 of the enemy bringing back useful information regarding the enemy's wire, trenches etc:-	AWF

WAR DIARY or INTELLIGENCE SUMMARY

Army Form C. 2118

(Erase heading not required.)

Place	Date 1917	Hour	Summary of Events and Information	Remarks and references to Appendices
Trenches	July 19th		Our artillery was active throughout the day on enemy trenches and back areas. We exploded a German Minenwerfer type and used it against the enemy with good effect. This was organised & carried out by Lt Cronin. A Coy of B/Yorkshires were made for carrying out a raid on the following night.	Artillery
Trenches	July 20th		Our trenches were heavily shelled with H.E. and trench mortars as the result of an evening bombardment. We suffered 3 O.R. killed & 9 wounded. At about 10.30 p.m. a raid was carried out by the parties of 9 inch mortar 2nd Bn Alba. at Sergt. P. White. The trenches were entered in I.B.A. and the enemy holes several being shot down. 2 dug-outs was bombed and two Lewis rifles brought back (Ref T.13 Plouvan). The battalion was relieved on night of 20th/21st July by 10th Lancs Fus and returned to support trenches HUDSON & HUSSAR (Ref. 57.3 N.W. & Plouvan).	C.O.P. Arty
Support Trenches	July 21st		Day devoted to cleaning of rifles, equipment etc. fitting new H. O.R. assaulted. Our casualties during 24 hours.	Arty
Support Trenches	July 22nd		Working parties provided for salving, improvement of trenches etc.	Arty

WAR DIARY
or
INTELLIGENCE SUMMARY
(Erase heading not required.)

Army Form C. 2118

Instructions regarding War Diaries and Intelligence Summaries are contained in F.S. Regs., Part II. and the Staff Manual respectively. Title Pages will be prepared in manuscript.

Place	Date	Hour	Summary of Events and Information	Remarks and references to Appendices
Gully (Shrapnel Valley)	23rd Sept		Working parties busied as on previous days. Our artillery was rather troopsome the day. Enemy shelled our trench at H11A at night with gun shells.	A.W.L.
Support trench	24th Sept		Working parties resumed. Our artillery was troopsome. Sector not relieved 10 to 1 to tonight. Saw news. During the relief the enemy fired some G in shells on our communication trench causing 5 O.R. casualties, one of them seriously.	A.W.L.
Trenches	25th Sept		Fairly quiet day, though some activity by T.M's on both sides.	A.W.L.
Trenches	26th Sept		Our artillery was active, engaging the enemy's defences opposite our front. Enemy replied vigorously.	A.W.L.
Trenches	27th Sept		A battalion of our right brigade, (the EAST YORKS) successfully raided the enemy line astride the railway (MAP FANDOOR 17th Div T.13) taking 14 prisoners, two M.Gs and one T.M. Enemy shown Germans taking 14 prisoners on night of 27th/28th returned to our Battalion was relieved on night of 27th/28th returned to our outpost line HUDSON and HUSSAR (map 51B N.W.)	A.W.L.

1875 Wt. W593 9,099 4/15 J.B.C. & A. A.D.S.S./Forms/C. 2118.

WAR DIARY or INTELLIGENCE SUMMARY

Army Form C. 2118

Place	Date	Hour	Summary of Events and Information	Remarks and references to Appendices
Support Trenches	July 28th to July 31st 1917		Quiet time spent in support lines, working parties provided both day & night for work in front and support lines. On the night of 31st July/1st August the battalion was relieved by 10th Bn. A.I.F. and moved returned to Lancaster Camp at ST NICHOLAS.	A.I.F.

D. R. Ashton
Major
Comdg 9th Battalion Inf

1-8-17

To O/c ...C.3.

153.

Herewith casualty Report to 155 Phase.

Regtl No:	Rank & Name	Date	Coy	Remarks
10434	Pte Fox P.10.	8-7-17	B	Wounded

W.A. Robertson
Capt & Adjt;
O/C (5) Bn York & Lancs

In the Field
8.7.17

To O/c A.I.S.3.
Base S

154

Herewith casualty report No. 154 please.

Reg'l: No:	Rank & Name	Coy.	Date.	Casualty:
14776	Cpl Luke. W.	C	20.7.17	Killed
13233	Pte Brown R.I.L.	C	do	Killed
38223	" Lamb. W.	C	do	Killed
44610	" Robinson J.	C	do	Wounded
45786	" McAllister C.	C	do	- do -
33691	" Weldon G.W.	C	do	- do -
29/404	" James A.	C	do	- do -
17986	Cpl Elliott J.	C	do	- do -
32463	Pte Rothwell G.S.	C	do	- do -
23839	" Davison S.	A	do	- do -
10651	" Foster O.C.	A	do	- do -
10134	" Long A.	B	do	Remains at duty.
7199	Cpl Robertson A		21.7.17	Wounded.

A Robertson
Capt & Adjt

Lieut C.W.
For O.C. 9 North'n Fusiliers

In the Field
22.7.17

To O i/c R.I.S.3.

Herewith Casualty Report No 155 phase.

Regt No.	Rank & Name	Coy	Date	Casualty
46182	Cpl Mickelgow H.C.	B	20.7.17	Wounded Rem'd Duty
13108	Pte Coates. D.	D	21.7.17	do do
12925	" Gascoyne. O.	A	do	Wounded
11430	" Denny J.W.	D	do	do
31876	" Anderson G.	C	do	do

W.A. Robertson
Capt & Adjt
for O.C. 9th North'n Fusiliers

In the Field
23.7.17

To O/c R.I.S.3.
Base ?

156.

Herewith Casualty report No 156 please.

Regtl No.	Rank & Name	Co	Date	Casualty
19/651	Pte Battye	C	25.7.17	Wounded
14817	" Thompson Jno	C	do	do
13577	" Brady. J.	A	24.7.17	do
16265	" Garsden. H.	A	25.7.17	do
3/20889	" Wilson. L	B	do	do

W.Robertson
Capt & Adjt

Lieut
for O.C. 9 North'd Fus:

In the Field.
26.7.17

00% L.P.S 3

Base

Herewith Casualty
report No 15. Please.

Regt No	A.L. Name	Co	Date	Casualty
10604	Willow E.		Dec 17	Wounded

W. Robertson
Capt & Adjt

For O.C. North...

In the field
14.4.17

O/c R.I.S.3

Herewith Casualty
Report No 158, please.

158

Regtl No.	Rank	Name	Coy	Date	Casualty
46643	Pte	Latterton.W.	B	30.7.17	Wounded
48490	"	Garnick.J.	B	do	do
23/1446	"	Cameron.W.	A	29.7.17	do

W.A. Robertson
Capt & Adjt
for Major
Comdg. 9th North'd Fus.

In the Field
31.7.17

SPECIAL ORDER OF THE DAY
By
FIELD-MARSHAL SIR DOUGLAS HAIG,
K.T., G.C.B., G.C.V.O., K.C.I.E.,
Commander-in-Chief, British Armies in France.

The following telegrams are published for the information of all ranks:—

FROM FIELD-MARSHAL SIR DOUGLAS HAIG, TO HIS MAJESTY THE KING OF THE BELGIANS.

21.7.1917.

I have the honour to express to your Majesty on the occasion of the National Festival of Belgium the unshaken determination of the British Armies under my command to fight on side by side with our gallant Allies until the deliverance of Belgium and the defeat of our common enemy are finally accomplished.

To FIELD-MARSHAL SIR DOUGLAS HAIG, FROM HIS MAJESTY THE KING OF THE BELGIANS.

21.7.1917.

I sincerely thank you for the good wishes you have expressed to me on the occasion of the National Festival of Belgium. I can assure you that the Belgian Army will continue to act in the closest co-operation with the Armies of the Allies in this War which it is resolved to fight till the entire liberation of Belgian territory is accomplished.

D. Haig. F.M.

Commander-in-Chief,
British Armies in France.

General Headquarters,
25th July, 1917.

SPECIAL ORDER OF THE DAY

BY

HIS MAJESTY THE KING.

OFFICERS, NON-COMMISSIONED OFFICERS AND MEN.

On the conclusion of my fourth visit to the British Armies in the Field, I leave you with feelings of admiration and gratitude for past achievements, and of confidence in future efforts.

On all sides I have witnessed the scenes of your triumphs.

The battlefields of the Somme, the Ancre, Arras, Vimy and Messines have shown me what great results can be attained by the courage and devotion of all arms and services under efficient commanders and staffs.

Nor do I forget the valuable work done by the various departments behind the fighting line, including those who direct and man the highly developed system of railways and other means of communication.

Your comrades too—the men and women of the industrial Army at Home—have claims on your remembrance for their untiring service in helping you to meet the enemy on terms which are not merely equal, but daily improving.

It was a great pleasure to the Queen to accompany me, and to become personally acquainted with the excellent arrangements for the care of the sick and wounded, whose welfare is ever close to her heart.

For the past three years, the Armies of the Empire and workers in the Home-lands behind them have risen superior to every difficulty and every trial.

The splendid successes already gained, in concert with our gallant Allies, have advanced us well on the way towards the completion of the task we undertook.

There are doubtless fierce struggles still to come, and heavy strains on our endurance to be borne.

But be the road before us long or short, the spirit and pluck which have brought you so far will never fail, and, under God's guidance, the final and complete victory of our just cause is assured.

GEORGE, R.I.

General Headquarters,
   British Armies in France.
     14th July, 1917.

War Diary

SECRET.   Copy No. I

OPERATION ORDER
9th Northumberland Fusiliers
++++++++++++++

Ref. Map.
PLOUVAIN
1/10,000.

18th July 1917.

1. Under cover of the creeping barrage arranged for the night of 19/20th July two patrols will push into WART TRENCH at a time to be notified later.

OBJECT. 2. (a) To obtain identification.
(b) To kill any enemy encountered.

STRENGTH 3. RIGHT COMPANY (A). will supply a patrol of nine O.R. under sergeant WHITE. These will be closely supported by a party of 1 N.C.O. and six O.R.

CENTRE COMPANY (B). will supply a patrol of nine O.R. under 2nd Lieut. ALLAN. These will be closely supported by a party of 1 N.C.O. and six O.R.

Right patrol will leave CUTHBERT at I.7.B.9.0. and will enter WART at I.8.A.35.20.
Left patrol. will leave CUTHBERT at I.7.B.7.3. and will enter WART at I.8.A.30.35.

LEWIS GUN. 4. Centre Company will push a Lewis Gun to I.8.A.0.6., and a party of four O.R. to engage any hostile Machine Guns on the Left.

INSTRUCTIONS 5. The parties will form up in front of our wire before zero and will advance under cover of the barrage, as near as possible to it.

At 0 + 3, when the barrage lifts the patrols will rush into WART, the supporting parties remaining about 40 yards behind.
The Right flanker of the Right patrol and the Left flanker of the Left patrol will wear white distinguishing marks on their Left Shoulder straps. The leader will wear white distinguishing marks on both shoulder straps.
The timekeeper of each party will wear white distinguishing marks on his right shoulder strap.

EQUIPMENT Rifles and fixed bayonets, and ten rounds in the magazine. Each man will carry 2 clips of five in his pocket, and 1 Bomb. The left flanker of the left patrol will carry 6 bombs. Box respirators will be carried, but no equipment.
Each patrol will carry 2 pairs of wire cutters.

PRISONERS & CASUALTIES. Any prisoners taken, or wounded men of the patrols will at once be handed to the supporting party, for immediate discharge to the rear. The supporting parties will each carry a stretcher.

RETURN. At 0 + 9 two golden rain rockets will be sent up from CUTHBERT to warn parties to return.
An orange light will be flashed from CUTHBERT to guide parties on their return.
The lewis gun will return at 0 + 12

(2).

STOKES MORTARS. 6. Stokes mortars will assist by forming a defensive flank from I.8.A.35.60 to I.8.A.0.9., and by bombarding trench junction round I.1.D.90.25 and WHIP from I.2.C.6.0. to I.2.C.4.3.

Machine Guns. 7. Machine guns will assist by directing overhead fire along road running through I.8.A. and B. and by firing on tracks behind.

LEFT COMPANY. 8. Left Company will assist by rifle-grenading and bombing enemy bomb stop in front of COKE, and by engaging with Lewis Gun Fire and hostile M.G!s that may open.

WIRE. 9. Holes will be punched in the wire in front of WART at the points of entry, on the 19th July, by the supporting Artillery.

10. The 50th Infantry Brigade will carry out a similar operation on the right.

Copy No. 1 to War Diary.
    2 to O.C.'A' Coy.
    3 to O.C.'B' Coy.
    4 to O.C.'C' Coy.
    5 to O.C.'D' Coy.
    6 to H.C.
    7 OC 12th Manchesters
    8 India Command

(Sd) J.S.ALLEN. Major,
O.C. 9th Northumberland Fusiliers

www.ingramcontent.com/pod-product-compliance
Lightning Source LLC
Chambersburg PA
CBHW080852010526
44117CB00014B/2240